FROM
Gileskirk
TO
Greyfriars

2

⚜Tales of a Scottish Grandfather⚜

FROM
Gileskirk
TO
Greyfriars

Mary Queen of Scots, John Knox & the
Heroes of Scotland's Reformation

Sir Walter Scott

Introduction by
GEORGE GRANT

CUMBERLAND HOUSE
NASHVILLE, TENNESSEE

Introduction copyright © 2001 by George Grant

Published by
CUMBERLAND HOUSE PUBLISHING, INC.
431 Harding Industrial Drive
Nashville, Tennessee 37211
www.cumberlandhouse.com

Cover design by Unlikely Suburban Design, Nashville, Tennessee

Library of Congress Cataloging-in-Publication Data

Scott, Walter, Sir, 1771–1832.
   [Tales of a grandfather]
   Tales of a Scottish grandfather / Sir Walter Scott ; introduction by George Grant.
      p. cm.
   Includes index.
   Originally published: London : Routledge, 1828.
   Contents: v. 2. From Gileskirk to Greyfriars : Mary Queen of Scots, John Knox & the heroes of Scotland's reformation.
   ISBN 1-58182-128-X (v. 2 : pbk. : alk. paper)
   1. Scotland—History. I. Title.
DA761.S55 2001
941.1—dc21   00-065775

978-1-68442-358-3 (hc)

CONTENTS

INTRODUCTION

A great passion for the ballads and legends of his native land was the genesis of Sir Walter Scott's (1771–1832) remarkable literary career—he simply wanted to share his gleeful appreciation for great stories, lively yarns, and heroic tales.

In his early career he was best known for his verse. His first narrative poem, *The Lay of the Last Minstrel* (1805), brought him huge popularity. Following this success, he wrote a series of romantic narrative poems, which included *Marmion* (1808), *The Lady of the Lake* (1810), *The Bridal of Triermain* (1813), and *The Lord of the Isles* (1815). In 1813 he was offered the poet laureateship of England, but he declined humbly, recommending Robert Southey for the post instead. He also published critical editions of the writings of the English poet John Dryden in 1808 and of the English satirist Jonathan Swift in 1814.

Not entirely satisfied that epic verse was the best means to communicate his passion for the legacy of Scotland, he turned his hand to writing novels. *Waverley* (1814) began a new series of triumphs. More than twenty novels followed in rapid succession, including *Guy Mannering* (1815), *Old Mortality* (1816), *The Heart of Midlothian* (1818), *Rob Roy* (1818), *The Bride of Lammermoor* (1819), *Ivanhoe* (1819), *Kenilworth* (1821), *Quentin Durward* (1823), and *The Fair Maid of Perth* (1828). Although he published this fiction anonymously, his authorship became an open secret.

Still not having exhausted his creativity, he turned to biography, literary criticism, contemporary affairs, and history. With every endeavor, he chalked up one stunning success after another. And so it was that he began this new series of works, near the end of his life, *Tales of a Scottish Grandfather*. Written for his often sickly grandson, the books demonstrate both his command of the history of his beloved land as well as his mastery of the craft of storytelling.

This second of four volumes recounts the momentous events during the Reformation. With the colorful figures of John Knox, George Buchanan, and Mary Queen of Scots on center stage, Scott was able to delineate the distinctive differences between Scottish history and that of all other nations.

The Protestant faith first appeared in Scotland at the beginning of the fifteenth century, when the Lollard followers of John Wyclif fled persecution in England and found their way across the border. Shortly thereafter, the ideas and books of Martin Luther began filtering into the university towns. At about the time Knox began teaching at St. Andrews University, George Wishart, a zealous Protestant, had begun his preaching and teaching ministry there. Knox, still a Catholic priest, was attracted to the beauty, goodness, and truth he saw in Wishart's message. He offered to serve as a bodyguard for the evangelist—but soon afterward, Wishart was arrested, condemned as a heretic, and burned at the stake. His martyrdom provoked Knox's dramatic conversion—he would never be the same again, and neither would Scotland nor the legions of men who came after, including Sir Walter Scott. In this volume Scott tells just why.

From the early struggles of Knox and those reforming pioneers to the days of the Covenanters and their struggle for spiritual independence, the improbable story of how Scotland was transformed from a cultural backwater to one of the most important centers of intellectual progress, creativity, and innovation in all of Christendom is ably and enthusiastically told by Scott.

Not surprisingly, *Tales of a Scottish Grandfather* proved to be incredibly popular and influential. But more, it proved to be the aptest means for Scott to retell the great stories and relate the great themes that had been his passion from his earliest days.

George Grant

FROM
Gileskirk
TO
Greyfriars

XXIX

Mary Queen of Scots

1542-1560

THE evil fortunes of Mary Stewart, who succeeded her father in the crown of Scotland, commenced at her very birth, and could scarce be considered as ceasing during the whole period of her life. Of all the unhappy princes of the line of Stewart, she was the most uniformly unfortunate. She was born 7th December 1542, and, in a few days after, became, by her father's death, the infant Queen of a distracted country.

Two parties strove, as is usual in minorities, to obtain the supreme power. Mary of Guise, the Queen-Mother, with Cardinal David Beaton, were at the head of that which favoured the alliance with France. Hamilton, Earl of Arran, the nearest male relation of the infant Queen, was chief of the other, and possessed more extended popularity; for the nobles dreaded the bold and ambitious character of the Cardinal, and the common people detested him, on account of his cruel persecution of the Reformers. The Earl of Arran, however, was but a fickle and timid man, with little, it would seem, to recommend him, besides his high birth. He was, however, preferred to the office of Regent.

Henry VIII. is said to have expressed much concern for the death of his nephew, saying, there would never again reign a King in Scotland so nearly related to him, or so dear to him, and blaming, not the late James V., but his evil counsellors, for the unfortunate dispute between them. At the same time, Henry formed a plan of uniting the kingdoms of England and Scotland by a marriage betwixt the infant Queen of Scotland and his only son, Edward VI., then a child. He took into his counsels the Earl of Glencairn and other Scottish nobles, made prisoners in the rout of Solway, and offered to set them at liberty, provided, on their return to Scotland, they would undertake to forward the match which he proposed. They were released accordingly, upon giving pledges that they would return in case the treaty should not be accomplished.

Archibald, Earl of Angus, with his brother, Sir George Douglas, took the same opportunity of returning into Scotland, after fifteen years' exile. They had been indebted to Henry for support and protection during that long space of time. He had even admitted them to be members of his Privy Council, and by the countenance he afforded them, had given great offence to the late King James. When, therefore, the influence of the Douglases, naturally attached to him by gratitude, was added to that of Glencairn and the others, who had been made prisoners at Solway, and to the general weight of the Protestants, favourable, of course, to an alliance with England, Henry must be considered as having a party in Scotland in every way favourable to his views.

But the impatient temper of the English monarch ruined his own scheme. He demanded the custody of the young Queen of Scotland till she should be of age to complete the marriage to be contracted by the present league, and he insisted that some of the strongest forts in the kingdom should be put into his hands. These proposals alarmed the national jealousy of the Scots, and the characteristic love of independence and liberty which we find that people have always displayed. The nation at large became persuaded that Henry VIII., under pretence of a union by marriage, nourished, like Edward I. in similar circumstances, the purpose of subduing the country. The exiled lords who had agreed to assist Henry's views could be of no use to him, in consequence of the extravagance of his propositions. They told Sir Ralph Sadler, the English ambassador, frankly, that the nation could not endure the surrender of the Queen's person to Henry's charge—that their own vassals would not take arms for them in such a cause—that the old women of Scotland, with their distaffs, nay, the very stones in the street, would arise and fight against it.

Henry was with difficulty prevailed upon to defer the time for giving to him the custody of Queen Mary's person, until she should be ten years old. But even this modified proposition excited the greatest jealousy; and Sir George Douglas, Henry's chief advocate, only ventured to recommend acquiescence in the King's proposal as a means of gaining time. He told the Scottish nobles of a certain king, who was so fond of an ass, that he insisted his chief physician should teach the animal to speak, upon pain of being himself put to death. The physician consented to undertake the case, but gave the King to understand that it would be ten years before the operation of his medicines could take effect. The King permitted him to set to work accordingly. Now, one of the physician's friends seeing him busy about the animal, expressed his wonder that so wise a man should undertake what was contrary to nature; to which the physician replied,—"Do you not see I have gained ten years' advantage? If I had refused the King's orders, I must have been instantly put to death; but as it is, I have the advantage of a long delay, during which the King may die, the ass may die, or I may die myself. In either of the three cases, I am freed from my trouble."—"Even so," said Sir George Douglas, "if we agree to this treaty we avoid a bloody and destructive war, and have a long period before us, during which the King of England, his son Prince Edward, or the infant Queen Mary, may one of them die, so that the treaty will be broken off." Moved by such reasons, a parliament, which consisted almost entirely of the lords of the English party, consented to the match with England, and the Regent Arran also agreed to it.

But while one part of the Scottish nobles adopted the resolution to treat with King Henry on his own terms, the Queen-Mother and Cardinal Beaton were at the head of another and still more numerous faction, who adhered to the old religion, and to the ancient alliance with France, and were, of course, directly opposed to the English match. The fickle temper of the Regent contributed to break off the treaty which he had subscribed. Within a fortnight after he had ratified the conditions of the match with England, he reconciled himself to the Cardinal and Queen-Mother, and joined in putting a stop to the proposed marriage.

The English King, if he could have been watchful and patient, might perhaps have brought the measure, which was alike important to both countries, once more to bear. But Henry, incensed at the Regent's double dealing, determined for immediate war. He sent a fleet and army into the Firth of Forth, which landed, and, finding no opposition, burnt the capital of Scotland, and its seaport, and plundered the country around. Sir Ralph Evers, and Sir Brian Latoun, were, at the same time, employed in making inroads on the Border, which were of the fiercest and most wasteful description. The account of the ravage is tremendous. In one foray they numbered 192 towers, or houses of defence, burnt or razed, 403 Scots slain, and 816 made prisoners; 10,386 cattle, 12,492 sheep, 1,296 horses, and 850 bolls of corn, driven away as spoil. Another list gives an account of the destruction of seven monasteries, or religious houses; sixteen castles or towers; five market-towns, two hundred and forty-three villages, thirteen mills, and three hospitals, all pulled down or burnt.

The exploits of the English leaders might gratify Henry's resentment, but they greatly injured his interest in Scotland, for the whole kingdom became united to repel the invaders; and even those who liked the proposed match with England best, were, to use an expression of the time, disgusted with so rough a mode of wooing. The Douglases themselves, bound to Henry by so many ties, were obliged, on seeing the distress and devastation of the country, to take part in the war against him, and soon found an opportunity to do so.

It seems Henry had conferred upon his two successful leaders, Evers and Latoun, all the lands which they had conquered, or should be able to conquer upon the Border, and, in particular, the fine counties of Merse and Teviotdale. "I will write the instrument of possession upon their own bodies, with sharp pens, and in blood-red ink," said the Earl of Angus, "because they destroyed the tombs of my ancestors at the abbey of Melrose." He accordingly urged Arran, the regent, or governor, as he was called, to move towards the frontiers, to protect them. Arran was with difficulty prevailed on to advance southward to Melrose, with scarce so many as five hundred men in his company. The English leaders were lying at Jedburgh with five thousand men. Three thousand of these were regular soldiers, paid by the King of England; the rest were Borderers, amongst whom there were many Scottish clans who had taken the red cross, and submitted themselves to the dominion of England. With these forces Evers and Latoun made a sudden march, to surprise the governor and his handful of men; but they failed, for the Scots retreated beyond the Tweed, to the hills near Galashiels.

The English then prepared to retire to Jedburgh, and the governor, acting by Angus's advice, followed them, and watched their motions. In the meantime succours began to come in to the Scottish army. A bold young man, Norman Leslie, the master of Rothes, was the first to come up with three hundred horse, from Fife, gallantly armed. Afterwards the Lord Buccleuch joined them with a few of his clan, who arrived at full speed, and assured them that the rest of the Scotts would be presently on the field. This Border chieftain was a man of great military sagacity, and knew the ground well. He advised the governor and Angus to draw up their men at the foot of a small eminence, and to send their horses to the rear. The English, seeing the horses of the Scots ascend the hill, concluded they were in flight, and turned hastily back to attack them, hurrying in confusion, as to an assured conquest. Thus they came in front of the Scottish army, who were closely and firmly drawn up, at the very moment when they themselves were in confusion from their hasty advance. As the Scots began to charge, the Earl of Angus, seeing a heron arise out of the marsh, cried out, "Oh, that I had my white hawk here, that we might all join battle at once!" The English, surprised and out of breath (and having the sun in their eyes as well as the smoke of the gunpowder which the wind blew in their faces), were completely defeated, and compelled to take to flight. The Scottish Borderers, who had joined them during their prosperity, perceiving their own countrymen to be victorious, threw away their red crosses (the distinction which they had assumed as subjects of England), and fell upon the English, for the purpose of helping those against whom they had come to the field, and making amends for their desertion of the Scottish cause. These renegades made a pitiful slaughter, and the Scots in general, provoked, probably, by the late ravages of the English, showed themselves so cruel to the vanquished that they seemed to deserve the severe blow which the nation soon afterwards received. Tradition says that a beautiful young maiden, called Lillyard, followed her lover from the little village of Maxton, and when she saw him fall in battle, rushed herself into the heat of the fight, and was killed, after slaying several of the English. From this female they call the field of battle Lillyard's Edge to this day.

This battle was fought in 1545. A thousand Englishmen were killed, together with their two leaders, of whom Evers was buried in the abbey of Melrose, which he had repeatedly plundered, and finally burnt. A great many prisoners were made. One was Thomas Read, an alderman of the city of London, whom we are surprised to meet with in such a predicament. This worthy citizen had, we are informed, refused to pay his share of a benevolence, as it was called, that is, of a sum of money which Henry demanded from the citizens of London. It seems that though the power of the King could not throw the alderman into jail until he paid the money, yet he could force him to serve as a soldier; and there is a letter to Lord Evers, directing that Read should be subjected to all the rigours and hardships of the service, that he might know what soldiers suffered when in the field, and be more ready another time to assist the King with money to pay them. It is to be supposed that the alderman had a large ransom to pay to the Scotsman who had the good luck to get him for a prisoner.

Henry VIII. was highly incensed at this defeat of Lillyard's Edge, or Ancram Moor, as it is frequently called, and vented his displeasure in menaces against the Earl of Angus, notwithstanding their connection by the Earl's marriage with the King's sister. Angus treated the threats of the English monarch with contempt. "Is our royal brother-in-law," he said, "angry with me for being a good Scotsman, and for revenging upon Ralph Evers the destruction of my ancestors' tombs at Melrose? They were better men than Evers, and I could in honour do no less. And will my royal brother-in-law take my life for that? Little does King Henry know the skirts of Cairntable (a mountain near Douglas Castle); I can keep myself there against all his English host."

The truth is, that at no period of their history had the Scottish people ever been more attached to France, and more alienated from England, than now; the proposed match between the young Queen and the English Prince of Wales being generally regarded with an abhorrence which was chiefly owing to the vindictive and furious manner in which Henry conducted the war. Of all the Scottish nobles who had originally belonged to the English party, Lennox alone continued friendly to Henry; and he being obliged to fly into England, the King caused him to marry Lady Margaret Douglas, daughter of his sister Margaret, by her second husband, the Earl of Angus, and of course the King's niece. Their son was the unhappy Henry, Lord Darnley, of whom we shall have much to say hereafter.

The King of France now sent a powerful body of auxiliary troops to the assistance of the Scots, besides considerable supplies of money, which enabled them to retaliate on the English, so that the Borders on both sides were fearfully wasted. A peace at length, in June 1546, ended a war in which both countries suffered severely, without either attaining any decisive advantage.

The Scottish affairs were now managed almost entirely by Cardinal Beaton, a statesman, as we before observed, of great abilities, but a bigoted Catholic, and a man of a severe and cruel temper. He had gained entire influence over the Regent Arran, and had prevailed upon that fickle nobleman to abandon the Protestant doctrines, reconcile himself to the Church of Rome, and consent to the persecution of the heretics, as the Protestants were still called. Many cruelties were exercised; but that which excited public feeling to the highest degree was the barbarous death of George Wishart.

This martyr to the cause of Reformation was a man of honourable birth, great wisdom and eloquence, and of primitive piety. He preached the doctrines of the Reformed religion with zeal and with success, and was for some time protected against the efforts of the vengeful Catholics by the barons who had become converts to the Protestant faith. At length, however, he fell into the hands of the Cardinal, being surrendered to him by Lord Bothwell, and was conveyed to the castle of St. Andrews, a strong fortress and palace belonging to the Cardinal as archbishop, and there thrown into a dungeon. Wishart was then brought to a public trial, for heresy, before the Spiritual Court, where the Cardinal presided. He was accused of preaching heretical doctrine, by two priests, called Lauder and Oliphant, whose outrageous violence was strongly contrasted with the patience and presence of mind shown by the prisoner. He appealed to the authority of the Bible against that of the Church of Rome; but his judges were little disposed to listen to his arguments, and he was condemned to be burnt alive. The place of execution was opposite to the stately castle of the Cardinal, and Beaton himself sat upon the walls, which were hung with tapestry, to behold the death of his heretical prisoner. The spot was also carefully chosen, that the smoke of the pile might be seen as far as possible, to spread the greater terror. Wishart was then brought out, and fastened to a stake with iron chains. He was clad in a buckram garment, and several bags of gunpowder were tied round his body to hasten the operation of the fire. A quantity of fagots were disposed around the pile. While he stood in expectation of his cruel death, he cast his eyes towards his enemy the Cardinal, as he sat on the battlements of the castle, enjoying the dreadful scene.

"Captain," he said to him who commanded the guard, "may God forgive yonder man, who lies so proudly on the wall—within a few days he shall be seen lying there in as much shame as he now shows pomp and vanity."

The pile was then fired, the powder exploded, the flames arose, and Wishart was dismissed by a painful death to a blessed immortality.

Perhaps the last words of Wishart, which seemed to contain a prophetic spirit, incited some men to revenge his death. At any rate, the burning of that excellent person greatly increased the public detestation against the Cardinal, and a daring man stood forth to gratify the general desire, by putting him to death. This was Norman Leslie, called the Master of Rothes, the same who led the men of Fife at the battle of Ancram Moor. It appears, that besides his share of the common hatred to the Cardinal as a persecutor, he had some private feud or cause of quarrel with him. With no more than sixteen men, Leslie undertook to assault the Cardinal in his own castle, amongst his numerous guards and domestics. It chanced that, as many workmen were still employed in labouring upon the fortifications of the castle, the wicket of the castle gate was open early in the morning, to admit them to their work. The conspirators took advantage of this, and obtained possession of the entrance. Having thus gained admittance, they seized upon the domestics of the Cardinal, and turned them one by one out of the castle, then hastened to the Cardinal's chamber, who had fastened the door. He refused them entrance, until they threatened to apply fire, when, learning that Norman Leslie was without, the despairing prelate at length undid the door, and asked for mercy. Melville, one of the conspirators, told him he should only have such mercy as he had extended to George Wishart, and the other servants of God, who had been slain by his orders. He then, with his sword pointed to his breast, bid the Cardinal say his prayers to God, for his last hour was come. The conspirators now proceeded to stab their victim, and afterwards dragged the dead body to the walls, to show it to the citizens of St. Andrews, his clients and dependents, who came in fury to demand what had become of their bishop. Thus his dead body really came to lie with open shame upon the very battlements of his own castle, where he had sat in triumph to behold Wishart's execution.[1]

---

[1] "It may now be pronounced, without fear of contradiction, that the assassination of Beaton was no sudden event, arising simply out of indignation for the fate of Wishart, but an act of long projected murder, encouraged, if not originated, by the English monarch; and, so far as the principal conspirators were concerned, committed from private and mercenary considerations."—TYTLER.

Many persons who disapproved of this most unjustifiable action were yet glad that this proud Cardinal, who had sold the country in some measure to France, was at length removed. Some individuals, who assuredly would not have assisted in the slaughter, joined those who had slain the Cardinal in the defence of the castle. The Regent hastened to besiege the place, which, supplied by England with money, engineers, and provisions, was able to resist the Scottish army for five months. France, however, sent to Scotland a fleet and an army, with engineers better acquainted with the art of attacking strong places than those of the Scottish nation. The castle was, therefore, surrendered. The principal defenders of it were sent to France, and there for some time employed as galley-slaves. The common people made a song upon the event, of which the burden was—

> "Priests, content ye now,
> And, priests, content ye now,
> Since Norman and his company
> Have fill'd the galleys fou."

Shortly after this tragical incident, King Henry VIII. of England died. But his impatient and angry spirit continued to influence the counsels of the nation under the Lord Protector Somerset, who resolved to take the same violent measures to compel the Scots to give their young Queen in marriage to Edward VI., of which Henry had set an example. A chosen and well-disciplined army of eighteen thousand men, well supplied with all necessaries, and supported by an armed fleet, invaded Scotland on the eastern frontier. The Scots assembled a force of almost double the number of the invaders, but, as usual, unaccustomed to act in union together, or to follow the commands of a single general. Nevertheless, the Scottish leaders displayed at the commencement of the campaign some military skill. They posted their army behind the river Esk, near Musselburgh, a village about six miles from Edinburgh, and there seemed determined to await the advance of the English.

The Duke of Somerset, Regent of England, and general of the invading army, was now in a state of difficulty. The Scots were too strongly posted to be attacked with hope of success, and it is probable the English must have retreated with dishonour, had not their enemies, in one of those fits of impatience which caused so many national calamities, abandoned their advantageous position.

Confiding in the numbers of his army, the Scottish Regent (Earl of Arran) crossed the Esk, and thus gave the English the advantage of the ground, they being drawn up on the top of a sloping eminence. The Scots formed in their usual order, a close phalanx. They were armed with broadswords of an admirable form and temper, and a coarse handkerchief was worn in double and triple folds round each man's neck,—"not for cold," says an old historian, "but for cutting." Especially, each man carried a spear eighteen feet long. When drawn up, they stood close together, the first rank kneeling on one knee, and pointing their spears towards the enemy. The ranks immediately behind stooped a little, and the others stood upright, presenting their lances over the heads of their comrades, and holding them with the butt-end placed against their foot, the point opposed to the breast of the enemy. So that the Scottish ranks were so completely defended by the close order in which they stood, and by the length of their lances, that to charge them seemed to be as rash as to oppose your bare hand to a hedgehog's bristles.

The battle began by the English cavalry, under the Lord Gray, rushing upon the close array of the Scots. They stood fast, menacing the horsemen with their pikes, and calling, "Come on, ye heretics!" The charge was dreadful; but as the spears of the English horse were much shorter than those of the Scottish infantry, they had greatly the worst of the encounter, and were beaten off with the loss of many men. The Duke of Somerset commanded Lord Gray to renew the charge, but Gray replied, he might as well bid him charge a castle-wall. By the advice of the Earl of Warwick, a body of archers and musketeers was employed instead of horsemen. The thick order of the Scots exposed them to insufferable loss from the missiles now employed against them, so that the Earl of Angus, who commanded the vanguard, made an oblique movement to avoid the shot; but the main body of the Scots unhappily mistook this movement for a flight, and were thrown into confusion. The van then fled also, and the English horse returning to the attack, and their infantry pressing forward, the victory was gained with very little trouble. The Scots attempted no further resistance, and the slaughter was very great, because the river Esk lay between the fugitives and any place of safety. Their loss was excessive. For more than five miles the fields were covered with the dead, and with the spears, shields, and swords which the flying soldiers had cast away, that they might run the faster. The day was equally disgraceful and disastrous; so that the field of Pinkie, as it was the last great defeat which the Scots received from the English, was also one of the most calamitous. It was fought on 10th September 1547.

It seemed to be decreed in those unhappy national wars, that the English should often be able to win great victories over the Scots, but that they should never derive any permanent advantage from their successes. The battle of Pinkie, far from paving the way to a marriage between Queen Mary and Edward VI., which was the object of Somerset's expedition, irritated and alarmed the Scots to such a degree, that they resolved to prevent the possibility of such a union, by marrying their young mistress with the Dauphin, that is, the eldest son of the King of France, and sending her to be bred up at the French court. A hasty assent of the Scottish Parliament was obtained to this, partly by the influence of gold, partly by the appearance of the French soldiers, partly, according to the reformer Knox, by the menaces of the Lord of Buccleuch, whom he describes as "a bloody man, who swore, with many deadly oaths, that they who would not consent should do what they would like worse."

By the match with France the great object of the English government was rendered unattainable. But the Scots had little occasion for triumph. The union with France, which they so hastily and rashly adopted, brought a new and long series of ruinous consequences upon the country.

Scotland, however, enjoyed the immediate advantage of a considerable auxiliary force of French soldiers, under an officer named D'Essé, who rendered material assistance in recovering several forts and castles which had fallen into the hands of the English after the battle of Pinkie, and in which they had left garrisons. The presence of these armed strangers gave great facilities for carrying into accomplishment the treaty with France. The Regent was gratified by the dukedom of Chatelherault, conferred on him by the French king, with a considerable pension, in order to induce him to consent to the match. The young Queen was embarked on board the French galleys in July 1548, accompanied by four young ladies of quality of her own age, destined to be her playfellows in childhood, and her companions when she grew up. They all bore the same name with their mistress, and were called the Queen's Maries.[1]

The infant Queen being thus transferred to France, her mother, Mary of Guise, the widow of James V., had the address to get herself placed at the head of affairs in Scotland. The Duke of Chatelherault, as we must now term the Earl of Arran, always flexible in his disposition, was prevailed upon to resign the office of Regent which was occupied by the Queen Dowager, who displayed a considerable degree of wisdom and caution in the administration of the kingdom. Most men wondered at the facility with which the Duke of Chatelherault, himself so near in relation to the throne, had given place to Mary of Guise; but none was so much offended as the Duke's natural brother, who had succeeded Beaton as archbishop of St. Andrews. He exclaimed with open indecency against the mean spirit of his brother, who had thus given away the power of Regent, when there was but a "squalling girl" betwixt him and the crown.

The Queen Regent, thus placed in authority, endeavoured to secure herself by diminishing the power of the Scottish nobles, and increasing that of the crown. For this purpose she proposed that a tax should be levied on the country at large, to pay hired soldiers to fight, instead of trusting the defence of the country to the noblemen and their retainers. This proposal was exceedingly ill received by the Scottish Parliament. "We will fight for our families and our country," they said, "better than any hirelings can do—Our fathers did so, and we will follow their example." The Earl of Angus being checked for coming to Parliament with a thousand horse, contrary to a proclamation of the Queen Regent, that none should travel with more than their usual household train, answered jestingly, "That the knaves would not leave him; and that he would be obliged to the Queen, if she could put him on the way of being rid of them, for they consumed his beef and his ale." She had equally bad success when she endeavoured to persuade the Earl to give her up his strong castle of Tantallon, under pretence of

---

[1] The Queen's Maries were four young ladies of high families in Scotland, viz. Livingston, Fleming, Seatoun, and Beatoun. After their return with the Queen to Scotland, one of them became the subject of a tragic ballad, which has

"Yestreen the Queen had four Maries,
The night she'll hae but three."
Sir W. Scott's *Poetical Works*.

putting a garrison there to defend it against the English. At first he answered indirectly, as if he spoke to a hawk which he held on his wrist and was feeding at the time, "The devil," said he, "is in the greedy gled [kite]! Will she never be full?" The Queen, not choosing to take this hint, continued to urge her request about the garrison. "The castle, madam," he replied, "is yours at command; but, by St. Bride of Douglas, I must be the captain, and I will keep it for you as well as any one you will put into it." The other nobles held similar opinions to those of Angus, and would by no means yield to the proposal of levying any hired troops, who, as they feared, might be employed at the pleasure of the Queen Regent to diminish the liberties of the kingdom.

The prevalence of the Protestant doctrines in Scotland strengthened the Scottish nobles in their disposition to make a stand against the Queen Regent's desire to augment her power. Many great nobles, and a still greater proportion of the smaller barons, had embraced the Reformed opinions; and the preaching of John Knox, a man of great courage, zeal, and talents, made converts daily from the Catholic faith.

The Queen Regent, though herself a zealous Catholic, had for some time tolerated, and even encouraged the Protestant party, because they supported her interest against that of the Hamiltons; but a course of politics had been adopted in France, by her brothers of the House of Guise, which occasioned her to change her conduct in this respect.

You may remember that Edward VI. of England succeeded to his father Henry. He adopted the Protestant faith, and completed the Reformation which his father began. But he died early, and was succeeded by his sister Mary of England, daughter of Henry VIII. by his first wife, Catherine of Arragon, whom he divorced under pretext of scruples of conscience. This Mary endeavoured to bring back the Catholic religion, and enforced the laws against heresy with the utmost rigour. Many persons were burnt in her reign, and hence she has been called the Bloody Queen Mary. She died, however, after a short and unhappy reign, and her sister Elizabeth ascended the throne with the general assent of the English nation. The Catholics of foreign countries, however, and particularly those of France, objected to Elizabeth's title to the crown. Elizabeth was Henry's daughter by his second wife, Anne Boleyn. Now, as the Pope had never consented either to the divorce of Queen Catherine, or to the marriage of Anne Boleyn, the Catholics urged that Elizabeth must be considered as illegitimate, and as having, therefore, no lawful right to succeed to the throne, which, as Henry

VIII. had no other child, must, they contended, descend upon Queen
Mary of Scotland, as the grand-daughter of Margaret, Henry's sister,
wife of James IV. of Scotland, and the next lawful heir, according to
their argument, to her deceased grand-uncle.

The court of France, not considering that the English themselves
were to be held the best judges of the title of their own Queen,
resolved, in an evil hour, to put forward this claim of the Scottish
Queen to the English crown. Money was coined, and plate manufac-
tured, in which Mary, with her husband Francis the Dauphin, assumed
the style, title, and armorial bearings of England, as well as Scotland;
and thus laid the first foundation for that deadly hatred between Elizabeth and Mary which, as you will hear by and by, led to such fatal consequences.

Queen Elizabeth, finding France was disposed to challenge her
title to the crown of England, prepared to support it with all the bravery and wisdom of her character. Her first labour was to re-establish
the Reformed religion upon the same footing that Edward VI. had
assigned to it, and to destroy the Roman Catholic establishments,
which her predecessor Mary had endeavoured to replace. As the
Catholics of France and Scotland were her natural enemies, and
attempted to set up the right of Queen Mary as preferable to her own,
so she was sure to find friends in the Protestants of Scotland, who
could not fail to entertain respect, and even affection, for a princess
who was justly regarded as the protectress of the Protestant cause
throughout all Europe.

When, therefore, these changes took place in England, the Queen
Regent, at the instigation of her brothers of the House of Guise, began
once more to persecute the Protestants in Scotland; while their leaders
turned their eyes to Elizabeth for protection, counsel, and assistance;
all of which she was easily disposed to render to a party whose cause
rested on the same grounds with her own. Thus, while France made a
vain pretence of claiming the kingdom of England in the name of Mary,
and appealed for assistance to the English Catholics, Elizabeth far more
effectually increased the internal dissensions of Scotland by espousing
the cause of the Protestants of that country.

These Scottish Protestants no longer consisted solely of a few stu-
dious or reflecting men, whose indulgence in speculation had led them
to adopt peculiar opinions in religion, and who could be dragged
before the spiritual courts, fined, imprisoned, plundered, banished, or

burnt, at pleasure. The Reformed cause had now been adopted by many of the principal nobility; and being the cause, at once, of national religion and legitimate freedom, it was generally embraced by those who were most distinguished for wisdom and public spirit.

Among the converts to the Protestant faith was a natural son of the late King James V., who, being designed for the Church, was at this time called Lord James Stewart, the Prior of St. Andrews, but was afterwards better known by the title of the Earl of Murray. He was a young nobleman of great parts, brave and skilful in war, and in peace a lover of justice, and a friend to the liberties of his country. His wisdom, good moral conduct, and the zeal he expressed for the Reformed religion, occasioned his being the most active person amongst the Lords of the Congregation, as the leaders of the Protestant party were now called.

The Queen Regent, more in compliance with the wishes of her brothers than her own inclination, which was gentle and moderate, began the quarrel by commanding the Protestant preachers to be summoned to a court of justice at Stirling, on 10th May 1599; but such a concourse of friends and favourers attended them, that the Queen was glad to put a stop to the trial, on condition that they should not enter the town. Yet she broke this promise, and had them proclaimed outlaws for not appearing, although they had been stopped by her own command. Both parties then prepared for hostilities; and an incident happened which heightened their animosity, while it gave to the course of the Reformation a peculiar colour of zealous passion.

The Protestants had made Perth their headquarters, where they had already commenced the public exercise of their religion. John Knox, whose eloquence gave him great influence with the people, had pronounced a vehement sermon against the sin of idolatry, in which he did not spare those reproaches which the Queen Regent deserved for her late breach of faith. When his discourse was finished, and while the minds of the hearers were still agitated by its effects, a friar produced a little glass case, or tabernacle, containing the images of saints, which he required the bystanders to worship. A boy who was present exclaimed, "That was gross and sinful idolatry!" The priest, as incautious in his passion as ill-timed in his devotion, struck the boy a blow; and the lad, in revenge, threw a stone, which broke one of the images. Immediately all the people began to cast stones, not only at the images, but at the fine painted windows, and, finally, pulled down the altars, defaced the ornaments of the church, and nearly destroyed the whole building.

The multitude next resolved to attack the splendid convent of the Carthusians. The Prior had prepared for defence; his garrison consisted of the Highland tenants belonging to some lands which the convent possessed in the district of Athole. These men were determined to make the most of the occasion, and demanded, that since they were asked to expose their lives for the good of the Church, they should be assured, that if they were killed, their families should retain possession of the lands which they themselves enjoyed. The Prior impolitically refused their request. They next demanded refreshments and good liquor, to encourage them to fight. But nothing was served out to them by the sordid churchman excepting salted salmon and thin drink; so that they had neither heart nor will to fight when it came to the push, and made little defence against the multitude, by whom the stately convent was entirely destroyed.

The example of the Reformers in Perth was followed in St. Andrews and other places; and we have to regret that many beautiful buildings fell a sacrifice to the fury of the lower orders, and were either totally destroyed or reduced to piles of shapeless ruins.

The Reformers of the better class did not countenance these extremities, although the common people had some reason for the line of violence they pursued, besides their own natural inclination to tumultuary proceedings. One great point in which the Catholics and Protestants differed was, that the former reckoned the churches as places hallowed and sacred in their own character, which it was a highly meritorious duty to ornament and adorn with every species of studied beauty of architecture. The Scottish Protestants, on the contrary, regarded them as mere buildings of stone and lime, having no especial claim to respect when the divine service was finished. The defacing, therefore, and even destroying, the splendid Catholic churches, seemed to the early Reformers the readiest mode of testifying their zeal against the superstitions of Popery. There was a degree of policy in pulling down the abbeys and monasteries, with the cells and lodgings made for the accommodation of the monks. "The true way to banish the rooks," said John Knox, "is to pull down their nests, and the rooks will fly off." But this maxim did not apply to the buildings used for public worship. Respecting these at least, it would have been better to have followed the example of the citizens of Glasgow, who drew out in arms when the multitude were about to destroy the High Church of that city, and, while they agreed with the more zealous in removing all the emblems of Popish worship, insisted that the building itself should remain uninjured, and be applied to the uses of a Protestant church.

On the whole, however, though many fine buildings were destroyed in Scotland, in the first fury of the Reformation, it is better that the country should have lost these ornaments than that they should have been preserved entire, with the retention of the corrupt and superstitious doctrines which had been taught in them.

The demolition of the churches and sacred buildings augmented the Queen Regent's displeasure against the Lords of the Congregation, and at length both parties took the field. The Protestant nobles were at the head of their numerous followers; the Queen chiefly relied upon a small but select body of French troops. The war was not very violently carried on, for the side of the Reformers became every day stronger. The Duke of Chatelherault, the first nobleman in Scotland, a second time espoused the cause of the Congregation; and Maitland of Lethington, one of the wisest statesmen in the kingdom, took the same course. At the same time, although the Lords found it easy to bring together large bodies of men, yet they had not the money or means necessary to keep them together for a long time, while the French veteran soldiers were always ready to take advantage when the Reformed leaders were obliged to diminish their forces. Their difficulties became greater when the Queen Regent showed her design to fortify strongly the town of Leith and the adjacent island of Inchkeith, and place her French soldiers in garrison there; so that, being in possession of that seaport, she might at all times, when she saw occasion, introduce an additional number of foreigners.

Unskilled in the art of conducting sieges, and totally without money, the Lords of the Congregation had recourse to the assistance of England: and for the first time an English fleet and army approached the territories of Scotland by sea and land, not with the purpose of invasion, as used to be the case of old, but to assist the nation in its resistance to the arms of France, and the religion of Rome.

The English army was soon joined by the Scottish Lords of the Congregation, and advancing to Leith, laid siege to the town, which was most valorously defended by the French soldiers, who displayed a degree of ingenuity in their defence, which for a long time resisted every effort of the besiegers. They were, however, blockaded by the English fleet, so that no provisions could be received by sea; and on

land being surrounded by a considerable army, provisions became so
scarce that they were obliged to feed upon horse-flesh.

In the meantime their mistress, the Queen Regent, had retired into
the castle of Edinburgh, where grief, fatigue, and disappointed expec-
tations, threw her into an illness, of which she died on 10th of June
1560. The French troops in Leith being now reduced to extremity,
Francis and Mary determined upon making peace in Scotland at the
expense of most important concessions to the Reformed party. They
agreed that, instead of naming a new Regent, the administration of
affairs should be conferred upon a council of government chosen by
Parliament; they passed an act of indemnity, as it is called, that is, an
act pardoning all offences committed during these wars; and they left
the subject of religion to be disposed of as the Parliament should determine, which was, in fact, giving the full power to the Reformed party.
All foreign troops, on both sides, were to be withdrawn accordingly.

England, and especially Queen Elizabeth, gained a great point by
this treaty, for it recognised, in express terms, the title of that princess
to the throne of England; and Francis and Mary bound themselves to
lay aside all claim to that kingdom, together with the arms and
emblems of English sovereignty which they had assumed and borne.

The Parliament of Scotland being assembled, it was soon seen that
the Reformers possessed the power and inclination to direct all its resolutions upon the subject of religion. They condemned unanimously
the whole fabric of Popery, and adopted, instead of the doctrines of the
Church of Rome, the tenets contained in a confession, or avowal of
faith, drawn up by the most popular of the Protestant divines. Thus the
whole religious constitution of the Church was at once altered.

There was one particular in which the Scottish Reformers greatly
differed from those of England. The English monarch, who abolished
the power of the Pope, had established that of the crown as the visible
Head of the Church of England. The meaning of this phrase is, not that
the King has the power of altering the religious doctrines of the
Church, but only that he should be the chief of the government in
Church affairs, as he was always in those of the State. On the contrary,
the Reformed ministers of Scotland renounced the authority of any
interference of the civil magistrate, whether subject or sovereign, in the
affairs of the Church, declaring it should be under the exclusive direction of a court of delegates chosen from its own members, assisted by a
certain number of the laity, forming what is called a General Assembly

of the Church. The Scottish Reformers disclaimed also the division of the clergy into the various ranks of bishops, deans, prebendaries, and other classes of the clerical order. They discarded this subordination of ranks, though retained in the English Protestant Church, maintaining that each clergyman entrusted with a charge of souls was upon a level in every respect with the rest of his brethren. They reprobated, in particular, the order of bishops, as holding a place in the National Council, or Parliament; and asserted, that meddling in secular affairs was in itself improper for their office, and naturally led to the usurpation over men's consciences, which had been the chief abomination of the Church of Rome. The laity of Scotland, and particularly the great nobility, saw with pleasure the readiness of the ministers to resign all those pretensions to worldly rank and consequence, which had been insisted upon by the Roman Catholic clergy, and made their self-denying abjuration of titles and worldly business a reason for limiting the subsistence which they were to derive from the funds of the Church, to the smallest possible sum of annual stipend, whilst they appropriated the rest to themselves without scruple.

It remained to dispose of the wealth lately enjoyed by the Catholic clergy, who were supposed to be possessed of half of the revenue of Scotland, so far as it arose from land. Knox and the other Reformed clergy had formed a plan for the decent maintenance of a National Church out of these extensive funds, and proposed, that what might be deemed more than sufficient for this purpose should be expended upon hospitals, schools, universities, and places of education. But the Lords, who had seized the revenues of the Church, were determined not to part with the spoil they had obtained; and those whom the preachers had found most active in destroying Popery were wonderfully cold when it was proposed to them to surrender the lands they had seized upon for their own use. The plan of John Knox was, they said, a "devout imagination," a visionary scheme, which showed the goodness of the preacher's intentions, but which it was impossible to carry into practice. In short, they retained by force the greater part of the Church revenues for their own advantage.

When Francis and Mary, who had now become King and Queen of France, heard that the Scottish Parliament had totally altered the religion, and changed the forms of the National Church from Catholic to Protestant, they were extremely angry; and had the King lived, it is most likely they would have refused to consent to this great innovation, and preferred rekindling the war by sending a new army of French into Scotland. But if they meditated such a measure, it was entirely prevented by the death of Francis II., on the 5th of December 1560.

During her husband's life, Mary had exercised a great authority in France, for she possessed unbounded influence over his mind. After his death, and the accession of Charles his brother, that influence and authority ceased. It must have been painful to a lofty mind like Mary's thus to endure coldness and neglect in the place where she had met with honour and obedience. She retired, therefore, from the court of France, and determined to return to her native kingdom of Scotland; a resolution most natural in itself, but which became the introduction to a long and melancholy tale of misfortunes.

XXX

A Good Start

1560-1565

Mary Stewart, the Queen Dowager of France and the hereditary Queen of Scotland, was accounted the most beautiful and accomplished woman of her time. Her countenance was lovely; she was tall, well-formed, elegant in all her motions, skilled in the exercises of riding and dancing, and possessed of all the female accomplishments which were in fashion at that period. Her education in France had been carefully attended to, and she had profited by the opportunities of instruction she enjoyed. She was mistress of several languages, and understood state-affairs, in which her husband had often followed her advice. The beauty of Mary was enhanced by her great condescension, and by the good-humour and gaiety which she sometimes carried to the verge of excess. Her youth, for she was only eighteen when she returned to Scotland, increased the liveliness of her disposition. The Catholic religion, in which she had been strictly educated, was a great blemish in the eyes of her people; but on the whole the nation expected her return with more hope and joy than Mary herself entertained at the thought of exchanging the fine climate of France, and the gaieties of its court, for the rough tempests and turbulent politics of her native country.

Mary set sail from France 15th August 1561. The English fleet was at sea, and there is great reason to believe that it had a purpose of intercepting the Queen of Scots, as a neighbour whose return was dreaded by Elizabeth. Occupied with anxious forebodings, the Queen remained on the deck of her galley, gazing on the coasts of France. Morning found her in the same occupation; and when they vanished from her eyes, she exclaimed in sorrow, "Farewell, farewell, happy France; I shall never see thee more!"

She passed the English fleet under cover of a mist, and arrived at Leith on the 19th August, where little or no preparation had been made for her honourable reception. Such of the nobles as were in the capital hastened, however, to wait upon their young Queen, and convey her to Holyrood, the palace of her ancestors. Horses were provided to bring her and her train to Edinburgh; but they were wretched ponies, and had such tattered furniture and accoutrements that poor Mary, when she thought of the splendid palfreys and rich appointments at the court of France, could not forbear shedding tears. The people were, however, in their way, rejoiced to see her; and about two hundred citizens of Edinburgh, each doing his best upon a three-stringed fiddle, played under her window all night, by way of welcome, a noisy serenade, which deprived her of sleep after her fatigue. She took it as it was meant, nevertheless, and expressed her thanks to the perpetrators of this mistuned and mistimed concert. Mary had immediately after her arrival a specimen of the religious zeal of her Reformed subjects. She had ordered mass to be performed by a Popish ecclesiastic in her own chapel, but the popular indignation was so much excited, that but for the interference of her natural brother, the Prior of St. Andrews, the priest would have been murdered on his own altar.

Mary behaved with admirable prudence at this early period of her reign. She enchanted the common people by her grace and condescension, and while she sate in council, usually employed in some female work, she gained credit for her wisdom among the statesmen whom she consulted. She was cautious of attempting anything contrary to the religion of her subjects, though different from her own; and guided by the advice of the Prior of St. Andrews, and of the sagacious Maitland, she made rapid progress in the affections of her people. She conferred on the Prior of St. Andrews, who had given up thoughts of the Church, the title and the earldom of Mar, which had been frequently bestowed on branches of the royal family.

With similar prudence, the Queen maintained all the usual intercourse of civility with Elizabeth; and while she refused to abandon her title to the crown of England, in the case of Elizabeth dying without heirs of her body, she expressed her anxious wish to live on the best terms with her sister sovereign, and her readiness to relinquish, during the life of the English Queen, any right of inheritance to the English crown which she might possess to her prejudice. Elizabeth was silenced, if not satisfied: and there continued to be a constant communication of apparent friendship between the two sovereigns, and an exchange of letters, compliments, and occasionally of presents, becoming their rank, with much profession of mutual kindness.

But there was one important class of persons to whom Mary's form of religion was so obnoxious that they could not be gained to any favourable thoughts of her. These were the preachers of the Reformed faith, who, recollecting Mary's descent from the family of Guise, always hostile to the Protestant cause, exclaimed against the Queen, even in the pulpit, with an indecent violence unfitting that place, and never spoke of her but as one hardened in resistance to the voice of true Christian instruction. John Knox himself introduced such severe expressions into his sermons, that Queen Mary condescended to expostulate with him personally, and to exhort him to use more mild language in the discharge of his duty. Nevertheless, though the language of these rough Reformers was too vehement, and though their harshness was impolitic, as tending unnecessarily to increase the Queen's dislike of them and their form of religion, it must be owned that their suspicions of Mary's sincerity were natural, and in all probability well founded. The Queen uniformly declined to ratify the religious system adopted by the Parliament in 1560, or the confiscation of the Church lands. She always seemed to consider the present state of things as a temporary arrangement, to which she was indeed willing to submit for the time, but with the reservation that it should be subjected to alterations when there was a fitting opportunity. Her brother, the newly-created Earl of Mar, however, who was at this time her principal counsellor, and her best friend, used his influence with the Protestant clergy in her behalf; some coldness in consequence arose between him and John Knox, which continued for more than a year.

The first troublesome affair in Queen Mary's reign seems to have arisen from her attachment to this brother and his interest. She had created him Earl of Mar, as we have said; but it was her purpose to confer on him, instead of this title, that of Earl of Murray, and with it great part of the large estates belonging to that northern earldom, which had become vested in the crown after the extinction of the heirs of the celebrated Thomas Randolph, who enjoyed it in the reign of the great Robert Bruce. The earldom of Murray had afterwards been held by a brother of the Earl of Douglas, but had again been forfeited to the crown on the fall of that great family in James the Second's time.

This exchange, however, could not be made, without giving offence to the Earl of Huntly, often mentioned as head of the most powerful family in the North, who had possessed himself of a considerable part of those domains which had belonged to the earldom of Murray. This Earl of Huntly was a brave man, and possessed of very great power in the Northern counties. He was one of the few remaining peers who continued attached to the Catholic religion, and, after the family of Hamilton, was the nearest in connection to the royal family.

It was believed, that if the Queen, instead of coming to Leith, had landed at Aberdeen, and declared herself determined to reinstate the Catholic religion, the Earl would have joined her with twenty thousand men for accomplishing that purpose. Mary, however, declined this proposal, which must have had the immediate consequence of producing a great civil war. The Earl of Huntly was, therefore, considered as hostile to the present government, and to the Earl of Mar, who had the principal management of affairs; and it was to be supposed, that possessed as Huntly was of great power, and a very numerous body of dependents and retainers, he would not willingly surrender to his political enemy any part of the domains which he possessed belonging to the earldom of Murray.

The Earl of Mar was, on his part, determined to break the strength of this great opponent; and Queen Mary, who appears also to have feared Huntly's power, and the use which he seemed disposed to make of it, undertook a personal journey to the north of Scotland, to enforce obedience to her commands. About the same time, Sir John Gordon, the Earl of Huntly's son, committed some feudal outrage, for which he was sentenced to temporary confinement. This punishment, though slight, was felt as another mark of disfavour to the house of Gordon, and increased the probability of their meditating resistance. It is difficult, or rather impossible, to say whether there were good grounds for suspecting Huntly of entertaining serious views to take arms against the crown. But his conduct was, to say the least, incautious and suspicious.

The young Queen advanced northward at the head of a small army, encamping in the fields, or accepting such miserable lodgings as the houses of the smaller gentry afforded. It was, however, a scene which awoke her natural courage, and, marching at the head of her soldiery, such was her spirit, that she publicly wished she had been a man, to sleep all night in the fields, and to walk armed with a jack and skull-cap of steel, a good Glasgow buckler at her back, and a broadsword by her side.

Huntly seems to have been surprised by the arrival of his sovereign, and undecided what to do. While he made all offers of submission, and endeavoured to prevail on the Queen to visit his house as that of a dutiful subject, a party of his followers refused her admission into the royal castle of Inverness, and attempted to defend that fortress against her. They were, however, compelled to surrender, and the governor was executed for treason.

Meantime, Sir John Gordon escaped from the prison to which the Queen had sentenced him, and placed himself at the head of the vassals of his house, who were now rising in every direction; while his father, the Earl of Huntly, considering the Queen as guided entirely by his enemy, the Earl of Mar, at length assumed arms in person.

Huntly easily assembled a considerable host, and advanced towards Aberdeen. The purpose of his enterprise was, perhaps, such as Buccleuch had entertained at the field of Melrose, —an attack rather upon the Queen's counsellors than on her person. But her brother, who had now exchanged his title of Mar for that of Murray, was as brave and as successful as Angus upon the former occasion, with this advantage, that he enjoyed the confidence of his sovereign. He was, however, in a state of great difficulty. The men on whom he could with certainty rely were few, being only those whom he had brought from the midland counties. He summoned, indeed, the northern barons in his neighbourhood, and they came; but with doubtful intentions, full of awe for the house of Gordon, and probably with the private resolution of being guided by circumstances.

Murray, who was an excellent soldier, drew up the men he could trust on an eminence called the hill of Fare, near Corrichie. He did not allow the northern clans to mix their doubtful succours with this resolute battalion, and the event showed the wisdom of his precaution.

Huntly approached, and encountered the northern troops, his allies and neighbours, who offered little or no resistance. They fled tumultuously towards Murray's main body, pursued by the Gordons, who threw away their spears, drew their swords, and advanced in disorder, as to an assured victory. In this tumult they encountered the resistance of Murray's firm battalion of spearmen, who received the attack in close order, and with determined resolution. The Gordons were repulsed in their turn; and those clans who had before fled, seeing they were about to lose the day, returned with sprigs of heather in their caps, which they used to distinguish them, fell upon the Gordons, and completed Murray's victory. Huntly, a bulky man, and heavily armed, fell from horseback in the flight, and was trodden to death, or, as others say, died afterwards of a broken heart. This battle was fought 28th October 1562. The body of Huntly, a man lately esteemed one of the bravest, wisest, and most powerful in Scotland, was afterwards brought into a court of justice, meanly arrayed in a doublet of coarse canvas, that the sentence of a traitor might be pronounced over the senseless corpse.

Sir John Gordon, the son of the vanquished Earl, was beheaded at Aberdeen, three days after the battle. Murray was placed in possession of the estates belonging to his new earldom, and the Queen returned, after having struck general terror into the minds of such barons as were thought refractory, by the activity of her measures, and the success of her arms.

Thus far the reign of Mary had been eminently prosperous; but a fatal crisis approached, which was eventually to plunge her into the utmost misery. She had no children by her deceased husband, the King of France, and her subjects were desirous that she should marry a second husband, a purpose which she herself entertained and encouraged. It was necessary, or politic at least, to consult Queen Elizabeth on the subject. That princess had declared her own resolution never to marry, and if she should keep this determination, Mary of Scotland was the next heir to the English crown. In expectation of this rich and splendid inheritance, it was both prudent and natural, that in forming a new marriage, Mary should desire to have the advice and approbation of the princess to whose realm she or her children might hope to succeed, especially if she could retain her favour.

Elizabeth of England was one of the wisest and most sagacious Queens that ever wore a crown, and the English to this day cherish her memory with well-deserved respect and attachment. But her conduct towards her kinswoman Mary, from beginning to end, indicated a degree of envy and deceit totally unworthy of her general character. Determined herself not to marry, it seems to have been Elizabeth's desire to prevent Mary also from doing so, lest she should see before her a lineage, not her own, ready to occupy her throne immediately after her death. She therefore adopted a mean and shuffling policy, recommending one match after another to her kinswoman, but throwing in obstacles whenever any of them seemed likely to take place. At first she appeared desirous that Mary should marry the Earl of Leicester, a nobleman, whom, though by no means distinguished by talents or character, she herself admired so much for his personal beauty as to say that, except for her vow never to marry, she would have chosen him for her own husband. It may be readily believed, that she had no design such a match as she hinted at should ever take place, and that if Mary had expressed any readiness to accept of Leicester, Elizabeth would have found ready means to break off the marriage.

This proposal, however, was not at all agreeable to Queen Mary. Leicester, if his personal merit had been much greater, was of too low a rank to pretend to the hand of a Queen of Scotland, and Queen Dowager of France, to whom the most powerful monarchs in Europe were at the same time paying suit.

The Archduke Charles, third son of the Emperor of Germany, was proposed on one side; the hereditary Prince of Spain was offered on another; the Duke of Anjou, who became afterwards Henry II. of France, also presented himself. But if Mary had accepted the hand of a foreign prince, she would in so doing have resigned her chance of succeeding to the English crown: nay, considering the jealousy of her Protestant subjects, she might have endangered her possession of that of Scotland. She was so much impressed by these considerations, that she went so far as to intimate that she might consent to the match with the Earl of Leicester, provided that Elizabeth would recognise her as next heir to the English crown, in case of her own decease without children. This, however, did not suit Elizabeth's policy. She did not desire Mary to be wedded to any one, far less to Leicester, her own personal favourite; and was therefore extremely unlikely to declare her sentiments upon the succession (a subject on which she always observed the most mysterious silence), in order to bring about the union of her rival with the man she herself preferred.

Meantime the views of Queen Mary turned towards a young nobleman of high birth, nearly connected both with her own family and that of Elizabeth. This was Henry Stewart Lord Darnley, eldest son of the Earl of Lennox. You may recollect that, after the battle of Flodden, the Earl of Angus married the Queen Dowager of Scotland; and, in the tumults which followed, was compelled to retire for a season to London. While Angus resided in England, his wife bore him a daughter, called Lady Margaret Douglas, who, when her parents returned to Scotland, continued to remain at the English court, under the protection of her uncle, King Henry. Again you must remember that during the regency of the Duke of Chatelherault, the Earl of Lennox attempted to place himself at the head of the English party in Scotland; but his efforts failing through want of power or of conduct, he also was compelled to retire to England, where Henry VIII., in acknowledgment of his unavailing aid, bestowed on him the hand of his niece, Lady Margaret Douglas, who, in right of her mother Margaret, had a claim of inheritance to the English crown.

The young Lord Darnley's father being of such high rank, and his parents having such pretensions, Mary imagined that in marrying him she would gratify the wishes of Elizabeth, who seemed to point out, though ambiguously, a native of Britain, and one not of royal rank, as her safest choice, and as that which would be most agreeable to herself. Elizabeth seemed to receive the proposal favourably, and suffered the young man, and his father Lennox, to visit the court of Scotland, in the hope that their presence might embroil matters further; and thinking that, in case the match should be likely to take place, she might easily break it off by recalling them as her subjects; a command which she supposed they would not dare to disobey, as enjoying all their lands and means of living in England.

Young Darnley was remarkably tall and handsome, perfect in all external and showy accomplishments, but unhappily destitute of sagacity, prudence, steadiness of character, and exhibiting only doubtful courage, though extremely violent in his passions. Had this young man possessed a very moderate portion of sense, or even of gratitude, we might have had a different story to tell of Mary's reign—as it was, you will hear a very melancholy one. Mary had the misfortune to look upon this young nobleman with partiality, and was the more willing to gratify her own inclinations in his favour, that she longed to put an end to the intrigues by which Queen Elizabeth had endeavoured to impose upon her, and prevent her marriage. Indeed, while the two queens used towards each other the language of the most affectionate cordiality, there was betwixt them neither plain dealing nor upright meaning, but great dissimulation, envy, and fear.

Darnley, in the meantime, endeavouring to strengthen the interest which he had acquired in the Queen's affections, had recourse to the friendship of a man, of low rank, indeed, but who was understood to possess particular influence over the mind of Mary. This was an Italian of humble origin, called David Rizzio, who had been promoted from being a menial in the Queen's family, to the confidential office of French secretary. His talents for music gave him frequent admission to Mary's presence, as she delighted in that art; and his address and arts of insinuation gained him a considerable influence over her mind. It was almost necessary that the Queen should have near her person some confidential officer, skilled at once in languages and in business, through whom she might communicate with foreign states, and with her friends in France in particular. No such agent was likely to be found in Scotland, unless she had chosen a Catholic priest, which would have given more offence to her Protestant subjects than even the employment of a man like Rizzio. Still the elevation of this person, a stranger, a Catholic, and a man of mean origin, to the rank of a minister of the crown—and, yet more, the personal familiarity to which the Queen condescended to admit him, and the airs of importance which this low-born foreigner pretended to assume, became the subject of offence to the proud Scottish nobles, and of vulgar scandal among the common people.

Darnley, anxious to strengthen his interest with the Queen on every hand, formed an intimacy with Rizzio, who employed all the arts of flattery and observance to gain possession of his favour, and unquestionably was serviceable to him in advancing his suit. The Queen, in the meanwhile, exerted herself to remove the obstacles to her union with Darnley, and with such success, that, with the approbation of far the greater part of her subjects, they were married at Edinburgh on the 29th July 1565.

XXXI

Foul Play

1565-1567

WHEN Elizabeth received news that this union was determined upon, she gave way to all the weakness of an envious woman. She remonstrated against the match, though, in fact, Mary could scarcely have made a choice less dangerous to England. She recalled Lennox and his son Darnley from Scotland—a mandate which they refused, or delayed, to obey. She committed the Countess of Lennox, the only one of the family within her reach, a prisoner to the Tower of London. Above all, she endeavoured to disturb the peace of Scotland, and the government of Mary and her new husband, by stirring up to insurrection those among the Scottish nobility to whom the match with Darnley was distasteful.

The Queen's brother, the Earl of Murray, was by far the most able and powerful of those who were displeased by Mary's marriage. Darnley and he were personal enemies; and besides, Murray was the principal of the Lords of the Congregation, who affected to see danger to the Protestant religion in Mary's choice of Darnley for a husband, and in the disunion which it was likely to create betwixt Scotland and England. Murray even laid a plan to intercept Darnley, seize his person, and either put him to death, or send him prisoner to England. A body of horse was for this purpose stationed at a pass under the hill of Bennarty, near Kinross, called the Parrot-well, to intercept the Queen and Darnley as they returned from a Convention of Estates held at Perth; and they only escaped the danger by a hasty march, commenced early in the morning.

After the marriage, Murray and his confederates, who were the Duke of Chatelherault, Glencairn, Argyle, Rothes, and others, actually took up arms. The Queen, in this emergency, assembled her subjects around her. They came in such numbers as showed her popularity. Darnley rode at their head in gilded armour, accompanied by the Queen herself, having loaded pistols at her saddle-bow. Unable to stand their ground, Murray and his accomplices eluded the pursuit of the royal army, and made a sudden march on Edinburgh, where they hoped to find friends. But the citizens not adopting their cause, and the castle threatening to fire on them, the insurgents were compelled to retreat, first to Hamilton, then to Dumfries, until they finally disbanded their forces in despair, and the leaders fled into England. Thus ended an insurrection which, from the hasty and uncertain manner in which the conspirators posted from one part of the kingdom to another, obtained the popular name of the Run-about Raid (or ride).

Elizabeth, who had encouraged Murray and his associates to rise against Mary, was by no means desirous to have the discredit of having done so, when she saw their attempt was unsuccessful. She caused Murray and the Abbot of Kilwinning to appear before her in presence of the ambassadors of France and Spain, who, interfering in Mary's behalf, had accused Elizabeth of fomenting the Scottish disturbances. "How say you," she exclaimed, "my Lord of Murray, and you his companion? Have you had advice or encouragement from me in your late undertaking?" The exiles, afraid to tell the truth, were contented to say, however falsely, that they had received no advice or assistance at her hands. "There you indeed speak truth," replied Elizabeth; "for neither did I, nor any in my name, stir you up against your Queen; your abominable treason may serve for example to my own subjects to rebel against me. Therefore get out of my presence; you are but unworthy traitors!" Mortified and disgraced, Murray and his companions again retired to the Border, where Queen Elizabeth, notwithstanding her pretended resentment, allowed them privately means of support, until times should permit them to return into Scotland, and renew disturbances there.

Mary had thus overcome her refractory subjects, but she soon found that she had a more formidable enemy in the foolish and passionate husband whom she had chosen. This headstrong young man behaved to his wife with great disrespect, both as a woman and as a queen, and gave himself up to intoxication, and other disgraceful vices. Although already possessed of more power than fitted his capacity or age, for he was but nineteen, he was importunate in his demands for obtaining what was called in Scotland the Crown Matrimonial; that is, the full equality of royal right in the crown with his consort. Until he obtained this eminence he was not held to be King, though called so in courtesy. He was only the husband of the Queen.

This crown matrimonial had been bestowed on Mary's first husband, Francis, and Darnley was determined to be possessed of the same rank. But Mary, whose bounty had already far exceeded his deserts, as well as his gratitude, was resolved not to make this last concession, at least without the advice and consent of the Parliament.

The childish impatience of Darnley made him regard with mortal hatred whatever interfered with the instant execution of his wishes; and his animosity on this occasion turned against the Italian secretary, once his friend, but whom he now esteemed his deadly foe, because he supposed that Rizzio encouraged the Queen in resisting his hasty ambition. His resentment against the unhappy stranger arose to such a height, that he threatened to poniard him with his own hand; and as Rizzio had many enemies, and no friends save his mistress, Darnley easily procured instruments, and those of no mean rank, to take the execution of his revenge on themselves.

The chief of Darnley's accomplices, on this unhappy occasion, was James Douglas, Earl of Morton, chancellor of the kingdom, tutor and uncle to the Earl of Angus (who chanced then to be a minor), and administrator, therefore, of all the power of the great house of Douglas. He was a nobleman of high military talent and great political wisdom; but although a pretender to sanctity of life, his actions show him to have been a wicked and unscrupulous man. Notwithstanding he was chancellor of the kingdom, and therefore bound peculiarly to respect the laws, he did not hesitate to enter into the young King's cruel and unlawful purpose. Lord Ruthven too, whose frame was exhausted by illness, nevertheless undertook to buckle on his armour for the enterprise; and they had no difficulty in finding other agents.

It would have been easy to have seized on Rizzio, and disposed of

him as the Scottish peers at the bridge of Lauder used the favourites of
James III. But this would not have accomplished the revenge of Darnley, who complained that the Queen showed this mean Italian more
civility than she did to himself, and therefore took the barbarous resolution of seizing him in her very presence.

While this savage plot was forming, Rizzio received several hints of
what was likely to happen. Sir James Melville was at pains to explain to
him the danger that was incurred by a stranger in any country, who
rose so high in the favour of the prince, as to excite the disgust of the
natives of the land. A French priest, who was something of an
astrologer, warned the secretary to beware of a bastard. To such counsels, he replied, "That the Scots were more given to threaten than to
strike; and as for the bastard (by whom he supposed the Earl of Murray
to be meant), he would take care that he should never possess power
enough in Scotland to do him any harm." Thus securely confident, he
continued at court, to abide his fate.

Those lords who engaged in the conspiracy did not agree to gratify
Darnley's resentment against Rizzio for nothing. They stipulated, as the
price of their assistance, that he should in turn aid them in obtaining
pardon and restoration to favour for Murray, and his accomplices in
the Run-about Raid; and intimation was despatched to these noblemen, apprising them of the whole undertaking, and desiring them to
be at Edinburgh on the night appointed for doing the deed.

Queen Mary, like her father, James V., was fond of laying aside the
state of a sovereign, and indulging in small private parties, quiet, as she
termed them, and merry. On these occasions, she admitted her
favourite domestics to her table, and Rizzio seems frequently to have
had that honour. On the 9th of March 1566 six persons had partaken
of supper in a small cabinet adjoining to the Queen's bedchamber, and
having no entrance save through it. Rizzio was of the number. About
seven in the evening, the gates of the palace were occupied by Morton,
with a party of two hundred men; and a select band of the conspirators, headed by Darnley himself, came into the Queen's apartment by a
secret staircase. Darnley first entered the cabinet, and stood for an
instant in silence, gloomily eyeing his victim. Lord Ruthven followed in
complete armour, looking pale and ghastly, as one scarcely recovered
from long sickness. Others crowded in after them, till the little closet
was full of armed men. While the Queen demanded the purpose of
their coming, Rizzio, who saw that his life was aimed at, got behind

her, and clasped the folds of her gown, that the respect due to her person might protect him. The assassins threw down the table, and seized on the unfortunate object of their vengeance, while Darnley himself took hold of the Queen, and forced Rizzio and her asunder. It was their intention, doubtless, to have dragged Rizzio out of Mary's presence, and to have killed him elsewhere; but their fierce impatience hurried them into instant murder. George Douglas, called the postulate of Arbroath, a natural brother of the Earl of Morton, set the example, by snatching Darnley's dagger from his belt, and striking Rizzio with it. He received many other blows. They dragged him through the bedroom and antechamber, and despatched him at the head of the staircase, with no less than fifty-six wounds. Ruthven, after all was over, fatigued with his exertions, sat down in the Queen's presence, and, begging her pardon for the liberty, called for a drink to refresh him, as if he had been doing the most harmless thing in the world.

The witnesses, the actors, and the scene of this cruel tragedy, render it one of the most extraordinary which history records. The cabinet and the bedroom still remain in the same condition in which they were at the time; and the floor near the head of the stair bears visible marks of the blood of the unhappy Rizzio. The Queen continued to beg his life with prayers and tears; but when she learned that he was dead, she dried her tears.—"I will now," she said, "study revenge."

The conspirators, who had committed the cruel action entirely or chiefly to gratify Darnley, reckoned themselves, of course, secure of his protection. They united themselves with Murray and his associates, who were just returned from England according to appointment, and agreed upon a course of joint measures. The Queen, it was agreed, should be put under restraint in Edinburgh Castle, or elsewhere; and Murray and Morton were to rule the state under the name of Darnley, who was to obtain the crown matrimonial, which he had so anxiously desired. But all this scheme was ruined by the defection of Darnley himself. As fickle as he was vehement, and as timorous as he had shown himself cruel, Rizzio was no sooner slain than Darnley became terrified at what had been done, and seemed much disposed to deny having given any authority for the crime.

Finding her weak-minded husband in a state between remorse and fear, Mary prevailed on him to take part against the very persons whom he had instigated to the late atrocious proceeding. Darnley and Mary escaped together out of Holyrood House, and fled to Dunbar, where the Queen issued a proclamation which soon drew many faithful followers around her. It was now the turn of the conspirators to tremble. That the Queen's conquest over them might be more certain, she pardoned the Earl of Murray, and those concerned in the Run-about Raid, as guilty of more venial offences than the assassins of Rizzio; and thus Murray, Glencairn, and others, were received into favour, while Morton, Ruthven, and his comrades fled in their turn to England. No Scottish subject, whatever his crime, could take refuge there without finding secret support, if not an open welcome. Such was Elizabeth's constant policy.

Queen Mary was now once more in possession of authority, but much disturbed and vexed by the silly conduct of her husband, whose absurdities and insolences were not abated by the consequences of Rizzio's death; so that the royal pair continued to be upon the worst terms with each other, though disguised under a species of reconciliation.

On the 19th of June 1566 Mary was delivered of a son, afterwards James VI. When news of this event reached London, Queen Elizabeth was merrily engaged in dancing; but upon hearing what had happened, she left the dance, and sat down, leaning her head on her hand, and exclaiming passionately to her ladies, "Do you not hear how the Queen of Scots is mother of a fair son, while I am but a barren stock!" But next morning she had recovered herself sufficiently to maintain her usual appearance of outward civility, received the Scottish ambassador with much seeming favour, and accepted with thanks the office of godmother to the young Prince, which he proffered to her in Queen Mary's name.

After a splendid solemnity at christening the heir of Scotland, Queen Mary seems to have turned her mind towards settling the disorders of her nobility; and, sacrificing her own justifiable resentment, she yielded so far as to grant pardon to all those concerned in the murder of Rizzio. Two men of low rank, and no more, had been executed for that crime. Lord Ruthven, the principal actor, had died in England, talking and writing as composedly of "the slaughter of David," as if it had been the most indifferent, if not meritorious, action possible. George Douglas, who struck the first blow, and Ker of Faldonside, another ruffian who offered his pistol at the Queen's bosom in the fray, were exempted from the general pardon. Morton and all the others were permitted to return, to plan new treasons and murders.

We are now come, my dear child, to a very difficult period in history. The subsequent events in the reign of Queen Mary are well known; but neither the names of the principal agents in those events, nor the motives upon which they acted, are at all agreed upon by historians. It has, in particular, been warmly disputed, and will probably long continue to be so, how far Queen Mary is to be considered as a voluntary party or actor in the tragical and criminal events of which I am about to tell you; or how far, being innocent of any foreknowledge of these violent actions, she was an innocent victim of the villainy of others. Leaving you, my dear child, when you come to a more advanced age, to study this historical point for yourself, I shall endeavour to give you an outline of the facts as they are admitted and proved on all sides.

James Hepburn, Earl of Bothwell, a man in middle age, had for several years played a conspicuous part in these troubled times. He had sided with the Queen Regent against the Reformed party, and was in general supposed to be attached rather to the reigning Queen than to any of the factions who opposed her. He was head of the powerful family of Hepburn, and possessed great influence in East Lothian and Berwickshire, where excellent soldiers could always be obtained. In his morals Bothwell was wild and licentious, irregular and daring in his ambition; and although his history does not show many instances of personal courage, yet in his early life he had the reputation of possessing it. He had been in danger on the occasion of Rizzio's murder, being supposed, from his regard for the Queen, to have been desirous of preventing that cruel insult to her person and authority. As this nobleman displayed great zeal for Mary's cause, she was naturally led to advance him at court, until many persons, and particularly the preachers of the Reformed religion, thought that she admitted to too great intimacy a man of so fierce and profligate a character; and a numerous party among her subjects accused the Queen of being fonder of Bothwell than was becoming.

A thoughtless action of Mary's seemed to confirm this suspicion. Bothwell, among other offices of authority, held that of Lord Warden of all the Marches, and was residing at the castle of Hermitage, a royal fortress which belonged to that office, in order to suppress some disorders on the Border. In October 1566, attempting with his own hand to seize a Border freebooter called John Elliot of the Park, he was severely wounded in the hand. The Queen, who was then at Jedburgh holding a court of justice, hastened through woods, morasses, and waters, to pay a visit to the wounded warden; and though the distance was twenty English miles, she went and returned from Hermitage Castle in the same day. This excursion might arise solely from Mary's desire to learn the cause and particulars of a great outrage on her lieutenant; but all those who wished ill to her, who were a numerous body, represented it as expressive of her anxiety for the safety of her lover.

In the meantime, the dissensions between Darnley and the Queen continued to increase; and while he must have been disliked by Mary from their numerous quarrels, and the affronts he put upon her, as well as from his share in the murder of Rizzio, those who had been concerned with him in that last crime, considered him as a poor mean-spirited wretch, who, having engaged his associates in so daring an act, had afterwards betrayed and deserted them. His latter conduct showed no improvement in either sense or spirit. He pretended he would leave the kingdom, and by this and other capricious resolutions, hastily adopted and abandoned, he so far alienated the affections of the Queen, that many of the unscrupulous and plotting nobles, by whom she was surrounded, formed the idea, that it would be very agreeable to Mary if she could be freed from her union with this unreasonable and ill-tempered young man.

The first proposal made to her was, that she should be separated from Darnley by a divorce. Bothwell, Maitland, Morton, and Murray, are said to have joined in pressing such a proposal upon the Queen, who was then residing at Craigmillar Castle, near Edinburgh; but she rejected it steadily. A conspiracy of a darker kind was then agitated, for the murder of the unhappy Darnley; and Bothwell seems to have entertained little doubt that Mary, thus rid of an unacceptable husband, would choose him for a successor. He spoke with the Earl of Morton on the subject of despatching Darnley, and represented it as an enterprise which had the approbation of the Queen. Morton refused to stir in a matter of so great consequence, unless he received a mandate under the Queen's hand. Bothwell undertook to procure him such a warrant, but he never kept his word. This was confessed by Morton at his death. When it was asked of him by the clergyman who received his confession, why he had not prevented the conspiracy, by making it public? he replied, that there was no one to whom he could confess it with safety. "The Queen," he said, "was herself in the plot; and if I had told Darnley, his folly was so great that I am certain he would have betrayed it to his wife, and so my own destruction would have been assured." But though he did not acknowledge more than I have told you, Morton was always supposed to have been one of the active conspirators; and it was universally believed that a daring and profligate relation of his, called Archibald Douglas, parson of Glasgow, was one of the actual murderers.[1] While these suspicions hung over Morton himself, he seems to have had no reason for believing Mary's guilt, excepting what Bothwell told him. It seems probable that Maitland of Lethington also knew the fatal and guilty secret. Morton and he, however, were both men of deep sagacity. They foresaw that Bothwell would render himself, and perhaps the Queen also, odious to the nation by the dark and bloody action which he meditated; and therefore they resolved to let him run his course, in the hope that he would come to a speedy fall, and that they themselves might succeed to the supreme power.

While these schemes were in agitation against his life, Darnley fell ill at Glasgow, and his indisposition proved to be the smallpox. The Queen sent her physician, and after an interval went herself to wait upon him, and an apparent reconciliation was effected between them. They came together to Edinburgh on the 31st January 1566-67. The King was lodged in a religious house called the Kirk-of-Field, just without the walls of the city.[2] The Queen and the infant Prince were accommodated in the palace of Holyrood. The reason assigned for their living separate was the danger of the child catching the smallpox. But the Queen showed much attention to her husband, visiting him frequently; and they never seemed to have been on better terms than when the conspiracy against Darnley's life was on the eve of being executed. Meanwhile Darnley and his groom of the chamber were alone during the night time, and separated from any other persons, when measures were taken for his destruction in the following horrible manner:—

On the evening of the 9th February, several persons, kinsmen, retainers, and servants of the Earl of Bothwell, came in secret to the Kirk-of-Field. They had with them a great quantity of gunpowder; and by means of false keys they obtained entrance into the cellars of the

---

[1] Douglas was twenty years afterwards brought to trial for his alleged participation in the murder of Darnley, and acquitted.—ARNOT's *Criminal Trials*.

[2] The Kirk-of-Field stood on part of the site of the College of Edinburgh.

building, where they disposed the powder in the vaults under Darn-ley's apartment, and especially beneath the spot where his bed was placed. About two hours after midnight upon the ensuing morning, Bothwell himself came disguised in a riding cloak, to see the execution of the cruel project. Two of his ruffians went in and took means of firing the powder, by lighting a piece of slow-burning match at one end, and placing the other amongst the gunpowder. They remained for some time watching the event, and Bothwell became so impatient, that it was with difficulty he was prevented from entering the house, to see whether the light had not been extinguished by some accident. One of his accomplices, by looking through a window, ascertained that it was still burning. The explosion presently took place, blew up the Kirk-of-Field, and alarmed the whole city. The body of Darnley was found in the adjoining orchard. The bed in which he lay had preserved him from all action of the fire, which occasioned a general belief that he and his chamber-groom, who was found in the same situation, had been strangled and removed before the house was blown up. But this was a mistake. It is clearly proved, by the evidence of those who were present at the event, that there were no means employed but gun-powder—a mode of destruction sufficiently powerful to have rendered any other unnecessary.

XXXII

The Long Goodbye

1567-1586

THE horrible murder of the unhappy Darnley excited the strongest suspicions, and the greatest discontent, in the city of Edinburgh, and through the whole kingdom. Bothwell was pointed out by the general voice as the author of the murder; and as he still continued to enjoy the favour of Mary, her reputation was not spared. To have brought this powerful criminal to an open and impartial trial, would have been the only way for the Queen to recover her popularity; and Mary made a show of doing this public justice, but under circumstances which favoured the criminal.

Lennox, father of the murdered Darnley, had, as was his natural duty, accused Bothwell of the murder of his son. But he received little countenance in prosecuting the accused. Everything seemed to be done as hastily as if it were determined to defeat the operations of justice. Lennox received information on the 28th of March that the 12th of April was appointed for the day of trial; and, at so short warning as fourteen days, he was summoned, as nearest relation of the murdered monarch, to appear as accuser, and to support the charge he had made against Bothwell. The Earl of Lennox complained that the time allowed him to prepare the charge and evidence necessary for convicting so powerful a criminal was greatly too short; but he could not get it extended.

It was a usual thing in Scotland for persons accused of crimes to come to the bar of a court of justice attended by all their friends, retainers, and dependents, the number of whom was frequently so great, that the judges and accusers were overawed, and became afraid to proceed in the investigation; so that the purposes of justice were for the time frustrated. Bothwell, conscious of guilt, was desirous to use this means of protection to the utmost. He appeared in Edinburgh with full five thousand attendants. Two hundred chosen musketeers kept close by his side, and guarded the doors of the court as soon as the criminal had entered. In such circumstances, there could be no chance of a fair trial. Lennox did not appear, saving by one of his vassals, who protested against the proceedings of the day. No charge was made,—no proof of innocence, of course, was required,—and a jury, consisting of nobles and gentlemen of the first rank, acquitted Bothwell of a crime of which all the world believed him to be guilty.

The public mind remained dissatisfied with this mockery of justice; but Bothwell, without regarding the murmurs of the people, hurried forward to possess himself of the situation which he had made vacant by the murder of Darnley. He convened a number of the principal nobility, at a feast given in a tavern, and prevailed on them to sign a bond, in which they not only declared Bothwell altogether innocent of the King's death, but recommended him as the fittest person whom her Majesty could choose for a husband. Morton, Maitland, and others, who afterwards were Mary's bitter enemies and accusers, subscribed this remarkable deed, either because they were afraid of the consequences of a refusal, or that they thought it the readiest and safest course for accomplishing their own purposes, to encourage Bothwell and the Queen to run headlong to their ruin, by completing a marriage which must be disgustful to the whole kingdom.

Murray, the most important person in Scotland, had kept aloof from all these proceedings. He was in Fife when the King was murdered, and, about three days before Bothwell's trial, he obtained leave of his sister the Queen to travel to France. Probably he did not consider that his own person would be safe, should Bothwell rise to be King.

The Earl of Bothwell, thus authorised by the apparent consent of the nobility, and, no doubt, thinking himself secure of the Queen's approbation, suddenly appeared at the bridge of Cramond, with a thousand horse, as Mary arrived there on her return from Stirling to Edinburgh. Bothwell took the Queen's horse by the bridle, and surrounding and disarming her attendants, he led her, as if by an appearance of force, to the strong castle of Dunbar, of which he was governor. On this occasion Mary seems neither to have attempted to resist, nor to have expressed that feeling of anger and shame which would have been proper to her as a queen and as a woman. Her attendants were assured by the officers of Bothwell, that she was carried off in consequence of her own consent; and considering that such an outrage was offered to a sovereign of her high rank and bold spirit, her tame submission and silence under it seem scarce otherwise to be accounted for. They remained at Dunbar ten days, after which they again appeared in Edinburgh, apparently reconciled; the Earl carefully leading the Queen's palfrey, and conducting her up to the castle, the government of which was held by one of his adherents.

Whilst these strange proceedings took place, Bothwell had been able to procure a sentence of divorce against his wife, a sister of the Earl of Huntly. On the 12th of May the Queen made a public declaration, that she forgave Bothwell the late violence which he had committed, and that, although she was at first highly displeased with him, she was now resolved not only to grant him her pardon, but also to promote him to further honours. She was as good as her word, for she created him Duke of Orkney; and, on the 15th of the same month, did Mary, with unpardonable indiscretion, commit the great folly of marrying this ambitious and profligate man, stained as he was with the blood of her husband.

The Queen was not long in discovering that by this unhappy marriage she had gotten a more ruthless and wicked husband than she had in the flexible Darnley. Bothwell used her grossly ill, and being disappointed in his plans of getting the young Prince into his keeping, used such upbraiding language to Mary, that she prayed for a knife with which to stab herself, rather than endure his ill-treatment.

In the meantime the public discontent rose high, and Morton, Maitland, and others, who had been privy to the murder of Darnley, placed themselves, notwithstanding, at the head of a numerous party of the nobility, who resolved to revenge his death, and remove Bothwell from his usurped power. They took arms hastily, and had nearly surprised the Queen and Bothwell, while feasting in the castle of the

Lord Borthwick, from whence they fled to Dunbar, the Queen being concealed in the disguise of a page.

The confederated lords marched towards Dunbar, and the Queen and Bothwell, having assembled an army, advanced to the encounter, and met them on Carberry Hill, not far from the place where the battle of Pinkie was fought. This was on the 15th of June 1567. Mary would have acted more wisely in postponing the threatened action, for the Hamiltons, in great force, were on their way to join her. But she had been accustomed to gain advantages by rapid and ready movements, and was not at first sufficiently aware what an unfavourable impression existed against her even in her own army. Many, if not most, of those troops who had joined the Queen, had little inclination to fight in Bothwell's cause. He himself, in a bravado, offered to prove his innocence of Darnley's murder, by a duel in the lists with any of the opposite lords who should affirm his guilt. The valiant Kirkaldy of Grange, Murray of Tullibardin, and Lord Lindsay of the Byres, successively undertook the combat; but Bothwell found exceptions to each of them, and, finally, it appeared that this wicked man had not courage to fight with any one in that quarrel. In the meantime the Queen's army began to disband, and it became obvious that they would not fight in her cause, while they considered it as the same with that of Bothwell. She therefore recommended to him to fly from the field of action; an advice which he was not slow in following, riding to Dunbar as fast as he could, and from thence escaping by sea.

Mary surrendered herself, upon promise of respect and kind treatment, to the laird of Grange, and was conducted by him to the headquarters of the confederate army. When she arrived there, the lords received her with silent respect; but some of the common soldiers hooted at and insulted her, until Grange, drawing his sword, compelled them to be silent. The lords adopted the resolution of returning to the capital, and conveying Mary thither, surrounded by their troops.

As the unhappy Queen approached Edinburgh, led as it were in triumph by the victors, the most coarse and insulting behaviour was used towards her by the lower classes. There was a banner prepared for this insurrection, displaying on the one side the portrait of Darnley, as he lay murdered under a tree in the fatal orchard, with these words embroidered, "Judge, and avenge my cause, O Lord!" and on the other side, the little Prince on his knees, holding up his hands, as if praying to Heaven to punish his father's murderers. As the Queen rode through the streets, with her hair loose, her garments disordered, covered with dust, and overpowered with grief, shame, and fatigue, this fatal flag was displayed before her eyes, while the voices of the rude multitude upbraided her with having been an accomplice in Darnley's murder. The same cries were repeated, and the same insulting banner displayed, before the windows of the Lord Provost's house, to which she was for a few hours committed as if a prisoner. The better class of craftsmen and citizens were at length moved by her sorrows, and showed such a desire to take her part, that the lords determined to remove her from the city, where respect to her birth and misfortunes seemed likely to create partisans, in spite of her own indiscretions, and the resentment of her enemies. Accordingly, on the next evening, being 16th June 1567, Mary, in disguised apparel, and escorted by a strong armed force, was conveyed from Holyrood to the castle of Lochleven, which stands on a little island, surrounded by the lake of the same name, and was there detained a prisoner.

The insurgent lords now formed themselves into a Secret Council, for managing the affairs of the nation. Their first attention was turned to securing Bothwell, although, perhaps, there may have been some even among their own number,—Morton, for example, and Maitland,—who had been participant with him in the murder of Darnley, who could not be very desirous that he should be produced on a public trial. But it was necessary to make a show of pursuing him, and many were sincerely desirous that he should be taken.

Kirkaldy of Grange followed Bothwell with two vessels, and had nearly surprised him in the harbour of Lerwick, the fugitive making his escape at one issue of the bay, while Grange entered at another; and Bothwell might even then have been captured, but that Grange's ship ran upon a rock, and was wrecked, though the crew escaped. Bothwell was only saved for a more melancholy fate. He took to piracy in the Northern Seas, in order to support himself and his sailors. He was in consequence assaulted and taken by some Danish ships of war. The Danes threw him into the dungeons of the castle of Malmay, where he died in captivity, about the end of the year 1576. It is said that this atrocious criminal confessed at his death that he had conducted the murder of Darnley, by the assistance of Murray, Maitland, and Morton, and that Mary was altogether guiltless of that crime. But there is little reliance to be placed on the declaration of so wicked a man, even if it were certain he had made it.

Meantime, poor Mary reaped the full consequences of Bothwell's guilt, and of her own infatuated attachment to him. She was imprisoned in a rude and inconvenient tower, on a small islet, where there was scarce room to walk fifty yards; and not even the intercession of Queen Elizabeth, who seems for the time to have been alarmed at the successful insurrection of subjects against their sovereign, could procure any mitigation of her captivity. There was a proposal to proceed against the Queen as an accomplice in Darnley's murder, and to take her life under that pretence. But the Lords of the Secret Council resolved to adopt somewhat of a gentler course, by compelling Mary to surrender her crown to her son, then an infant, and to make the Earl of Murray regent during the child's minority. Deeds to this purpose were drawn up, and sent to the castle of Lochleven, to be signed by the Queen. Lord Lindsay, the rudest, most bigoted, and fiercest of the confederated lords, was deputed to enforce Mary's compliance with the commands of the Council. He behaved with such peremptory brutality as had perhaps been expected, and was so unmanly as to pinch with his iron glove the arm of the poor Queen, to compel her to subscribe the deeds.

If Mary had any quarter to which, in her disastrous condition, she might look for love and favour, it was to her brother Murray. She may have been criminal—she had certainly been grossly infatuated—yet she deserved her brother's kindness and compassion. She had loaded him with favours, and pardoned him considerable offences. Unquestionably she expected more favour from him than she met with. But Murray was ambitious; and ambition breaks through the ties of blood, and forgets the obligations of gratitude. He visited his imprisoned sister and benefactress in Lochleven Castle, but it was not to bring her comfort; on the contrary, he pressed all her errors on her with such hard-hearted severity, that she burst into floods of tears, and abandoned herself to despair.

Murray accepted of the regency, and in doing so broke all remaining ties of tenderness betwixt himself and his sister. He was now at the head of the ruling faction, consisting of what were called the King's Lords; while such of the nobility as desired that Mary, being now freed from the society of Bothwell, should be placed at liberty, and restored to the administration of the kingdom, were termed the Queen's Party. The strict and sagacious government of Murray imposed silence and submission for a time upon this last-named faction; but a singular incident changed the face of things for a moment, and gave a gleam of hope to the unfortunate captive.

Sir William Douglas, the laird of Lochleven, owner of the castle where Mary was imprisoned, was a half-brother by the mother's side of the Regent Murray. This baron discharged with severe fidelity the task of Mary's jailor; but his youngest brother, George Douglas, became more sensible to the Queen's distress, and perhaps to her beauty, than to the interests of the Regent, or of his own family. A plot laid by him for the Queen's deliverance was discovered, and he was expelled from the island in consequence. But he kept up a correspondence with a kinsman of his own, called Little Douglas, a boy of fifteen or sixteen, who had remained in the castle. On Sunday, the 2d May 1568, this Little William Douglas, contrived to steal the keys of the castle while the family were at supper. He let Mary and her attendant out of the tower when all had gone to rest—locked the gates of the castle to prevent pursuit—placed the Queen and her waiting-woman in a little skiff, and rowed them to the shore, throwing the keys of the castle into the lake in the course of their passage. Just when they were about to set out on this adventurous voyage, the youthful pilot had made a signal, by a light in a particular window visible at the upper end of the lake, to intimate that all was safe. Lord Seaton and a party of the Hamiltons were waiting at the landing-place. The Queen instantly mounted, and hurried off to Niddry Castle, in West Lothian; she proceeded next day to Hamilton. The news flew like lightning throughout the country, and spread enthusiasm everywhere. The people remembered Mary's gentleness, grace, and beauty,—they remembered her misfortunes also—and if they reflected on her errors, they thought they had been punished with sufficient severity. On Sunday, Mary was a sad and helpless captive in a lonely tower. On the Saturday following, she was at the head of a powerful confederacy, by which nine earls, nine bishops, eighteen lords, and many gentlemen of high rank, engaged to defend her person and restore her power. But this gleam of success was only temporary.

It was the Queen's purpose to place her person in security in the castle of Dumbarton, and her army, under the Earl of Argyle, proposed to carry her thither in a species of triumph. The Regent was lying at Glasgow with much inferior forces; but, with just confidence in his own military skill, as well as the talents of Morton, and the valour of Kirkaldy, and other experienced soldiers, he determined to meet the Queen's Lords in their proposed march, and to give them battle.

On 13th May 1568 Murray occupied the village of Langside, which lay full in the march of the Queen's army. The Hamiltons, and other gentlemen of Mary's troop, rushed forth with ill-considered valour to dispute the pass. They fought, however, with obstinacy, after the Scottish manner; that is, they pressed on each other front to front, each fixing his spear in his opponent's target, and then endeavouring to bear him down, as two bulls do when they encounter each other. Morton decided the battle by attacking the flank of the Hamiltons, while their column was closely engaged in the front. The measure was decisive, and the Queen's army was completely routed.

Queen Mary beheld this final and fatal defeat from a castle called Crookstane, about four miles from Paisley, where she and Darnley had spent some happy days after their marriage, and which, therefore, must have been the scene of bitter recollections. It was soon evident that there was no resource but in flight, and, escorted by Lord Herries and a few faithful followers, she rode sixty miles before she stopped at the abbey of Dundrennan, in Galloway. From this place she had the means of retreating either to France or England, as she should ultimately determine. In France she was sure to have been well received; but England afforded a nearer, and, as she thought, an equally safe place of refuge.

Forgetting, therefore, the various causes of emulation which existed betwixt Elizabeth and herself, and remembering only the smooth and flattering words which she had received from her sister sovereign, it did not occur to the Scottish Queen that she should incur any risk by throwing herself upon the hospitality of England. It may also be supposed, that poor Mary, amongst whose faults want of generosity could not be reckoned, judged of Elizabeth according to the manner in which she would herself have treated the Queen of England in the same situation. She therefore resolved to take refuge in Elizabeth's kingdom, in spite of the opposition of her wiser attendants. They kneeled and entreated in vain. She entered the fatal boat, crossed the Solway, and delivered herself up to a gentleman named Lowther, the English deputy-warden. Much surprised, doubtless, at the incident, he sent express to inform Queen Elizabeth; and receiving the Scottish Queen with as much respect as he had the means of showing, lodged her in Carlisle Castle.

Queen Elizabeth had two courses in her power, which might be more or less generous, but were alike just and lawful. She might have received Queen Mary honourably, and afforded her the succour she petitioned for; or, if she did not think that expedient, she might have allowed her to remain in her dominions, at liberty to depart from them freely, as she had entered them voluntarily.

But Elizabeth, great as she was upon other occasions of her reign, acted on the present from mean and envious motives. She saw in the fugitive who implored her protection a princess who possessed a right of succession, to the crown of England, which, by the Catholic part of her subjects at least, was held superior to her own. She remembered that Mary had been led to assume the arms and titles of the English monarchy, or rather, that the French had assumed them in her name, when she was in childhood. She recollected that Mary had been her rival in accomplishments; and certainly she did not forget that she was her superior in youth and beauty; and had the advantage, as she had expressed it herself, to be the mother of a fair son, while she remained a barren stock. Elizabeth, therefore, considered the Scottish Queen not as a sister and friend in distress, but as an enemy, over whom circumstances had given her power, and determined upon reducing her to the condition of a captive.

In pursuance of the line of conduct to which this mean train of reasoning led, the unfortunate Mary was surrounded by English guards; and, as Elizabeth reasonably doubted that if she were left upon the Border, the fugitive Queen might obtain aid from her adherents in Scotland, she was removed to Bolton Castle, in Yorkshire. But some pretext was wanting for a conduct so violent, so ungenerous, and so unjust, and Elizabeth contrived to find one.

The Regent Murray, upon Mary's flight to England, had endeavoured to vindicate his conduct in the eyes of Queen Elizabeth, by alleging that his sister had been accessory to the murder of her husband Darnley, in order that she might marry her paramour Bothwell. Now, although this, supposing it to be true, was very criminal conduct, yet Elizabeth had not the least title to constitute herself judge in the matter. Mary was no subject of hers, nor, according to the law of nations, had the English Queen any right to act as umpire in the quarrel between the Scottish sovereign and her subjects. But she extorted, in the following manner, a sort of acquiescence in her right to decide, from the Scottish Queen.

The messengers of Queen Elizabeth informed Mary, that their mistress regretted extremely that she could not at once admit her to her presence, nor give her the affectionate reception which she longed to afford her, until her visitor stood clear, in the eyes of the world, of the scandalous accusations of her Scottish subjects. Mary at once undertook to make her innocence evident to Elizabeth's satisfaction; and this the Queen of England pretended to consider as a call upon herself to act as umpire in the quarrel betwixt Mary and the party by which she had been deposed and exiled. It was in vain that Mary remonstrated, that, in agreeing to remove Elizabeth's scruples, she acted merely out of respect to her opinion, and a desire to conciliate her favour, but not with the purpose of constituting the English Queen her judge in a formal trial. Elizabeth was determined to keep the advantage which she had attained, and to act as if Mary had, of her full free will, rendered her rival the sole arbiter of her fate.

The Queen of England accordingly appointed commissioners to hear the parties, and consider the evidence which was to be laid before them by both sides. The Regent Murray appeared in person before these commissioners, in the odious character of the accuser of his sister, benefactress, and sovereign. Queen Mary also sent the most able of her adherents, the Bishop of Ross, Lord Herries, and others, to plead the case on her side.

The Commission met at York in October 1568. The proceedings commenced with a singular attempt to establish the obsolete question of the alleged supremacy of England over Scotland. "You come hither," said the English commissioners to the Regent and his assistants, "to submit the differences which divide the kingdom of Scotland to the Queen of England, and therefore I first require of you to pay her Grace the homage due to her." The Earl of Murray blushed and was silent. But Maitland of Lethington answered with spirit—"When Elizabeth restored to Scotland the earldom of Huntingdon, with Cumberland, Northumberland, and such other lands as Scotland did of old possess in England, we will do such homage for these territories as was done by the ancient sovereigns of Scotland who enjoyed them. As to the crown and kingdom of Scotland, they are more free than those of England, which lately paid Peter-pence to Rome."

This question being waived, they entered on the proper business of the Commission. It was not without hesitation that Murray was induced to state his accusation in explicit terms, and there was still greater difficulty in obtaining from him any evidence in support of the odious charges of matrimonial infidelity, and accession to the murder of her husband, with which that accusation charged Mary. It is true, the Queen's conduct had been unguarded and imprudent, but there was no arguing from thence that she was guilty of the foul crime charged. Something like proof was wanted, and at length a box of letters and papers was produced, stated to have been taken from a servant of Bothwell, called Dalgleish. These letters, if genuine, certainly proved that Mary was a paramour of Bothwell while Darnley was yet alive, and that she knew and approved of the murder of that ill-fated young man. But the letters were alleged by the Queen's commissioners to be gross forgeries, devised for the purpose of slandering their mistress. It is most remarkable that Dalgleish had been condemned and executed without a word being asked him about these letters, even if it had been only to prove that they had been found in his possession. Lord Herries and the Bishop of Ross did not rest satisfied with defending the Queen; they charged Murray himself with having confederated with Bothwell for the destruction of Darnley.

At the end of five months' investigation, the Queen of England informed both parties that she had, on the one hand, seen nothing which induced her to doubt the worth and honour of the Earl of Murray, while, on the other hand, he had, in her opinion, proved nothing of the criminal charges which he had brought against his sovereign. She was therefore, she said, determined to leave the affairs of Scotland as she had found them.

To have treated both parties impartially, as her sentence seemed intended to imply her desire to do, the Queen ought to have restored Mary to liberty. But while Murray was sent down with the loan of a large sum of money, Mary was retained in that captivity which was only to end with her life.

Murray returned to Scotland, having had all the advantage of the conference at York. His coffers were replenished, and his power confirmed, by the favour of Queen Elizabeth; and he had little difficulty in scattering the remains of the Queen's Lords, who, in fact, had never been able to make head since the battle of Langside, and the flight of their mistress.

In the meantime some extraordinary events took place in England. The Duke of Norfolk had formed a plan to restore Queen Mary to liberty, and was in recompense to be rewarded with her hand in marriage. The Regent Murray had been admitted into the secret of this plot, although it may be supposed the object was not very acceptable to him. Many of the great nobles had agreed to join in the undertaking, particularly the powerful Earls of Westmoreland and Northumberland. The plot of Norfolk was discovered and proved against him chiefly by the declarations of Murray, who meanly betrayed the secret entrusted to him; Norfolk was in consequence seized upon, committed to confinement, and, a few months afterwards, upon the discovery of some new intrigues, was tried and executed.

But before this catastrophe, Northumberland and Westmoreland rushed into a hasty rebellion, which they were unable to conduct with sufficient vigour. Their troops dispersed without a battle before the army which Queen Elizabeth sent against them. Westmoreland found a secure refuge among the Scottish Borderers, who were favourable to the cause of Mary. They assisted him in his escape to the sea-coast, and he finally made his way to Flanders, and died in exile. Northumberland was less fortunate. A Borderer, named Hector Armstrong of Harlaw, treacherously betrayed him to the Regent Murray, who refused indeed to deliver him up to Queen Elizabeth, but detained him prisoner in that same lonely castle of Lochleven, which had been lately the scene of Mary's captivity.

All these successive events tended to establish the power of Murray, and to diminish the courage of such lords as remained attached to the opposite party. But it happens frequently, that when men appear most secure of the object they have been toiling for, their views are suddenly and strangely disappointed. A blow was impending over Murray from a quarter which, if named to the haughty Regent, he would probably have despised, since it originated in the resentment of a private man.

After the battle of Langside, six of the Hamiltons, who had been most active on that occasion, were sentenced to die, as being guilty of treason against James VI., in having espoused his mother's cause. In this doom there was little justice, considering how the country was divided between the claims of the mother and the son. But the decree was not acted upon, and the persons condemned received their pardon through the mediation of John Knox with the Regent.

One of the individuals thus pardoned was Hamilton of Bothwellhaugh, a man of a fierce and vindictive character. Like others in his condition, he was punished by the forfeiture of his property, although his life was spared. His wife had brought him, as her portion, the lands of Woodhouselee, near Roslin, and these were bestowed by Murray upon one of his favourites. This person exercised the right so rudely, as to turn Hamilton's wife out of her own house undressed, and unprotected from the fury of the weather. In consequence of this brutal treatment, she became insane, and died. Her husband vowed revenge, not on the actual author of his misfortune, but upon the Regent Murray, whom he considered as the original cause of it, and whom his family prejudices induced him to regard as the usurper of the sovereign power, and the oppressor of the name and house of Hamilton. There is little doubt that the Archbishop of St. Andrews, and some others of his name, encouraged Bothwellhaugh in this desperate resolution.

The assassin took his measures with every mark of deliberation. Having learnt that the Regent was to pass through Linlithgow on a certain day, he secretly introduced himself into an empty house belonging to the Archbishop of St. Andrews, which had in front a wooden balcony looking upon the street. Bothwellhaugh hung a black cloth on the wall of the apartment where he lay, that his shadow might not be seen from without, and spread a mattrass on the floor, that the sound of his feet might not be heard from beneath. To secure his escape he fastened a fleet horse in the garden behind the house, and pulled down the lintel stones from the posts of the garden door, so that he might be able to pass through it on horseback. He also strongly barricaded the front door of the house, which opened to the street of the town. Having thus prepared all for concealment until the deed was done, and for escape afterwards, he armed himself with a loaded carabine, shut himself up in the lonely chamber, and waited the arrival of his victim.

Some friend of Murray transmitted to him a hint of the danger which he might incur, in passing through the street of a place in which he was known to have enemies, and advised that he should avoid it by going round on the outside of the town; or, at least, by riding hastily past the lodging which was more particularly suspected, as belonging to the Hamiltons. But the Regent, thinking that the step recommended would have an appearance of timidity, held on his way through the crowded street. As he came opposite the fatal balcony, his horse being somewhat retarded by the number of spectators, Bothwellhaugh had time to take a deliberate aim. He fired the carabine, and the Regent fell, mortally wounded. The ball, after passing through his body, killed the horse of a gentleman who rode on his right hand. His attendants rushed furiously at the door of the house from which the shot had issued; but Bothwellhaugh's precautions had been so securely taken that they were unable to force their entrance till he had mounted his good horse, and escaped through the garden gate. He was notwithstanding pursued so closely, that he had very nearly been taken; but after spur and whip had both failed, he pricked his horse with his dagger, compelled him to take a desperate leap over a ditch, which his pursuers were unable to cross, and thus made his escape.

The Regent died in the course of the night, leaving a character which has been, perhaps, too highly extolled by one class of authors, and too much depreciated by another, according as his conduct to his sister was approved or condemned.

The murderer escaped to France. In the civil wars of that country an attempt was made to engage him, as a known desperado, in the assassination of the Admiral Coligni; but he resented it as a deadly insult. He had slain a man in Scotland, he said, from whom he had sustained a mortal injury; but the world could not engage him to attempt the life of one against whom he had no personal cause of quarrel.

The death of Murray had been an event expected by many of Queen Mary's adherents. The very night after it happened, Scott of Buccleuch and Ker of Fairniehirst broke into England, and ravaged the frontier with more than their wonted severity. When it was remarked by one of the sufferers under this foray, that the Regent would punish the party concerned in such illegal violence, the Borderer replied contemptuously, that the Regent was as cold as his bridle-bit. This served to show that their leaders had been privy to Bothwellhaugh's action, and now desired to take advantage of it, in order to give grounds for war between the countries. But Queen Elizabeth was contented to send a small army to the frontier, to burn the castles and ravage the estates of the two clans which had been engaged in the hostile inroad; a service which they executed with much severity on the clans of Scott and Ker, without doing injury to those other Borderers against whom their mistress had no complaint.

Upon the death of Murray, Lennox was chosen Regent. He was the father of the murdered Darnley, yet showed no excessive thirst of vengeance. He endeavoured to procure a union of parties, for the purpose of domestic peace. But men's minds on both sides had become too much exasperated against each other. The Queen's party was strengthened by Maitland of Lethington and Kirkaldy of Grange joining that faction, after having been long the boast of that of the King. Lethington we have often mentioned as one of the ablest men in Scotland, and Kirkaldy was certainly one of the bravest. He was, besides, Governor of Edinburgh Castle, and his declaring that he held that important place for the Queen gave great spirit to Mary's adherents. At the same time, they were deprived of a stronghold of scarcely inferior consequence, by the loss of Dumbarton Castle in the following extraordinary manner.

This fortress is one of the strongest places in the world. It is situated on a rock, which rises almost perpendicularly from a level plain to the height of several hundred feet. On the summit of this rock the buildings are situated, and as there is only one access from below, which rises by steps, and is strongly guarded and fortified, the fort might be almost held to be impregnable, that is, impossible to be taken. One Captain Crawford of Jordanhill, a distinguished adherent of the King's party, resolved, nevertheless, to make an attempt on this formidable castle.

He took advantage of a misty and moonless night to bring to the foot of the castle-rock the scaling-ladders which he had provided, choosing for his terrible experiment the place where the rock was highest, and where less pains were taken to keep a regular guard. This choice was fortunate; for the first ladder broke with the weight of the men who attempted to mount, and the noise of the fall must have betrayed them had there been any sentinel within hearing. Crawford, assisted by a soldier who had deserted from the castle, and was acting as his guide, renewed the attempt in person, and having scrambled up to a projecting ledge of rock where there was some footing, contrived to make fast the ladder, by tying it to the roots of a tree, which grew about midway up the rock. Here they found a small flat surface, sufficient, however, to afford footing to the whole party, which was, of course, very few in number. In scaling the second precipice, another accident took place:—One of the party, subject to epileptic fits, was seized by one of these attacks, brought on perhaps by terror, while he was in the act of climbing up the ladder. His illness made it impossible for him either to ascend or descend. To have slain the man would have been a cruel expedient, besides that the fall of his body might have alarmed the garrison. Crawford caused him, therefore, to be tied to the ladder, which they turned, and thus mounted with ease. When the party gained the summit, they slew the sentinel ere he had time to give the alarm, and easily surprised the slumbering garrison, who had trusted too much to the security of their castle to keep good watch.

This exploit of Crawford may compare with anything of the kind which we read of in history.

Hamilton, the Archbishop of St. Andrews, was made prisoner in Dumbarton, where he had taken refuge, as he was particularly hated by the King's party. He was now in their hands, and, as they had formerly proclaimed him a traitor, they now without scruple put him to death as such. This cruel deed occasioned other violences, by way of retaliation, which, in turn, led to fresh acts of bloodshed. All natural ties were forgotten in the distinction of Kingsmen and Queensmen; and, as neither party gave quarter to their opponents, the civil war assumed a most horrible aspect. Fathers, and sons, and brothers, took opposite sides, and fought against each other. The very children of the towns and villages formed themselves into bands for King James or Queen Mary, and fought inveterately with stones, sticks, and knives.

In the midst of this confusion, each party called a parliament, which was attended only by the lords of their own side. The Queen's Parliament met at Edinburgh, under protection of the castle, and its governor Kirkaldy. The King's faction had a much more numerous assembly, assuming the same denomination, at Stirling, where they produced the young King, to give authority to their proceedings. The boy, with natural childishness, taking notice of a rent in the carpet which covered the table at which the clerks sat, observed, "there was a hole in the Parliament." These words were remarked afterwards, as if they had contained a sort of prophecy of the following singular event:—

Kirkaldy devised an enterprise, by which, if successful, he would have put a complete stop to the proceedings of the King's Parliament, nay, to the civil war itself. He sent for Buccleuch and Fairniehirst, already noticed as zealous partisans of Mary, desiring them to bring a large party of their best horsemen, and joined with them the Lord Claud Hamilton, with a detachment of infantry. The whole were guided by a man of the name of Bell, who knew the town of Stirling, being a native of that place. On the 4th of September 1571 he introduced the party, consisting of about five hundred men, into the middle of the town, at four in the morning, without even a dog barking at them. They then raised the alarm, crying out, "God and the Queen! think on the Archbishop of Saint Andrews! all is our own!" According to the directions they had received, they sent parties to the different houses of which the King's Lords had taken possession, and made them prisoners without resistance, except on the part of Morton, whose obstinate valour obliged them to set fire to his lodgings. He then reluctantly surrendered himself to Buccleuch, who was his near connection. But his resistance had gained some time, and the assailants had scattered themselves in quest of plunder. At this moment, Mar brought a party of musketeers out of the castle, and placing them behind the walls of a house which he had commenced building on the castle-hill, he opened a heavy and unexpected fire upon the Queens-men. These being already in disorder, were struck with panic in the moment of victory, and began to fly. The scene was now completely changed, and they who had been triumphant the moment before, were glad to surrender to their own captives. Lennox the Regent had been mounted behind Spens of Wormeston, who had made him captive. He was a particular object of vengeance to the Hamiltons, who longed to requite the death of the Archbishop of St. Andrews. He was killed, as was believed, by Lord Claud Hamilton's orders, and Spens, who most honourably endeavoured to protect his prisoner, was slain at the same time. The Queen's party retreated out of Stirling without much loss, for the Borderers carried off all the horses, upon which the opposite party might have followed them. Kirkaldy received the news of the Regent's death with much dissatisfaction, abusing those who commanded the party as disorderly beasts, who neither knew how to gain a victory, nor how to use it. Had he placed himself at the head of the detachment, as he had earnestly desired to do, it is probable that the Raid of Stirling might have ended the war. As it fell out, the quarrel was only embittered, if possible, by the death of Lennox.

The Earl of Mar was named Regent on the King's side. He was a man of fair and moderate views, and so honourably desirous of restoring the blessing of peace to his country, that the impossibility of attaining his object is said to have shortened his life. He died 29th October 1572, having been Regent little more than one year.

The Earl of Morton was next made Regent. We have seen that this nobleman, however respectable for courage and talents, was nevertheless of a fierce, treacherous, and cruel disposition. He had been concerned in Rizzio's murder, and was at least acquainted with that of Darnley. It was to be expected that he would continue the war with the same ferocious cruelty by which it had been distinguished, instead of labouring, like Mar, to diminish its violence. This fell out accordingly. Each party continued to execute their prisoners; and as skirmishes were daily fought, the number of persons who fell by the sword, or died upon the gibbet, was fearfully great. From the family name of Morton, these were called the Douglases' wars.

After these hostilities had existed for about five years, the Duke of Chatelherault, and the Earl of Huntly, the two principal nobles who had supported the Queen's cause, submitted themselves to the King's authority, and to the sway of the Regent. Kirkaldy of Grange, assisted by the counsels of Maitland of Lethington, continued to maintain the castle of Edinburgh against Morton. But Queen Elizabeth, who became now desirous of ending the Scottish dissensions, sent Sir William Drury from Berwick with a considerable number [1,500] of regular forces, and, what was still more needful, a large train of artillery, which formed a close siege around the castle of Edinburgh. The garrison were, however, much more distressed for provisions than by the shot of the English batteries. It was not till after a valiant defence, in the course of which one of the springs which supplied the fortress with water was dried up, and the other became choked with ruins, that the gallant Kirkaldy was compelled to capitulate.

After a siege of thirty-three days he surrendered to the English general, who promised that his mistress should intercede with the Regent for favourable treatment to the governor and his adherents. This might the rather have been expected, because Morton and Kirkaldy had been at one time great friends. But the Regent was earnest in demanding the life of his valorous opponent; and Elizabeth, with little regard to her general's honour or her own, abandoned the prisoners to Morton's vengeance. Kirkaldy and his brother were publicly executed, to the great regret even of many of the King's party themselves. Maitland of Lethington, more famed for talents than integrity, despaired of obtaining mercy where none had been extended to Kirkaldy, and put a period to his existence by taking poison. Thus ended the civil wars of Queen Mary's reign, with the death of the bravest soldier, and of the ablest statesman, in Scotland; for such were Kirkaldy and Maitland.

From the time of the surrender of Edinburgh Castle, 29th May 1573, the Regent Morton was in complete possession of the supreme power in Scotland. As Queen Elizabeth had been his constant friend during the civil wars, he paid devoted attention to her wishes when he became the undisputed ruler of the kingdom.

Morton even went so far as to yield up to the justice, or the revenge, of the English Queen, that unfortunate Earl of Northumberland, who, as I formerly mentioned, had raised a rebellion in England, and flying into Scotland, had been confined by the Regent Murray in Lochleven Castle. The surrender of this unfortunate nobleman to England was a great stain, not only on the character of Morton, but on that of Scotland in general, which had hitherto been accounted a safe and hospitable place of refuge for those whom misfortune or political faction had exiled from their own country. It was the more particularly noticed, because when Morton himself had been forced to fly to England, on account of his share in Rizzio's murder, he had been courteously received and protected by the unhappy nobleman whom he had now delivered up to his fate. It was an additional and aggravating circumstance, that it was a Douglas who betrayed a Percy; and when the annals of their ancestors were considered, it was found that while they presented many acts of open hostility, many instances of close and firm alliance, they never till now had afforded an example of any act of treachery exercised by the one family against the other. To complete the infamy of the transaction, a sum of money was paid to the Regent on this occasion, which he divided with Douglas of Lochleven. Northumberland was beheaded at York, 1572.

In other respects, Scotland derived great advantage from the peace with England, as some degree of repose was highly necessary to this distracted country. The peace now made continued, with little interruption, for thirty years and upwards.

On one occasion, however, a smart action took place betwixt the Scots and English, which, though of little consequence, I may here tell you of, chiefly because it was the last considerable skirmish—with the exception of a deed of bold daring, of which I shall speak by and by—which the two nations had, or, it is to be hoped, ever will have, with each other.

It was the course adopted for preserving peace upon the Border, that the wardens on each side used to meet on days appointed, and deliver up to each other the malefactors who had committed aggressions upon either country, or else make pecuniary reparation for the trespasses which they had done. On the 7th July 1575, Carmichael, as warden for the Scottish Middle Marches, met Sir John Foster, the English officer on the opposite frontier, each being, as usual, accompanied by the guards belonging to their office, as well as by the armed clans inhabiting their jurisdiction. Foster was attended by the men of Tynedale, in greater numbers than those of the Scottish Borderers, all well armed with jack and spear, as well as bows and arrows. The meeting was at first peaceful. The wardens commenced their usual business of settling delinquencies; and their attendants began to traffic with each other, and to engage in sports and gaming. For, notwithstanding their habitual incursions, a sort of acquaintance was always kept up between the Borderers on both sides, like that which takes place betwixt the outposts of two contending armies.

During this mutual friendly intercourse, a dispute arose between the two wardens, Carmichael desiring delivery of an English depredator, for whom Foster, on the other hand, refused to be responsible. They both arose from their seats as the debate grew warm, and Sir John Foster told Carmichael, contemptuously, he ought to match himself with his equals. The English Borderers immediately raised their war-cry of "To it, Tynedale!" and without further ceremony shot a flight of arrows among the Scots, who, few in number, and surprised, were with difficulty able to keep their ground. A band of the citizens of Jedburgh arrived just in time to support their countrymen, and turn the fate of the day; for most of them having firearms, the old English long-bow no more possessed its ancient superiority. After a smart action, the English were driven from the field; Sir John Foster, with many of the English gentlemen, being made prisoners, were sent to the Regent Morton to be at his disposal. Sir George Heron of Chipchase, and other persons of condition, were slain on the English side. The Scots lost but one gentleman of name.

Morton, afraid of Queen Elizabeth's displeasure, though the offence had been given by the English, treated the prisoners with distinction, and dismissed them, not only without ransom, but with presents of falcons, and other tokens of respect. "Are you not well treated?" said a Scotsman to one of these liberated prisoners, "since we give you live hawks for dead herons?"

This skirmish, called the Raid of the Redswair, took place on the mountainous ridge of the Carter. It produced no interruption of concord between the two countries, being passed over as a casual affray. Scotland, therefore, enjoyed the blessings of peace and tranquillity during the greater part of Morton's regency.

But the advantages which the kingdom derived from peace, were in some measure destroyed by the corrupt and oppressive government of the Regent, who turned his thoughts almost entirely to amassing treasure, by every means in his power. The extensive property, which formerly belonged to the Roman Catholic Church, was a mine out of which Morton and the other great nobles contrived to work for themselves a great deal of wealth. This they did chiefly by dealing with those who were placed in the room of the abbots and priors as commendators, by which word the Scots distinguished a layman who obtained possession of an ecclesiastical benefice. To these commendators the nobles applied, and, by fair means or force, compelled them to make over and transfer to them the property of the abbacies, or at least to grant it to them in long leases for a trifling rent. That you may understand how this sort of business was managed, I will give you a curious instance of it:—

In August 1570 Allan Stewart, commendator of the abbacy of Crossraguel, in Ayrshire, was prevailed on to visit the Earl of Cassilis, who conveyed him, partly against his will, to a lonely tower, which overhangs the sea, called the Black Vault of Denure, the ruins of which are yet visible. He was treated for some time kindly; but as his arms and servants were removed from him, he soon saw reason to consider himself less as a friendly guest than as a prisoner, to whom some foul play intended. At length the Earl conveyed his guest into a private chamber, in which there was no furniture of any kind excepting a huge clumsy iron grate or gridiron, beneath which was a fire of charcoal. "And now, my lord abbot," said the Earl of Cassilis, "will you be pleased to sign these deeds?" And so saying, he laid before him leases and other papers, transferring the whole lands of the abbacy of Crossraguel to the Earl himself. The commendator refused to yield up the property or to subscribe the deeds. A party of ruffians then entered, and seizing the unhappy man, stripped him of his clothes, and forcibly stretched him on the iron bars, where he lay, scorched by the fire beneath, while they basted him with oil, as a cook bastes the joint of meat which she roasts upon a spit. The agony of such torture was not to be endured. The poor man cried pitifully, begging they would put him to instant death, rather than subject him to this lingering misery, and offered his purse, with the money it contained, to any who would in mercy shoot him through the head. At length he was obliged to promise to subscribe whatever the Earl wished, rather than endure the excessive torture any longer. The letters and leases being then presented to him, he signed them with his half-roasted hand, while the Earl all the while exclaimed, with the most impudent hypocrisy, "Benedicite! you are the most obstinate man I ever saw, to oblige me to use you thus: I never thought to have treated any one as your stubbornness has made me treat you." The commendator was afterwards delivered by a party commanded by Hamilton of Bargany, who attacked the Black Vault of Denure for the purpose of his liberation. But the wild, savage, and ferocious conduct of the Earl shows in what manner the nobles obtained grants of the church lands from those who had possession of them for the time.

The Earl of Morton, however, set the example of another and less violent mode of appropriating Church revenues to his own purposes. This was by reviving the order of bishops, which had been discarded from the Presbyterian form of Church government. For example, on the execution of the Archbishop of St. Andrews, he caused Douglas, Rector of St. Andrews, to be made archbishop in his place; but then he allowed this nominal prelate only a small pension out of the large revenues of the bishopric, and retained possession of all the rest of the income for his own advantage, though the rents were levied in the bishop's name.

These and other innovations gave great distress to John Knox, the bold and inflexible father of the Scottish Reformation. He saw with pain that the Protestant nobles were likely to diminish even the scanty subsistence which had hitherto been supplied to the Scottish clergy, out of the ample funds belonging originally to the Church of Rome. He was also jealous of the republican equality of the clergy, when he beheld the Church of Scotland innovated upon by this new introduction of bishops, though with limited incomes and diminished power. For these and other reasons he had more than once bitterly rebuked the Regent Morton; but when this remarkable man died, the Regent, who attended his funeral, pronounced over his coffin an eulogium never to be forgotten.—"There lies he," said Morton, "who never feared the face of man."

In the State as in the Church, the Regent displayed symptoms of a vindictive, avaricious, and corrupt disposition. Although the civil wars were ended, he resolved to avenge upon the Hamiltons the continued support which that powerful family had given to the Queen's party, and the obstacles which they had thrown in the way of his own exaltation. He proceeded to act against them as public enemies, drove them out of Scotland, and seized upon their estates. The Earl of Arran, eldest brother of the family, to whom the estates actually belonged, was insane, and in a state of confinement; but this did not prevent Morton from declaring that the earldom and the lands belonging to it were forfeited,—an abuse of law which scandalised all honest men.

It was not only by confiscation that Morton endeavoured to amass wealth. He took money for the offices which he had it in his power to bestow. Even in administering justice, his hands were not pure from bribes; to dispense the behests of law from favour or love of gain is one of the greatest crimes of which a public man can be guilty.

It is told of Morton, in a history of the family of Somerville, that a nobleman of that house having a great and important cause to be decided, in which the influence of the Regent might assuredly occasion it to be determined as he himself should think fit, he followed, by the advice of an ancient and experienced acquaintance of the Regent, the following singular course:—Lord Somerville waited on the Earl of Morton, and recommended his case to his favourable opinion,—a kind of personal solicitation which was then much in use. Having spoken with the Regent for a short time, he turned to depart, and, opening his purse, as if to take out some money to give to the ushers and attendants, as was the custom upon such occasions, he left the purse on the table as though he had forgot it. Morton called after him,—"My lord, your purse—you have forgotten your purse!"—but Lord Somerville hastened away without turning back. He heard nothing more of the purse, which he had taken care should be pretty full of gold; but Lord Morton that day decided the cause in his favour.

Instances of such base profligacy by degrees alienated from Morton even the affections of his best friends, and his government at length became so unpopular, that a universal wish was entertained that the King would put an end to the Regency by taking the government into his own hands.

These opinions prevailed so generally, that Morton, on the 12th March 1578, resigned his office of Regent, and retired to reside in his castle of Dalkeith, as a private man, leaving the affairs of state to be administered by a council of nobles, twelve in number. But accustomed to be at the head of the government, he could not long remain inactive. He burst from his seclusion in the gloomy fortress, which the people called the Lion's Den, and using a mixture of craft and force, expelled the new counsellors; and once more, after the old Douglas's fashion, obtained the supreme management of public affairs. But the sovereign was no longer a child. He was now begin-ning to think and act for himself; and it is necessary you should know something of his character.

James VI. was but an infant when he was placed on the throne of his mother. He was now only a boy of fourteen, very good-natured, and with as much learning as two excellent schoolmasters could cram him with. In fact, he had more learning than wisdom; and yet, in the course of his future life, it did not appear that he was without good sense so much, as that he was destitute of the power to form manly purposes, and the firmness necessary to maintain them. A certain childishness and meanness of mind rendered his good sense useless, and his learning ridiculous. Even from his infancy he was passionately addicted to favourites, and already, in his thirteenth or fourteenth year, there were two persons so high in his good graces that they could bring him to do anything they pleased

The first was Esme Stewart of Aubigny, a nephew of the late Earl of Lennox, and his heir. The King not only restored this young man to the honours of his family, but created him Duke of Lennox, and raised him with too prodigal generosity to a high situation in the state. There was nothing in the character of this favourite either to deserve such extreme preferment or to make him unworthy of it. He was a gallant young gentleman, who was deeply grateful to the King for his bounty, and appears to have been disposed to enjoy it without injuring any one.

Very different was the character of the other favourite of James VI. This was Captain James Stewart, a second son of the family of Ochiltree. He was an unprincipled, abandoned man, without any wisdom except cunning, and only distinguished by the audacity of his ambition and the boldness of his character.

The counsels of these two favourites increased the King's natural desire to put an end to the sway of Morton, and Stewart resolved that the pretext for his removal should also be one which should bring him to the block. The grounds of accusation were artfully chosen. The Earl of Morton, when he resigned the regency, had obtained a pardon under the great seal for all crimes and offences which he had or might have committed against the King; but there was no mention, in that pardon, of the murder of Henry Darnley, the King's father; and in counselling, if not in committing that murder, the Earl of Morton had certainly participated. The favourite Stewart took the office of accuser upon himself; and entering the King's chamber suddenly when the Privy Council were assembled, he dropped on his knees before James, and accused the Earl of Morton of having been concerned in the murder of the King's father. To this Morton, with a haughty smile, replied, that he had prosecuted the perpetrators of that offence too severely to make it probable that he himself was one of them. All he demanded was a fair inquiry.

Upon this public accusation, the Earl, so lately the most powerful man in Scotland, was made prisoner, and appointed to abide a trial. The friends he had left earnestly exhorted him to fly. His nephew, the Earl of Angus, offered to raise his men, and protect him by force. Morton refused both offers, alleging he would wait the event of a fair investigation. The Queen of England interfered in Morton's behalf with such partial eagerness, as perhaps prejudiced James still more against the prisoner, whom he was led to believe to be more attached to Elizabeth's service than to his own.

Meantime the accuser, Stewart, was promoted to the earldom of Arran, vacant by the forfeiture of the Hamiltons. Morton, who had no knowledge of this preferment, was astonished when he heard that the charge ran against him in the name of James, Earl of Arran. When it was explained to him who it was that now enjoyed the title, he observed, "Is it even so? then I know what I have to expect." It was supposed that he recollected an old prophecy, which foretold "that the Bloody Heart" (the cognisance of the Douglases) "should fall by the mouth of Arran;" and it was conjectured that the fear of some one of the Hamiltons accomplishing that prophecy had made him the more actively violent in destroying that family. If so, his own tyrannical oppression only opened the way for the creation of an Arran different from those whom he had thought of.

The trial of Morton appears to have been conducted with no attention to the rules of impartial justice; for the servants of the accused person were apprehended, and put to the torture, in order to extort from them confessions which might be fatal to their master. Morton protested against two or three persons who were placed upon his jury, as being his mortal enemies; but they were nevertheless retained. They brought in a verdict, finding that he was guilty, art and part, of the murder of Henry Darnley. A man is said to be art and part of a crime when he contrives the manner of the deed, and concurs with and encourages those who commit the crime, although he does not put his own hand to the actual execution of it. Morton heard the verdict with indignation, and struck his staff against the ground as he repeated the words, "Art and part! art and part! God knoweth the contrary." On the morning after his sentence he awoke from a profound sleep—"On former nights," he said, "I used to lie awake, thinking how I might defend myself; but now my mind is relieved of its burden." Being conjured by the clergyman who attended him to confess all he knew of Henry Darnley's murder, he told them, as we have noticed elsewhere, that a proposal had been made to him by Bothwell to be accessory to the deed, but that he had refused to assent to it without an order under the Queen's hand, which Bothwell promised to procure, but could not, or at least did not, do so. Morton admitted that he had kept the secret, not knowing, he said, to whom to discover it: for if he had told it Queen Mary, she was herself one of the conspirators; if to Darnley, he was of a disposition so fickle that the Queen would work it out of him, and then he, Morton, was equally undone. He also admitted, that he knew that his friend, dependent, and kinsman, Archibald Douglas, was present at the murder, whom, notwithstanding, he never brought to justice, but, on the contrary, continued to favour. Upon the whole, he seems to allow, that he suffered justly for concealing the crime, though he denied having given counsel or assistance to its actual execution. "But it is all the same," he said; "I should have had the same doom, whether I were as innocent as St. Stephen, or as guilty as Judas."

As they were about to lead the Earl to execution, Captain Stewart, his accuser, now Earl of Arran, came to urge his subscribing a paper containing the purport of his confession. Morton replied, "I pray you trouble me not; I am now to prepare for death, and cannot write in the state in which I am." Arran then desired to be reconciled to him, pretending he had only acted from public and conscientious motives. "It is no time to count quarrels now;" said the Earl—"I forgive you and all others."

This celebrated man died by a machine called the *Maiden*, which he himself had introduced into Scotland from Halifax, in Yorkshire. The criminal who suffered by this engine, was adjusted upon planks, in a prostrate state, his neck being placed beneath a sharp axe, heavily loaded with lead, which was suspended by a rope brought over a pulley. When the signal was given, the rope was cast loose, and the axe, descending on the neck of the condemned person, severed, of course, the head from the body. Morton submitted to his fate with the most Christian fortitude; and in him died the last of those terrible Douglases, whose talents and courage rendered them the pride of their country, but whose ambition was often its scourge. No one could tell what became of the treasures he had amassed, and for the sake of which he sacrificed his popularity as a liberal, and his conscience as an honest, man. He was, or seemed to be, so poor, that when going to the scaffold, he borrowed money from a friend, that he might bestow a parting alms upon the mendicants who solicited his charity. Some have thought that his mass of wealth lies still concealed among the secret vaults of his castle of Dalkeith, now belonging to the Duke of Buccleuch. But Hume of Godscroft, who writes the history of the Douglas family, says that large sums were expended by the Earl of Angus, the nephew of Morton, in maintaining a number of exiles, who, like the Earl himself, were banished from Scotland, and at length, when paying away some money for this purpose, he was heard to say, "The last of it is now gone, and I never looked that it should have done so much good." This Godscroft believed to allude to the final expenditure of the treasures of the Regent Morton.

After the death of Morton, his faults and crimes were in a great measure forgotten, when it was observed that Arran (that is, Captain Stewart) possessed all the late Regent's vices of corruption and oppression, without his wisdom or his talents. Lennox, the King's other favourite, was also unpopular, chiefly because he was unacceptable to the clergy, who, although he avowedly professed the Protestant religion, were jealous of his retaining an attachment to the Catholic faith. This suspicion arose from his having been educated in France. They publicly preached against him as "a great Champion called his Grace, who, if he continued to oppose himself to religion, should have little grace in the end."

A plot was formed among the discontented nobles to remove the King's favourites from the court; and this was to be accomplished by forcibly seizing on the person of the King himself, which, during the minority of the prince, was the ordinary mode of changing an administration in the kingdom of Scotland.

On the 23d August 1582 the Earl of Gowrie invited the King to his castle at Ruthven, under pretext of hunting; he was joined by the Earl of Mar, Lord Lindsay, the Tutor of Glamis, and other noblemen, chiefly such as had been friendly to the Regent Morton, and who were, like him, attached to Queen Elizabeth's faction. When the King saw so many persons gather round him whom he knew to be of one way of thinking, and that hostile to his present measures, he became apprehensive of their intentions, and expressed himself desirous of leaving the castle.

The nobles gave him to understand that he would not be permitted to do so; and when James rose and went towards the door of the apartment, the Tutor of Glamis, a rude stern man, placed his back against it, and compelled him to return. Affronted at this act of personal restraint and violence, the King burst into tears. "Let him weep on," said the Tutor of Glamis fiercely; "better that bairns (children) weep, than bearded men." These words sank deep into the King's heart, nor did he ever forget or forgive them.

The insurgent lords took possession of the government, and banished the Duke of Lennox to France, where he died brokenhearted at the fall of his fortunes. James afterwards recalled his son to Scotland, and invested him with his father's fortune and dignities. Arran, the King's much less worthy favourite, was thrown into prison, and closely guarded. The King himself, reduced to a state of captivity, like his grandfather, James V., when in the hands of the Douglases, temporised, and watched an opportunity of escape. His guards consisted of a hundred gentlemen, and their commander, Colonel Stewart, a relation of the disgraced and imprisoned Arran, was easily engaged to do what the King wished.

James, with the purpose of recovering his freedom, made a visit to St. Andrews, and, when there, affected some curiosity to see the castle. But no sooner had he entered it than he caused the gates to be shut, and excluded from his presence the nobles who had been accessary to what was called the Raid of Ruthven.

The Earl of Gowrie and his accomplices, being thus thrust out of office, and deprived of the custody of the King's person, united in a fresh plot for regaining the power they had lost, by a new insurrection. In this, however, they were unsuccessful. The King advanced against them with considerable forces; Gowrie was made prisoner, tried and executed at Stirling, 4th May 1584. Angus and the other insurgents fled to England, the ordinary refuge of Scottish exiles. The execution of Gowrie gave rise long afterwards to that extraordinary event in Scottish history called the Gowrie Conspiracy, of which I shall give you an account by and by.

The upstart Earl of Arran was now restored to power, and indeed raised higher than ever, by that indiscriminate affection which on this and other occasions induced James to heap wealth and rank without bounds upon his favourites. This worthless minister governed everything at court and throughout the kingdom; and, though ignorant as well as venal and profligate, he was raised to the dignity of Lord Chancellor, the highest law-office in the state, and that in which sagacity, learning, and integrity were chiefly required.

One day when the favourite was bustling into the Court of Justice, at the head of his numerous retinue, an old man, rather meanly dressed, chanced to stand in his way. As Arran pushed rudely past him, the man stopped him, and said, "Look at me, my lord,—I am Oliver Sinclair!" Oliver Sinclair, you remember, was the favourite of James V., and had exercised during his reign as absolute a sway in Scotland as Arran now enjoyed under his grandson, James VI. In presenting himself before the present favourite in his neglected condition, he gave Arran an example of the changeful character of court favour. The lesson was a striking one; but Arran did not profit by it.

The favourite's government became so utterly intolerable that, in the year 1585, the banished lords found a welcome reception in Scotland, and marching to Stirling at the head of ten thousand men, compelled James to receive them into his counsels; and, by using their victory with moderation, were enabled to maintain the power which they had thus gained. Arran, stripped of his earldom and ill-gotten gains, and banished from the court, was fain to live privately and miserably among the wilds of the north-west of Ayrshire, afraid of the vengeance of his numerous enemies.

The fate which he apprehended from their enmity befell him at length; for, in 1596, seeing, or thinking he saw, some chance of regaining the King's favour, and listening, as is said, to the words of some idle soothsayer, who pretended that his head was about to be raised higher than ever, Stewart (for he was an earl no longer) ventured into the southern country of Dumfries. Here he received a hint to take care of his safety, since he was now in the neighbourhood of the Douglases, whose great leader, the Earl of Morton, he had been the means of destroying; and in particular, he was advised to beware of James Douglas of Torthorwald, the Earl's near kinsman [nephew]. Stewart replied haughtily, he would not go out of his road for him or all of the name of Douglas. This was reported to Torthorwald, who, considering the expression as a defiance, immediately mounted, with three servants, and pursued the disgraced favourite. When they overtook him, they thrust a spear through his body, and killed him[1] on the spot without resistance. His head was cut off, placed on the point of a lance, and exposed from the battlements of the tower of Torthorwald; and thus, in some sense, the soothsayer's prophecy was made good, as his head was raised higher than before, though not in the way he had been made to hope. His body was left for several days on the place where he was killed, and was mangled by dogs and swine. So ended this worthless minion, by a death at once bloody and obscure.

---

[1] Sir James Douglas was killed on the High Street of Edinburgh, 1608, by Captain William Stewart, a nephew of the chancellor, who ran him through the body to revenge his uncle's death.

XXXIII

From Kingdom to Empire

1586-1603

I DARESAY you are wondering all this time what became of Queen Mary. We left her, you know, in the hands of Queen Elizabeth, who had refused to decide anything on the question of her guilt or innocence. This was in 1568–69; and undoubtedly, by every rule of law or justice, Mary ought then to have been set at liberty. She had been accused of matters which Elizabeth herself had admitted were not brought home to her by proof, and of which, even if they had been proved, the Queen of England had no right to take cognisance. Nevertheless, Elizabeth continued to treat Mary as guilty, though she declined to pronounce her so, and to use her as her subject, though she was an independent sovereign, who had chosen England for a retreat, in the hope of experiencing that hospitable protection which would have been given to the meanest Scottish subject, who, flying from the laws of his own country, sought refuge in the sister kingdom. When you read English history, you will see that Elizabeth was a great and glorious Queen, and well deserved the title of the Mother of her country; but her conduct towards Queen Mary casts a deep shade over her virtues, and leads us to reflect what poor frail creatures even the wisest of mortals are, and of what imperfect materials that which we call human virtue is found to consist.

Always demanding her liberty, and always having her demand evaded or refused, Mary was transported from castle to castle,[1] and placed under the charge of various keepers, who incurred Elizabeth's most severe resentment when they manifested any of that attention to soften the rigours of the poor Queen's captivity, which mere courtesy, and compassion for fallen greatness, sometimes prompted. The very furniture and accommodations of her apartments were miserably neglected, and the expenses of her household were supplied as grudgingly as if she had been an unwelcome guest, who could depart at pleasure, and whom, therefore, the entertainer endeavours to get rid of by the coldness and discomfort of the reception afforded. It was, upon one occasion, with difficulty that the Queen Dowager of France, and actual Queen of Scotland, obtained the accommodation of a down bed, which a complaint in her limbs, the consequence of damp and confinement, rendered a matter of needful accommodation rather than of luxury. When she was permitted to take exercise, she was always strongly guarded, as if she had been a criminal; and if any one offered her a compliment, or token of respect, or any word of comfort, Queen Elizabeth, who had her spies everywhere, was sure to reproach those who were Mary's guardians for the time, with great neglect of their duty, in permitting such intercourse.

During this severe captivity on the one part, and the greatest anxiety, doubt, and jealousy on the other, the two Queens still kept up a sort of correspondence. In the commencement of this intercourse, Mary endeavoured, by the force of argument, by the seductions of flattery, and by appeals to the feelings of humanity, to soften towards her the heart of Elizabeth. She tried also to bribe her rival into a more humane conduct towards her, by offering to surrender her crown and reside abroad if she could but be restored to her personal freedom. But Elizabeth had injured the Queen of Scotland too deeply to venture the consequences of her resentment, and thought herself, perhaps, compelled to continue the course she had commenced, from the fear that

---

[1] On her own solicitations, for the recovery of health, Mary was allowed visits to Buxton; but all the while a prisoner; the waters there were of little avail when air, exercise, and amusement were denied. Her forced removals were, in 1568, from Carlisle to Bolton,—1569, to Tutbury, Wingfield, Tutbury, Ashby-de-la-Zouche, Coventry,—1570, to Tutbury, Chatsworth, Sheffield,—1577, to Chatsworth,—1578, to Sheffield,—1584, to Wingfield,—1585, to Tutbury, Chartley, Tixhall, Chartley,—1586 (25th September), to Fotheringay.

once at liberty, Mary might have pursued measures of revenge, and that she herself would find it impossible to devise any mode of binding the Scottish Queen to perform, when at large, such articles as she might consent to when in bondage.

Despairing at length of making any favourable impression, upon Elizabeth, Mary, with more wit than prudence, used her means of communicating with the Queen of England to irritate and provoke her; yielding to the not unnatural, though certainly the rash and impolitic purpose, of retaliating some part of the pain to which she was herself subjected upon the person whom she justly considered as the authoress of her calamities.

Being for a long time under the charge of the Earl of Shrewsbury, whose lady was a woman of a shrewish disposition, Mary used to report to Elizabeth that the countess had called her old and ugly; had said she was grown as crooked in her temper as in her body, with many other scandalous and abusive expressions, which must have given exquisite pain to any woman, and more especially to a Queen so proud as Elizabeth, and desirous, even in old age, of being still esteemed beautiful. Unquestionably these reproaches added poignancy to the hatred with which the English sovereign regarded Queen Mary.

But, besides these female reasons for detesting her prisoner, Elizabeth had cause to regard the Queen of Scots with fear as well as envy and hatred. The Catholic party in England were still very strong, and they considered the claim of Mary to the throne of England as descended from the Princess Margaret, daughter of Henry VII., to be preferable to that of the existing Queen, who was, in their judgment, illegitimate, as being the heir of an illegal marriage betwixt Henry VIII. and Anne Boleyn. The Popes also, by whom Elizabeth was justly regarded as the great prop of the Reformed religion, endeavoured to excite against her such of her subjects as still owned obedience to the see of Rome. At length, in 1570-71, Pius V., then the reigning Pope, published a bull, or sentence of excommunication, by which he deprived Queen Elizabeth (as far as his sentence could) of her hopes of heaven, and of her kingdom upon earth, excluded her from the privileges of Christians, and delivered her over as a criminal to whomsoever should step forth to vindicate the Church, by putting to death its greatest enemy. The zeal of the English Catholics was kindled by this warrant from the head of their Church. One of them [named Felton] was found bold enough to fix a copy of the sentence of excommunication upon the door of the Bishop of London, and various plots were entered into among the Papists for dethroning Elizabeth, and transferring the kingdom of England to Mary, a sovereign of their own religion, and in their eyes the lawful successor to the crown.

As fast as one of these conspiracies was discovered, another seemed to form itself; and as the Catholics were promised powerful assistance from the King of Spain, and were urged forward by the impulse of enthusiasm, the danger appeared every day more and more imminent. It cannot be doubted that several of these plots were communicated to Mary in her imprisonment; and, considering what grounds she had to complain of Elizabeth, it would have been wonderful if she had betrayed to her jailer the schemes which were formed to set her at liberty. But these conspiracies coming so closely the one after the other, produced one of the most extraordinary laws that was ever passed in England; declaring that if any rebellion, or any attempt against Queen Elizabeth's person, should be meditated by, or for, any person pretending a right to the crown, the Queen might grant a commission to twenty-five persons, who should have power to examine into, and pass sentence upon, such offences; and, after judgment given, a proclamation was to be issued, depriving the persons in whose behalf the plots or rebellion had been made of all right to the throne; and it was enacted that they might be prosecuted to the death. The hardship of this enactment consisted in its rendering Mary, against whom it was levelled, responsible for the deeds of others, as well as for her own actions; so that if the Catholics arose in rebellion, although without warrant from Mary, or even against her inclination, she was nevertheless rendered liable to lose her right of succession to the crown, and indeed to forfeit her life. Nothing short of the zeal of the English Government for the Reformed religion, and for the personal safety of Elizabeth, could have induced them to consent to a law so unjust and so oppressive.

This act was passed in 1585, and in the following year a pretext was found for making it the ground of proceedings against Mary. Anthony Babington, a young gentleman of fortune and of talents, but a zealous Catholic, and a fanatical enthusiast for the cause of the Scottish Queen, had associated with himself five resolute friends and adherents, all men of condition, in the desperate enterprise of assassinating Queen Elizabeth, and setting Mary at liberty. But their schemes were secretly betrayed to Walsingham, the celebrated minister of the

Queen of England. They were suffered to proceed as far as was thought safe, then seized, tried, and executed.

It was next resolved upon, that Mary should be brought to trial for her life, under pretence of her having encouraged Babington and his companions in their desperate purpose. She was removed to the castle of Fotheringay, and placed under two keepers, Sir Amias Paulet and Sir Drew Drury, whose well-known hatred of the Catholic religion was supposed to render them inclined to treat their unfortunate captive with the utmost rigour. Her private cabinet was broken open and stripped of its contents, her most secret papers were seized upon and examined, her principal domestics were removed from her person, her money and her jewels were taken from her. Queen Elizabeth then proceeded to name Commissioners, in terms of the Act of Parliament which I have told you of. They were forty in number, of the most distinguished of her statesmen and nobility, and were directed to proceed to the trial of Mary for her alleged accession to Babington's conspiracy.

On the 14th October 1586 these Commissioners held their court in the great hall of Fotheringay Castle. Mary, left to herself, and having counsel of no friend, advocate, or lawyer, made, nevertheless, a defence becoming her high birth and distinguished talents. She refused to plead before a court composed of persons who were of a degree inferior to her own; and when at length she agreed to hear and answer the accusation brought against her, she made her protest that she did so, not as owning the authority of the court, but purely in vindication of her own character.

The attorney and solicitor for Queen Elizabeth stated the conspiracy of Babington, as it unquestionably existed, and produced copies of letters which Mary was alleged to have written, approving the insurrection, and even the assassination of Elizabeth. The declarations of Naue and Curle, two of Mary's secretaries, went to confirm the fact of her having had correspondence with Babington, by intervention of a priest called Ballard. The confessions of Babington and his associates were then read, avowing Mary's share in their criminal undertaking.

To these charges Mary answered, by denying that she ever had any correspondence with Ballard, or that she had ever written such letters as those produced against her. She insisted that she could only be affected by such writings as bore her own hand and seal, and not by copies. She urged that the declarations of her secretaries were given in private, and probably under the influence of fear of torture, or hope of reward, of which, indeed, there is every probability. Lastly, she pleaded that the confessions of the conspirators could not affect her, since they were infamous persons, dying for an infamous crime. If their evidence was designed to be used, they ought to have been pardoned, and brought forward in person, to bear witness against her. Mary admitted that, having for many years despaired of relief or favour from Queen Elizabeth, she had, in her distress, applied to other sovereigns, and that she had also endeavoured to procure some favour for the persecuted Catholics of England; but she denied that she had endeavoured to purchase liberty for herself, or advantage for the Catholics, at the expense of shedding the blood of any one; and declared, that if she had given consent in word, or even in thought, to the murder of Elizabeth, she was willing, not only to submit to the doom of men, but even to renounce the mercy of God.

The evidence which was brought to convict the Queen of Scotland was such as would not now affect the life of the meanest criminal; yet the Commission had the cruelty and meanness to declare Mary guilty of having been accessary to Babington's conspiracy, and of having contrived and endeavoured the death of Queen Elizabeth, contrary to the statute made for security of the Queen's life. And the Parliament of England approved of and ratified this iniquitous sentence.

It was not perhaps to be expected that James VI. should have had much natural affection for his mother, whom he had never seen since his infancy, and who had, doubtless, been represented to him as a very bad woman, and as one desirous, if she could have obtained her liberty, of dispossessing him of the crown which he wore, and resuming it herself. He had, therefore, seen Mary's captivity with little of the sympathy which a child ought to feel for a parent. But, upon learning these proceedings against her life, he must have been destitute of the most ordinary feelings of human nature, and would have made himself a reproach and scandal throughout all Europe, if he had not interfered in her behalf. He therefore sent ambassadors, first, Sir William Keith, and after him the Master of Gray, to intercede with Queen Elizabeth, and to use both persuasion and threats to preserve the life of his mother. The friendship of Scotland was at this moment of much greater importance to England than at any previous period of her history. The King of Spain was in the act of assembling a vast navy and army (boastingly called the Invincible Armada), by which he proposed to invade and conquer England; and if James VI. had been disposed to open the ports and harbours of Scotland to the Spanish fleets and armies, he might have greatly facilitated this formidable invasion, by diminishing the risk which the Armada might incur from the English fleet.

It therefore seems probable, that had James himself been very serious in his interposition, or had his ambassador been disposed to urge the interference committed to his charge with due firmness and vigour, it could scarce have failed in being successful, at least for a time. But the Master of Gray, as is now admitted, privately encouraged Elizabeth and her ministers to proceed in the cruel path they had chosen, and treacherously gave them reason to believe, that though, for the sake of decency, James found it necessary to interfere in his mother's behalf, yet, in his secret mind, he would not be very sorry that Mary, who, in the eyes of a part of his subjects, was still regarded as sovereign of Scotland, should be quietly removed out of the way. From the intrigues of this treacherous ambassador, Elizabeth was led to trust that the resentment of the King for his mother's death would neither be long nor violent; and, knowing her own influence with a great part of the Scottish nobility, and the zeal of the Scots in general for the Reformed religion, she concluded that the motives arising out of these circumstances would prevent James from making common cause against England with the King of Spain.

At any other period in the English history, it is probable that a sovereign attempting such an action as Elizabeth meditated, might have been interrupted by the generous and manly sense of justice and humanity peculiar to a free and high-minded people like those of England. But the despotic reign of Henry VIII. had too much familiarised the English with the sight of the blood of great persons, and even of queens, poured forth by the blow of the executioner, upon the slightest pretexts; and the idea that Elizabeth's life could not be in safety while Mary existed, was, in the deep sentiment of loyalty and affection which they entertained for their Queen (and which the general tenour of her reign well deserved), strong enough to render them blind to the gross injustice exercised upon a stranger and a Catholic.

Yet with all the prejudices of her subjects in her own favour, Elizabeth would fain have had Mary's death take place in such a way as that she herself should not appear to have any hand in it. Her ministers were employed to write letters to Mary's keepers, insinuating what a good service they would do to Elizabeth and the Protestant religion, if

Mary could be privately assassinated. But these stern guardians, though strict and severe in their conduct towards the Queen, would not listen to such persuasions; and well was it for them that they did not, for Elizabeth would certainly have thrown the whole blame of the deed upon their shoulders, and left them to answer it with their lives and fortunes. She was angry with them, nevertheless, for their refusal, and called Paulet a precise fellow, loud in boasting of his fidelity, but slack in giving proof of it.

As, however, it was necessary, from the scruples of Paulet and Drury, to proceed in all form, Elizabeth signed a warrant for the execution of the sentence pronounced on Queen Mary, and gave it to Davison, her secretary of state, commanding that it should be sealed with the great seal of England. Davison laid the warrant, signed by Elizabeth, before the Privy Council, and next day the great seal was placed upon it. Elizabeth, upon hearing this, affected some displeasure that the warrant had been so speedily prepared, and told the secretary that it was the opinion of wise men that some other course might be taken with Queen Mary. Davison, in this pretended change of mind, saw some danger that his mistress might throw the fault of the execution upon him after it had taken place. He therefore informed the Keeper of the Seals what the Queen had said, protesting he would not venture farther in the matter. The Privy Council, having met together, and conceiving themselves certain what were the Queen's real wishes, determined to save her the pain of expressing them more broadly, and resolving that the blame, if any might arise, should be common to them all, sent off the warrant for execution with their clerk Beale. The Earls of Kent and Shrewsbury, with the High Sheriff of the county, were empowered and commanded to see the fatal mandate carried into effect without delay.

Mary received the melancholy intelligence with the utmost firmness. "The soul," she said, "was undeserving of the joys of Heaven, which would shrink from the blow of an executioner. She had not," she added, "expected that her kinswoman would have consented to her death, but submitted not the less willingly to her fate." She earnestly requested the assistance of a priest; but this favour, which is granted to the worst criminals, and upon which Catholics lay particular weight, was cruelly refused. The Queen then wrote her last will, and short and affectionate letters of farewell to her relations in France. She distributed among her attendants such valuables as had been left her, and desired them to keep them for her sake. This occupied the evening before the day appointed for the fatal execution.

On the 8th February 1587 the Queen, still maintaining the same calm and undisturbed appearance which she had displayed at her pretended trial, was brought down to the great hall of the castle, where a scaffold was erected, on which were placed a block and a chair, the whole being covered with black cloth. The Master of her Household, Sir Andrew Melville, was permitted to take a last leave of the mistress whom he had served long and faithfully. He burst into loud lamentations, bewailing her fate, and deploring his own in being destined to carry such news to Scotland. "Weep not, my good Melville," said the Queen, "but rather rejoice; for thou shalt this day see Mary Stewart relieved from all her sorrows." She obtained permission, with some difficulty, that her maids should be allowed to attend her on the scaffold. It was objected to, that the extravagance of their grief might disturb the proceedings; she engaged for them that they would be silent.

When the Queen was seated in the fatal chair, she heard the death warrant read by Beale, the Clerk to the Privy Council, with an appearance of indifference; nor did she seem more attentive to the devotional exercises of the Dean of Peterborough, in which, as a Catholic, she could not conscientiously join. She implored the mercy of Heaven, after the form prescribed by her own Church. She then prepared herself for execution, taking off such parts of her dress as might interfere with the deadly blow. The executioners offered their assistance, but she modestly refused it, saying, she had neither been accustomed to undress before so many spectators, nor to be served by such grooms of the chamber. She quietly chid her maids, who were unable to withhold their cries of lamentation, and reminded them that she had engaged for their silence. Last of all Mary laid her head on the block, and the executioner severed it from her body with two strokes of his axe. The headsman held it up in his hand, and the Dean of Peterborough cried out, "So perish all Queen Elizabeth's enemies!" No voice, save that of the Earl of Kent, could answer *Amen!* the rest were choked with sobs and tears.

Thus died Queen Mary, aged a little above forty-four years. She was eminent for beauty, for talents, and accomplishments, nor is there reason to doubt her natural goodness of heart, and courageous manliness of disposition. Yet she was, in every sense, one of the most unhappy princesses that ever lived, from the moment when she came into the world, in an hour of defeat and danger, to that in which a bloody and violent death closed a weary captivity of eighteen years.

Queen Elizabeth, in the same spirit of hypocrisy which had characterised all her proceedings towards Mary, no sooner knew that the deed was done, than she hastened to deny her own share in it. She pretended, that Davison had acted positively against her command in laying the warrant before the Privy Council; and that she might seem the more serious in her charge, she caused him to be fined in a large sum of money, and deprived him of his offices, and of her favour for ever. She sent a special ambassador to King James, to apologise for "this unhappy accident," as she chose to term the execution of Queen Mary.

James at first testified high indignation, with which the Scottish nation was well disposed to sympathise. He refused to admit the English envoy to his presence, and uttered menaces of revenge. When a general mourning was ordered for the departed Queen, the Earl of Argyle appeared at the court in armour, as if that were the proper way of showing the national sense of the treatment which Mary had received. But James's hopes and fears were now fixed upon the succession to the English crown, which would have been forfeited by engaging in a war with Elizabeth. Most of his ancestors, indeed, would have set that objection at defiance, and have broken into the English frontier at the head of as large an army as Scotland could raise; but James was by nature timorous and unwarlike. He was conscious that the poor and divided country of Scotland was not fit, in its own strength, to encounter a kingdom so wealthy and so unanimous as England. On the other hand, if James formed an alliance with the Spanish monarch, he considered that he would probably have been deserted by the Reformed part of his subjects; and, besides, he was aware that Philip of Spain himself laid claim to the Crown of England; so that to assist that prince in his meditated invasion would have been to rear up an important obstacle to the accomplishment of his own hopes of the English succession. James, therefore, gradually softening towards Queen Elizabeth, affected to believe the excuses which she offered; and in a short time they were upon as friendly a footing as they had been before the death of the unfortunate Mary.

James was now in full possession of the Scottish kingdom, and showed himself to as much, or greater advantage, than at any subsequent period of his life. After the removal of the vile James Stewart from his counsels, he acted chiefly by the advice of Sir John Maitland, the Chancellor, a brother of that Maitland of Lethington whom we have so often mentioned. He was a prudent and good minister; and as it was James's nature, in which there was a strange mixture of wisdom and of weakness, to act with sagacity, or otherwise, according to the counsels which he received, there now arose in Britain, and even in Europe, a more general respect for his character, than was afterwards entertained when it became better known.

Besides, James's reign in Scotland was marked with so many circumstances of difficulty, and even of danger, that he was placed upon his guard, and compelled to conduct himself with the strictest attention to the rules of prudence; for he had little chance of overawing his turbulent nobility, but by maintaining the dignity of the royal character. If the King had possessed the ability of distributing largesses among his powerful subjects, his influence would have been greater; but this was so far from being the case, that his means of supporting his royal state, excepting an annuity allowed to him by Elizabeth of five thousand pounds yearly, were in the last degree precarious. This was owing in a great measure to the plundering of the revenue of the crown during the civil wars of his minority, and the regency of the Earl of Morton. The King was so dependent that he could not even give an entertainment without begging poultry and venison from some of his more wealthy subjects; and his wardrobe was so ill-furnished that he was obliged to request the loan of a pair of silk hose from the Earl of Mar, that he might be suitably apparelled to receive the Spanish ambassador.

There were also peculiarities in James's situation which rendered it embarrassing. He had extreme difficulty in his necessary intercourse with the Scottish clergy, who possessed a strong influence over the minds of the people, and sometimes used it in interference with public affairs. Although they had not, like the bishops of England and other countries, a seat in Parliament, yet they did not the less intermeddle with politics, and often preached from the pulpit against the King and his measures. They used this freedom the more boldly, because they asserted that they were not answerable to any civil court for what they might say in their sermons, but only to the spiritual courts, as they were called; that is, the Synods and General Assemblies of the Church, composed chiefly of clergymen like themselves, and who, therefore, were not likely to put a check upon the freedom of speech used by their brethren.

Upon one occasion, which occurred 17th December 1596, disputes of this kind between the King and the Church came to such a height that the rabble of the city, inflamed by the violence of some of the sermons which they heard, broke out into tumult, and besieged the door of the Tolbooth, where James was sitting in the administration of justice, and threatened to break it open. The King was saved by the intervention of the better disposed part of the inhabitants, who rose in arms for his protection. Nevertheless he left Edinburgh the next day in great anger, and prepared to take away the privileges of the city, as a punishment for the insolence of the rioters. He was appeased with much difficulty, and, as it seemed, was by no means entirely satisfied; for he caused the High Street to be occupied by a great number of the Border and Highland clans. The citizens, terrified by the appearance of these formidable and lawless men, concluded that the town was to be plundered, and the alarm was very great. But the King, who only desired to frighten them, made the magistrates a long harangue upon the excesses of which he complained, and admitted them to pardon, upon their submission.

Another great plague of James the Sixth's reign was the repeated insurrections of a turbulent nobleman, called Francis Stewart, Earl of Bothwell,—a different person, of course, from James Hepburn, who bore that title in the reign of Queen Mary. This second Earl of Bothwell was a relation of the King's, and made several violent attempts to get possession of his person, with the purpose of governing the state, as the Douglases did of old, by keeping the King prisoner. But although he nearly succeeded on one or two occasions, yet James was always rescued from his hands, and was finally powerful enough to banish Bothwell altogether from the country. He died in contempt and exile.

But by far the greatest pest of Scotland at that time was the deadly feuds among the nobility and gentry, which eventually led to the most bloody consequences, and were perpetuated from father to son; while the King's good nature, which rendered him very ready to grant pardons to those who had committed such inhuman outrages, made the evil still more frequent. The following is a remarkable instance:—

The Earl of Huntly, head of the powerful family of Gordon, and the man of greatest consequence in the north of Scotland, had chanced to have some feudal differences with the Earl of Murray, son-in-law of the Regent-earl of the same name, in the course of which, John Gordon, a brother of Gordon of Cluny, was killed by a shot from Murray's castle of Darnaway. This was enough to make the two families irreconcilable enemies, even if they had been otherwise on friendly terms. Murray was so handsome and personable a man, that he was generally known by the name of the Bonnie Earl of Murray. About 1591-92 an accusation was brought against Murray, for having given some countenance or assistance to Stewart, Earl of Bothwell, in a recent treasonable exploit. James, without recollecting, perhaps, the hostility between the two earls, sent Huntly with a commission to bring the Earl of Murray to his presence. Huntly probably rejoiced in the errand, as giving him an opportunity of avenging himself on his feudal enemy. He beset the house of Donibristle, on the northern side of the Forth, and summoned Murray to surrender. In reply, a gun was fired, which mortally wounded one of the Gordons. The assailants proceeded to set fire to the house; when Dunbar, Sheriff of the county of Moray, said to the Earl, "Let us not stay to be burned in the flaming house; I will go out foremost, and the Gordons, taking me for your lordship, will kill me, while you escape in the confusion." They rushed out among their enemies accordingly, and Dunbar was slain. But his death did not save his friend, as he had generously intended. Murray indeed escaped for the moment, but as he fled towards the rocks by the seashore, he was traced by the silken tassels attached to his headpiece, which had taken fire as he broke out from among the flames. By this means the pursuers followed him down amongst the cliffs near the sea, and Gordon of Buckie, who is said to have been the first that overtook him, wounded him mortally. As Murray was gasping in the last agony, Huntly came up; and it is alleged by tradition, that Gordon pointed his dirk against the person of his chief, saying, "By Heaven, my lord, you shall be as deep in as I," and so compelled him to wound Murray whilst he was dying. Huntly, with a wavering hand, struck the expiring earl on the face. Thinking of his superior beauty, even in that moment of parting life, Murray stammered out the dying words, "You have spoiled a better face than your own."

After this deed of violence, Huntly did not choose to return to Edinburgh, but departed for the North. He took refuge for the moment in the castle of Ravenscraig, belonging to the Lord Sinclair, who told him, with a mixture of Scottish caution and Scottish hospitality, that he was welcome to come in, but would have been twice as welcome to have passed by. Gordon of Buckie, when a long period had elapsed, avowed his contrition for the guilt he had incurred.

Soon afterwards, three lords, the Earls of Huntly and Errol, who had always professed the Catholic religion, and the young Earl of Angus, who had become a convert to that faith, were accused of corresponding with the King of Spain, and of designing to introduce Spanish troops into Scotland for the restoration of the Catholic religion. The story which was told of this conspiracy does not seem very probable. However, the King ordered the Earl of Argyle to march against the Popish lords, with the northern forces of Lord Forbes and others, who were chiefly Protestants, and entered into the war with the religious emulation which divided the Reformers from the Catholics. Argyle likewise levied great bands of the Western Highlanders, who cared but little about religion, but were extremely desirous of plunder.

The army of Argyle, about ten thousand strong, encountered the forces of Huntly and Errol at Glenlivat, on the 3d of October 1594. The shock was very smart. But the Gordons and Hays, though far inferior in numbers, were gentlemen, well mounted, and completely armed, and the followers of Argyle had only their plaids and bonnets. Besides, the two earls had two or three pieces of cannon, of which the Highlanders, unaccustomed to anything of the kind, were very apprehensive. The consequence of the encounter was, that though the cavalry had to charge up a hill, encumbered with rocks and stones, and although the Highlanders fought with great courage, the small body of Huntly and Errol, not amounting to above fifteen hundred horse, broke, and dispersed with great loss the numerous host opposed to them. On the side of Argyle there was some treachery; the Grants, it is said, near neighbours, and some of them dependents, of the Gordons, joined their old friends in the midst of the fray. The Chief of MacLean and his followers defended themselves with great courage, but were at length completely routed. This was one of the occasions on which the Highland irregular infantry were found inferior to the compact charge of the cavaliers of the Lowland counties, with their long lances, who beat them down, and scattered them in every direction.

Upon learning Argyle's defeat, the King himself advanced into the north with a small army, and restored tranquillity by punishing the insurgent earls.

We have before mentioned, that in those wild days the very children had their deadly feuds, carried weapons, and followed the bloody example of their fathers. The following instance of their early ferocity occurred in September 1595. The scholars of the High School of Edinburgh, having a dispute with their masters about the length of their holidays, resolved to stand out for a longer vacation. Accordingly, they took possession of the school in that sort of mutinous manner, which in England is called *Barring-out,* and resisted the admission of the masters. Such foolish things have often occurred in public schools elsewhere; but what was peculiar to the High School boys of Edinburgh was, that they defended the school with sword and pistol, and when Bailie MacMorran, one of the magistrates, gave directions to force the entrance, three of the boys fired, and killed him on the spot. There were none of them punished, because it was alleged that it could not be known which of them did the deed; but rather because two of them were gentlemen's sons. So you see the bloodthirsty spirit of the times descended even to children.

To do justice to James VI., he adopted every measure in his power to put an end to these fatal scenes of strife and bloodshed. Wise laws were made for preventing the outrages which had been so general; and in order to compose the feuds amongst the nobles, James invited the principal lords, who had quarrels, to a great banquet, where he endeavoured to make them agree together, and caused them to take each other's hands and become friends on the spot. They obeyed him; and proceeding himself at their head, he made them walk in procession to the cross of Edinburgh,[1] still hand in hand, in token of perfect reconciliation, whilst the provost and magistrates danced before them for joy, to see such a prospect of peace and concord. Perhaps this reconciliation was too hasty to last long in every instance; but upon the whole, the authority of the law gradually gained strength, and the passions of men grew less fierce as it became more unsafe to indulge them.

I must now fulfil my promise, and in this place, tell you of another exploit on the Borders, the last that was performed there, but certainly not the least remarkable for valour and conduct.

The English and Scottish Wardens, or their deputies, had held a day of truce for settling Border disputes, and, having parted friends, both, with their followers, were returning home. At every such meeting it was the general rule on the Borders that there should be an absolute truce for twenty-four hours, and that all men who attended the Warden on either side to the field should have permission to ride home again undisturbed.

---

[1] "A collation of wine and sweetmeats was prepared at the public Cross, and there they, King and nobles, drank to each other with all the signs of reciprocal forgiveness and of future friendship."—ROBERTSON.

Now, there had come to the meeting, with other Border men, a notorious depredator, called William Armstrong, but more commonly known by the name of Kinmont Willie. This man was riding home on the north or Scottish side of the Liddell, where that stream divides England and Scotland, when some of the English who had enmity against him, or had suffered by his incursions, were unable to resist the temptation to attack him. They accordingly dashed across the river, pursued Kinmont Willie more than a mile within Scotland, made him prisoner, and brought him to Carlisle Castle.

As the man talked boldly and resolutely about the breach of truce in his person, and demanded peremptorily to be set at liberty, Lord Scrope told him scoffingly, that before he left the castle he should bid him "Farewell," meaning, that he should not go without his leave. The prisoner boldly answered, "That he would not go without bidding him good-night."

The Lord of Buccleuch, who was Warden, or Keeper, of Liddesdale, demanded the restoration of Kinmont Willie to liberty, and complained of his being taken and imprisoned as a breach of the Border laws, and an insult done to himself. Lord Scrope refused, or at least evaded, giving up his prisoner. Buccleuch then sent him a challenge, which Lord Scrope declined to accept on the ground of his employment in the public service. The Scottish chief, therefore, resolved to redress by force the insult which his country as well as himself had sustained on the occasion. He collected about three hundred of his best men, and made a night march to Carlisle Castle. A small party of chosen men dismounted, while the rest remained on horseback, to repel any attack from the town. The night being misty and rainy, the party to whom that duty was committed approached the foot of the walls, and tried to scale them by means of ladders which they had brought with them for the purpose. But the ladders were found too short. They then, with mining instruments which they had provided, burst open a postern, or wicket-door, and entered the castle. Their chief had given them strict orders to do no harm save to those who opposed them, so that the few guards, whom the alarm brought together, were driven back without much injury. Being masters of the castle, the trumpets of the Scottish Warden were then blown, to the no small terror of the inhabitants of Carlisle, surprised out of their quiet sleep by the sounds of invasion at so early an hour. The bells of the castle rang out; those of the Cathedral and Moot-hall answered;

drums beat to arms; and beacons were lighted, to alarm the warlike country around.

In the meanwhile, the Scottish party had done the errand they came for. They had freed Kinmont Willie from his dungeon. The first thing Armstrong did was to shout a good-night to Lord Scrope, asking him, at the same time, if he had any news for Scotland. The Borderers strictly obeyed the commands of their chief, in forbearing to take any booty. They returned from the castle, bringing with them their rescued countryman, and a gentleman named Spenser, an attendant on the constable of the castle. Buccleuch dismissed him, with his commendations to Salkeld the constable, whom he esteemed, he said, a better gentleman than Lord Scrope, bidding him say it was the Warden of Liddesdale who had done the exploit, and praying the constable, if he desired the name of a man of honour, to issue forth and seek a revenge. Buccleuch then ordered the retreat, which he performed with great leisure, and re-entered Scotland at sunrise in honour and safety. "There had never been a more gallant deed of vassalage done in Scotland," says an old historian, "no, not in Wallace's days."

Queen Elizabeth, as you may imagine, was dreadfully angry at this insult, and demanded that Buccleuch should be delivered up to the English, as he had committed so great an aggression upon their frontier during the time of peace. The matter was laid before the Scottish Parliament. King James himself pleaded the question on the part of Elizabeth, willing, it may be supposed, to recommend himself to that princess by his tameness and docility. The Secretary of State replied in defence of Buccleuch; and the Scottish Parliament finally voted that they would refer the question to commissioners, to be chosen for both nations, and would abide by their decision. But concerning the proposed surrender of Buccleuch to England, the President declared, with a loud voice, that it would be time enough for Buccleuch to go to England when the King should pass there in person.

Buccleuch finally ended the discussion by going to England at the King's personal request, and on the understanding that no evil was to be done to him. Queen Elizabeth desired to see him personally, and demanded of him how he dared commit such aggression on her territory. He answered undauntedly, that he knew not that thing which a man dared NOT do. Elizabeth admired the answer, and treated this powerful Border chief with distinction during the time he remained in England, which was not long.

But the strangest adventure of James's reign was the event called the Gowrie Conspiracy, over which there hangs a sort of mystery, which time has not even yet completely dispelled. You must recollect that there was an Earl of Gowrie condemned and executed when James was but a boy. This nobleman left two sons, bearing the family name of Ruthven, who were well educated abroad, and accounted hopeful young men. The King restored to the eldest the title and estate of Gowrie, and favoured them both very much.

Now, it chanced in the month of August 1600 that Alexander Ruthven, the younger of the two brothers, came early one morning to the King, who was then hunting in the Park of Falkland, and told him a story of his having seized a suspicious-looking man, a Jesuit, as he supposed, with a large pot of gold under his cloak. This man Ruthven said he had detained prisoner at his brother's house, in Perth, till the King should examine him, and take possession of the treasure. With this story he decoyed James from the hunting-field, and persuaded him to ride with him to Perth, without any other company than a few noblemen and attendants, who followed the King without orders.

When they arrived at Perth, they entered Gowrie House, the mansion of the Earl, a large massive building, having gardens which stretched down to the river Tay. The Earl of Gowrie was, or seemed, surprised, to see the King arrive so unexpectedly, and caused some entertainment to be hastily prepared for his Majesty's refreshment. After the King had dined, Alexander Ruthven pressed him to come with him to see the prisoner in private; and James, curious by nature, and sufficiently indigent to be inquisitive after money, followed him from one apartment to another, until Ruthven led him into a little turret, where there stood—not a prisoner with a pot of gold—but an armed man, prepared, as it seemed, for some violent enterprise.

The King started back, but Ruthven snatched the dagger which the man wore, and, pointing it to James's breast, reminded him of his father the Earl of Gowrie's death, and commanded him, upon pain of death, to submit to his pleasure. The King replied that he was but a boy when the Earl of Gowrie suffered, and upbraided Ruthven with ingratitude. The conspirator, moved by remorse or some other reason, assured the King that his life should be safe, and left him in the turret with the armed man, who, not very well selected to aid in a purpose so desperate, stood shaking in his armour, without assisting either his master or the King.

Let us now see what was passing below, during this strange scene betwixt the King and Ruthven. The attendants of James had begun to wonder at his absence, when they were suddenly informed by a servant of the Earl of Gowrie, that the King had mounted his horse, and had set out on his return to Falkland. The noblemen and attendants rushed into the courtyard of the mansion, and called for their horses, the Earl of Gowrie at the same time hurrying them away. Here the porter interfered, and said the King could not have left the house, since he had not passed the gate, of which he had the keys. Gowrie, on the other hand, called the man a liar, and insisted that the King had departed.

While the attendants of James knew not what to think, a half smothered, yet terrified voice, was heard to scream from the window of a turret above their heads,—"Help! Treason! Help! my Lord of Mar!" They looked upwards, and beheld James's face in great agitation pushed through the window, while a hand was seen grasping his throat, as if some one behind endeavoured by violence to draw him back.

The explanation was as follows:—The King when left alone with the armed man, had, it seems, prevailed upon him to open the lattice window. This was just done when Alexander Ruthven again entered the turret, and, swearing that there was no remedy, but the King must needs die, he seized on him, and endeavoured by main force to tie his hands with a garter. James resisted, in the extremity of despair, and dragging Ruthven to the window, now open, called out to his attendants in the manner we have described. His retinue hastened to his assistance. The greater part ran to the principal staircase, of which they found the doors shut, and immediately endeavoured to force them open. Meantime a page of the King's, called Sir John Ramsay, discovered a back stair which led him to the turret, where Ruthven and the King were still struggling. Ramsay stabbed Ruthven twice with his dagger, James calling to him to strike high, as he had a doublet of proof on him. Ramsay then thrust Ruthven, now mortally wounded, towards the private staircase, where he was met by Sir Thomas Erskine and Sir Hugh Herries, two of the royal attendants, who despatched him with their swords. His last words were,—"Alas! I am not to blame for this action."

This danger was scarcely over, when the Earl of Gowrie entered the outer chamber, with a drawn sword in each hand, followed by seven attendants, demanding vengeance for the death of his brother. The King's followers, only four in number, thrust James, for the safety of his person, back into the turret-closet, and shut the door; and then engaged in a conflict, which was the more desperate, that they fought four to eight, and Herries was a lame and disabled man. But Sir John Ramsay having run the Earl of Gowrie through the heart, he dropped dead without speaking a word, and his servants fled. The doors of the great staircase were now opened to the nobles, who were endeavouring to force their way to the King's assistance.

In the meantime a new peril threatened the King and his few attendants. The slain Earl of Gowrie was provost of the town of Perth, and much beloved by the citizens. On hearing what had happened, they ran to arms, and surrounded the mansion-house, where this tragedy had been acted, threatening, that if their provost were not delivered to them safe and sound, the King's green coat should pay for it. Their violence was at last quieted by the magistrates of the town, and the mob were prevailed on to disperse.

The object of this strange conspiracy is one of the darkest in history, and what made it stranger, the armed man who was stationed in the turret could throw no light upon it. He proved to be one Henderson, steward to the Earl of Gowrie, who had been ordered to arm himself for the purpose of taking a Highland thief, and was posted in the turret by Alexander Ruthven, without any intimation what he was to do; so that the whole scene came upon him by surprise. The mystery seemed so impenetrable, and so much of the narrative rested upon James's own testimony, that many persons of that period, and even some historians of our own day, have thought that it was not a conspiracy of the brothers against the King, but of the King against the brothers; and that James, having taken a dislike to them, had contrived the bloody scene, and then thrown the blame on the Ruthvens, who suffered in it. But, besides the placability and gentleness of James's disposition, and besides the consideration that no adequate motive can be assigned, or even conjectured, for his perpetrating such an inhospitable murder, it ought to be remembered that the King was naturally timorous, and could not even look at a drawn sword without shuddering; so that it is contrary to all reason and probability to suppose that he could be the deviser of a scheme, in which his life was repeatedly exposed to the most imminent danger. However, many of the clergy refused to obey James's order to keep a day of solemn thanksgiving for the King's deliverance, intimating, without hesitation, that they greatly doubted the truth of his story. One of them being pressed by the King very hard, said—"That doubtless he must believe it, since his majesty said he had seen it; but that, had he seen it himself, he would not have believed his own eyes." James was much vexed with this incredulity, for it was hard not to obtain credit after having been in so much danger.

Nine years after the affair, some light was thrown upon the transaction by one Sprot, a notary-public, who, out of mere curiosity, had possessed himself of certain letters, said to have been written to the Earl of Gowrie by Robert Logan of Restalrig, a scheming, turbulent, and profligate man. In these papers, allusion was repeatedly made to the death of Gowrie's father, to the revenge which was meditated, and to the execution of some great and perilous enterprise. Lastly, there was intimation that the Ruthvens were to bring a prisoner by sea to Logan's fortress of Fast Castle, a very strong and inaccessible tower, overhanging the sea, on the coast of Berwickshire. This place he recommends as suitable for keeping some important prisoner in safety and concealment, and adds, he had kept Bothwell there in his utmost distresses, let the King and his council say what they would.

All these expressions seemed to point at a plot, not affecting the King's life, but his personal liberty, and make it probable, that when Alexander Ruthven had frightened the King into silence and compliance, the brothers intended to carry him through the gardens, and put him on board of a boat, and so conveying him down the Firth of Tay, and round the northeast coast of Fife, might, after making a private signal, which Logan alludes to, place their royal prisoner in security in Fast Castle. The seizing upon the person of the King was a common enterprise among the Scottish nobles, and the father of the Ruthvens had lost his life for such an attempt. Adopting this as their intention, it is probable that Queen Elizabeth was privy to the scheme; and perhaps having found it suit her policy to detain the person of Mary in captivity, she might have formed some similar plan for obtaining the custody of her son.

I must not conclude this story without observing, that Logan's bones were brought into a court of justice, for the purpose of being tried after death, and that he was declared guilty, and a sentence of forfeiture pronounced against him. But it has not been noticed that Logan, a dissolute and extravagant man, was deprived of great part of his estate before his death, and that the King, therefore, could have no lucrative object in following out this ancient and barbarous form of process. The fate of Sprot, the notary, was singular enough. He was condemned to be hanged for keeping these treasonable letters in his possession, without communicating them to the Government; and he suffered death accordingly, asserting to the last that the letters were genuine, and that he had only preserved them from curiosity. This fact he testified even in the agonies of death; for, being desired to give a sign of the truth and sincerity of his confession, after he was thrown off from the ladder, he is said to have clapped his hands three times. Yet some persons continue to think, that what Sprot told was untrue, and that the letters were forgeries; but it seems great incredulity to doubt the truth of a confession which brought to the gallows the man who made it; and, of late years, the letters produced by Sprot are regarded as genuine by the best judges of these matters. When so admitted, they render it evident that the purpose of the Gowrie Conspiracy was to make King James a prisoner in the remote and inaccessible tower of Fast Castle, and perhaps ultimately to deliver him up to Queen Elizabeth.

We now approach the end of this collection of Tales. King James VI. of Scotland married the daughter of the King of Denmark, called Ann of Denmark. They had a family, which recommended them very much to the English people, who were tired of seeing their crown pass from one female to another, without any prospect of male succession. They began, therefore, to turn their eyes towards James as the nearest heir of King Henry VIII., and the rightful successor, when Queen Elizabeth should fail. She was now old, her health broken, and her feelings painfully agitated by the death of Essex, her principal favourite. After his execution, she could scarcely be said ever to enjoy either health or reason. She sat on a pile of cushions, with her finger in her mouth, attending, as it seemed, to nothing, saving to the prayers which were from time to time read in her chamber.

While the Queen of England was thus struggling out the last moments of life, her subjects were making interest with her successor James, with whom even Cecil himself, the Prime Minister of England, had long kept up a secret correspondence. The breath had no sooner left Elizabeth's body than the near relation and godson of the late Queen, Sir Robert Carey, got on horseback, and, travelling with a rapidity which almost equalled that of the modern mail-coach, carried to the Palace of Holyrood the news, that James was King of England, France, and Ireland, as well as of his native dominions of Scotland.

James arrived in London on the 7th of May 1603, and took possession of his new realms without the slightest opposition; and thus the island of Great Britain, so long divided into the separate kingdoms of England and Scotland, became subject to the same prince. Here, therefore, must end the TALES of your GRANDFATHER so far as they relate to the History of Scotland, considered as a distinct and separate kingdom.

XXXIV

Progress of Civilisation
in Society

1603

THE kind reception which the former Tales, written for your amusement and edification, have met with, induces me, my dear little boy,
to make an attempt to bring down my historical narrative to a period,
when the union of England and Scotland became as complete, in the
intimacy of feelings and interests, as law had declared and intended
them to be, and as the mutual advantage of both countries had long,
though in vain, required. The importance of events, however, and the
desire to state them clearly, have induced me for the present to stop
short at the period of the Union of the Kingdoms.

We left off, you may recollect, when James, the sixth of that name
who reigned in Scotland, succeeded, by the death of Queen Elizabeth, to the throne of England, and thus became sovereign of the
whole island of Britain. Ireland also belonged to his dominions,
having been partly subdued by the arms of the English, and partly
surrendered to them by the submission of the natives. There had
been, during Elizabeth's time, many wars with the native lords and
chiefs of the country; but the English finally obtained the undisturbed and undisputed possession of that rich and beautiful island.
Thus the three kingdoms, formed by the Britannic Islands, came into

the possession of one sovereign, who was thus fixed in a situation of strength and security, which was at that time the lot of few monarchs in Europe.

King James's power was the greater, that the progress of human society had greatly augmented the wisdom of statesmen and counsellors, and given strength and stability to those laws which preserve the poor and helpless against the encroachments of the wealthy and the powerful.

But Master Littlejohn may ask me what I mean by the Progress of Human Society; and it is my duty to explain it as intelligibly as I can.

If you consider the lower order of animals, such as birds, dogs, cattle, or any class of the brute creation, you will find that they are, to every useful purpose, deprived of the means of communicating their ideas to each other. They have cries, indeed, by which they express pleasure or pain—fear or hope—but they have no formed speech, by which, like men, they can converse together. God Almighty, who called all creatures into existence in such manner as best pleased him, has imparted to those inferior animals no power of improving their situation, or of communicating with each other. There is, no doubt, a difference in the capacity of these inferior classes of creation. But though one bird may build her nest more neatly than one of a different class, or one dog may be more clever and more capable of learning tricks than another, yet, as it wants language to explain to its comrades the advantages which it may possess, its knowledge dies with it; thus birds and dogs continue to use the same general habits proper to the species, which they have done since the creation of the world. In other words, animals have a certain limited degree of sense termed instinct, which teaches the present race to seek their food, and provide for their safety and comfort, in nearly the same manner as their parents did before them since the beginning of time, but does not enable them to communicate to their successors any improvements, or to derive any increase of knowledge from the practice of their predecessors. Thus you may remark, that the example of the swallow, the wren, and other birds, which cover their nests with a roof to protect them against the rain, is never imitated by other classes, who continue to construct theirs in the same exposed and imperfect manner since the beginning of the world.

Another circumstance, which is calculated to prevent the inferior animals from rising above the rank in nature which they are destined to hold, is the short time during which they remain under the care of their parents. A few weeks gives the young nestlings of every season strength and inclination to leave the protection of the parents; the tender attachment which has subsisted while the young bird was unable to provide for itself without assistance is entirely broken off, and in a week or two more they probably do not know each other. The young of the sheep, the cow, and the horse, attend and feed by the mother's side for a certain short period, during which they are protected by her care, and supported by her milk; but they have no sooner attained the strength necessary to defend themselves, and the sense to provide for their wants, than they separate from the mother, and all intercourse between the parent and her offspring is closed for ever.

Thus each separate tribe of animals retains exactly the same station in the general order of the universe which was occupied by its predecessors; and no existing generation either is, or can be, much better instructed, or more ignorant than that which preceded or that which is to come after it.

It is widely different with mankind. God, as we are told in Scripture, was pleased to make man after his own image. By this you are not to understand that the Creator of heaven and earth has any visible form or shape, to which the human body bears a resemblance; but the meaning is, that as the God who created the world is a spirit invisible and incomprehensible, so he joined to the human frame some portion of an essence resembling his own, which is called the human soul, and which, while the body lives, continues to animate and direct its motions, and on the dissolution of the bodily form which it has occupied, returns to the spiritual world, to be answerable for the good and evil of its works upon earth. It is therefore impossible that man, possessing this knowledge of right and wrong, proper to a spiritual essence resembling those higher orders of creation whom we call angels, and having some affinity, though at an incalculable distance, to the essence of the Deity himself, should have been placed under the same limitations in point of progressive improvement with the inferior tribes, who are neither responsible for the actions which they perform under directions of their instinct, nor capable, by any exertion of their own, of altering or improving their condition in the scale of creation. So far is this from being the case with man, that the bodily organs of the human frame bear such a correspondence with the properties of his soul, as to give him the means, when they are properly used, of enlarging his powers, and becoming wiser and more skilful from hour to hour, as long as his life permits; and not only is this the case, but tribes and nations of men assembled together for the purpose of mutual protection and defence, have the same power of alteration and improvement, and may, if circumstances are favourable, go on by gradual steps from being a wild horde of naked barbarians, till they become a powerful and civilised people.

The capacity of amending our condition by increase of knowledge, which, in fact, affords the means by which man rises to be the lord of creation, is grounded on the peculiar advantages possessed by the human race. Let us look somewhat closely into this, my dear boy, for it involves some truths equally curious and important.

If man, though possessed of the same immortal essence or soul, which enables him to choose and refuse, to judge and condemn, to reason and conclude, were to be without the power of communicating to his fellow-men the conclusions to which his reasoning had conducted him, it is clear that the progress of each individual in knowledge could be only in proportion to his own observation and his own powers of reasoning. But the gift of speech enables any one to communicate to others whatever idea of improvement occurs to him, and thus, instead of dying in the bosom of the individual by whom it was first thought of, it becomes a part of the stock of knowledge proper to the whole community, which is increased and rendered generally and effectually useful by the accession of further information, as opportunities occur, or men of reflecting and inventive minds arise in the state. This use of spoken language, therefore, which so gloriously distinguishes man from the beasts that perish, is the primary means of introducing and increasing knowledge in infant communities.

Another early cause of the improvement in human society is the incapacity of children to act for themselves, rendering the attention and protection of parents to their offspring necessary for so long a period. Even where the food which the earth affords without cultivation, such as fruits and herbs, is most plentifully supplied, children remain too helpless for many years to be capable of gathering it, and providing for their own support. This is still more the case where food must be procured by hunting, fishing, or cultivating the soil, occupations requiring a degree of skill and personal strength which children cannot possess until they are twelve or fourteen years old. It follows, as a law of nature, that instead of leaving their parents at an early age, like the young of birds or quadrupeds, the youth of the human species necessarily remain under the protection of their father and mother for many years, during which they have time to acquire all the knowledge the parents are capable of teaching. It arises also from this wise arrangement that the love and affection between the offspring and the parents, which among the brute creation is the produce of mere instinct, and continues for a very short time, becomes in the human race a deep and permanent feeling, founded on the attachment of the parents, the gratitude of the children, and the effect of long habit on both.

For these reasons, it usually happens, that children feel no desire to desert their parents, but remain inhabitants of the same huts in which they were born, and take up the task of labouring for subsistence in their turn, when their fathers and mothers are disabled by age. One or two such families gradually unite together, and avail themselves of each other's company for mutual defence and assistance. This is the earliest stage of human society; and some savages have been found in this condition so very rude and ignorant, that they may be said to be little wiser or better than a herd of animals. The natives of New South Wales, for example, are, even at present, in the very lowest scale of humanity, and ignorant of every art which can add comfort or decency to human life. These unfortunate savages wear no clothes, construct no cabins or huts, and are ignorant even of the manner of chasing animals or catching fish, unless such of the latter as are left by the tide, or which are found on the rocks; they feed upon the most disgusting substances, snakes, worms, maggots, and whatever trash falls in their way. They know indeed how to kindle a fire—in that respect only they have stepped beyond the deepest ignorance to which man can be subjected—but they have not learned how to boil water; and when they see Europeans perform this ordinary operation, they have been known to run away in great terror. Voyagers tell us of other savages who are even ignorant of the use of fire, and who maintain a miserable existence by subsisting on shell-fish eaten raw.

And yet, my dear boy, out of this miserable and degraded state, which seems worse than that of the animals, man has the means and power to rise into the high place for which Providence hath destined him. In proportion as opportunities occur, these savage tribes acquire the arts of civilised life; they construct huts to shelter them against the weather; they invent arms for destroying the wild beasts by which they are annoyed, and for killing those whose flesh is adapted for food; they domesticate others, and use at pleasure their milk, flesh, and skins; and they plant fruit-trees and sow grain as soon as they discover that the productions of nature most necessary for their comfort may be increased by labour and industry. Thus the progress of human society, unless it is interrupted by some unfortunate circumstances, continues to advance, and every new generation, without losing any of the advantages already attained, goes on to acquire others which were unknown to the preceding one.

For instance, when three or four wandering families of savages have settled in one place, and begun to cultivate the ground, and collect their huts into a hamlet or village, they usually agree in choosing some chief to be their judge, and the arbiter of their disputes in time of peace, their leader and captain when they go to war with other tribes. This is the foundation of a monarchical government. Or, perhaps, their public affairs are directed by a council, or senate, of the oldest and wisest of the tribe—this is the origin of a republican state. At all events, in one way or other, they put themselves under something resembling a regular government, and obtain the protection of such laws as may prevent them from quarrelling with one another.

Other important alterations are introduced by time. At first, no doubt, the members of the community store their fruits and the produce of the chase in common. But shortly after, reason teaches them that the individual who has bestowed labour and trouble upon anything so as to render it productive, acquires a right of property, as it is called, in the produce, which his efforts have in a manner called into existence. Thus it is soon acknowledged, that he who has planted a tree has the sole right of consuming its fruit; and that he who has sown a field of corn has the exclusive title to gather in the grain. Without the labour of the planter and husbandman, there would have been no apples or wheat, and therefore, these are justly entitled to the fruit of their labour. In like manner, the state itself is conceived to acquire a right of property in the fields cultivated by its members, and in the forests and waters where they have of old practised the rights of hunting and fishing. If men of a different tribe enter on the territory of a neighbouring nation, war ensues between them and peace is made by agreeing on both sides to reasonable conditions. Thus a young state extends its possessions; and by its communications with other tribes lays the foundation of public laws for the regulation of their behaviour to each other in peace and in war.

Other arrangements arise not less important, tending to increase the difference between mankind in their wild and original state, and that which they assume in the progress of civilisation. One of the most remarkable is the separation of the citizens into different classes of society, and the introduction of the use of money. I will try to render these great changes intelligible to you.

In the earlier stages of society, every member of the community may be said to supply all his wants by his own personal labour. He acquires his food by the chase—he sows and reaps his own grain—he gathers his own fruit—he cuts the skin which forms his dress so as to fit his own person—he makes the sandals or buskins which protect his feet. He is, therefore, better or worse accommodated exactly in proportion to the personal skill and industry which he can apply to that purpose. But it is discovered in process of time, that one man has particular dexterity in hunting, being, we shall suppose, young, active, and enterprising; another, older and of a more staid character, has peculiar skill in tilling the ground, or in managing cattle and flocks; a third, lame perhaps, or infirm, has a happy talent for cutting out and stitching together garments, or for shaping and sewing shoes. It becomes, therefore, for the advantage of all, that the first man shall attend to nothing but hunting, the second confine himself to the cultivation of the land, and the third remain at home to make clothes and shoes. But then it follows as a necessary consequence, that the huntsman must give to the man who cultivates the land a part of his venison and skins, if he desires to have grain of which to make bread, or a cow to furnish his family with milk; and that both the hunter and the agriculturist must give a share of the produce of the chase, and a proportion of the grain to the third man, to obtain from him clothes and shoes. Each is thus accommodated with what he wants a great deal better, and more easily, by every one following a separate occupation, than they could possibly have been, had each of the three been hunter, farmer, and tailor, in his own person, practising two of the trades awkwardly and unwillingly, instead of confining himself to that which he perfectly understands, and pursues with success. This mode of accommodation is called barter, and is the earliest kind of traffic by which men exchange their property with each other and satisfy their wants by parting with their superfluities.

But in process of time, barter is found inconvenient. The husbandman, perhaps, has no use for shoes when the shoemaker is in need of corn, or the shoemaker may not want furs or venison when the hunter desires to have shoes. To remedy this, almost all nations have intro-duced the use of what is called *money*; that is to say, they have fixed on some particular substance capable of being divided into small portions, which, having itself little intrinsic value applicable to human use, is nevertheless received as a representative of the value of all commodi-ties. Particular kinds of shells are used as money in some countries; in others, leather, cloth, or iron, are employed; but gold and silver, divided into small portions, are used for this important purpose almost all over the world.

That you may understand the use of this circulating representative of the value of commodities, and comprehend the convenience which it affords, let us suppose that the hunter, as we formerly said, wanted a pair of shoes, and the shoemaker had no occasion for venison, but wanted some corn, while the husbandman, not desiring to have shoes, stood in need of some other commodity. Here are three men, each desirous of some article of necessity, or convenience, which he cannot obtain by barter, because the party whom he has to deal with does not want the commodity which he has to offer in exchange. But supposing the use of money introduced, and its value acknowledged, these three persons are accommodated by means of it in the amplest manner pos-sible. The shoemaker does not want the venison which the hunter offers for sale, but some other man in the village is willing to purchase it for five pieces of silver—the hunter sells his commodity, and goes to the shoemaker, who, though he would not barter the shoes for the venison which he did not want, readily sells them for the money, and, going with it to the farmer, buys from him the quantity of corn he needs; while the farmer, in his turn, purchases whatever he is in want of, or if he requires nothing at the time, lays the pieces of money aside, to use when he has occasion.

The invention of money is followed by the gradual rise of trade. There are men who make it their business to buy various articles, and sell them again for profit; that is, they sell them somewhat dearer than they bought them. This is convenient for all parties; since the original proprietors are willing to sell their commodities to those store-keepers, or shop-keepers, at a low rate, to be saved the trouble of hawking them about in search of a customer; while the public in general are equally willing to buy from such intermediate dealers, because they are sure to be immediately supplied with what they want.

The numerous transactions occasioned by the introduction of money, together with other circumstances, soon destroy the equality of ranks which prevails in an early stage of society. Some men hoard up quantities of gold and silver, become rich, and hire the assistance of others to do their work; some waste or spend their earnings, become poor, and sink into the capacity of servants. Some men are wise and skilful, and, distinguishing themselves by their exploits in battle and their counsels in peace, rise to the management of public affairs. Others, and much greater numbers, have no more valour than to follow where they are led, and no more talent than to act as they are commanded. These last sink, as a matter of course, into obscurity, while the others become generals and statesmen. The attainment of learning tends also to increase the difference of ranks. Those who receive a good education by the care of their parents, or possess so much strength of mind and readiness of talent as to educate themselves, become separated from the more ignorant of the community, and form a distinct class and condition of their own; holding no more communication with the others than is absolutely necessary.

In this way the whole order of society is changed, and instead of presenting the uniform appearance of one large family, each member of which has nearly the same rights, it seems to resemble a confederacy or association of different ranks, classes, and conditions of men, each rank filling up a certain department in society, and discharging a class of duties totally distinct from those of the others. The steps by which a nation advances from the natural and simple state which we have just described, into the more complicated system in which ranks are distinguished from each other, are called the progress of society, or of civilisation. It is attended, like all things human, with much of evil as well as good; but it seems to be a law of our moral nature, that, faster or slower, such alterations must take place, in consequence of the inventions and improvements of succeeding generations of mankind.

Another alteration, productive of consequences not less important, arises out of the gradual progress towards civilisation. In the early state of society, every man in the tribe is a warrior, and liable to serve as such when the country requires his assistance; but in progress of time the pursuit of the military art is, at least on all ordinary occasions, confined to bands of professional soldiers, whose business it is to fight the battles of the state, when required, in consideration of which they are paid by the community, the other members of which are thus left to the uninterrupted pursuit of their own peaceful occupations. This alteration is attended with more important consequences than we can at present pause to enumerate.

We have said that those mighty changes which bring men to dwell in castles and cities instead of huts and caves, and enable them to cultivate the sciences and subdue the elements, instead of being plunged in ignorance and superstition, are owing primarily to the reason with which God has graciously endowed the human race; and in a second degree to the power of speech, by which we enjoy the faculty of communicating to each other the result of our own reflections.

But it is evident that society, when its advance is dependent upon oral tradition alone, must be liable to many interruptions. The imagination of the speaker, and the dulness or want of comprehension of the hearer, may lead to many errors: and it is generally found that knowledge makes but very slow progress until the art of writing is discovered, by which a fixed, accurate, and substantial form can be given to the wisdom of past ages. When this noble art is attained, there is a sure foundation laid for the preservation and increase of knowledge. The record is removed from the inaccurate recollection of the aged, and placed in a safe, tangible, and imperishable form, which may be subjected to the inspection of various persons, until the sense is completely explained and comprehended, with the least possible chance of doubt or uncertainty.

By the art of writing, a barrier is fixed against those violent changes so apt to take place in the early stages of society, by which all the fruits of knowledge are frequently destroyed, as those of the earth are by a hurricane. Suppose, for example, a case, which frequently happens in the early history of mankind, that some nation which has made considerable progress in the arts, is invaded and subdued by another which is more powerful and numerous, though more ignorant than themselves. It is clear, that in this case, as the rude and ignorant victors would set no value on the knowledge of the vanquished, it would, if entrusted only to the memory of the individuals of the conquered people, be gradually lost and forgotten. But if the useful discoveries made by the ancestors of the vanquished people were recorded in writing, the manuscripts in which they were described, though they might be neglected for a season, would, if preserved at all, probably attract attention at some more fortunate period. It was thus, when the empire of Rome, having reached the utmost height of its grandeur, was broken down and conquered by numerous tribes of ignorant though brave barbarians, that those admirable works of classical learning, on which such value is justly placed in the present day, were rescued from total destruction and oblivion by manuscript copies preserved by chance in the old libraries of churches and convents. It may indeed be taken as an almost infallible maxim, that no nation can make any great progress in useful knowledge or civilisation until their improvement can be rendered stable and permanent by the invention of writing.

Another discovery, however, almost as important as that of writing, was made during the fifteenth century. I mean the invention of printing. Writing with the hand must be always a slow, difficult, and expensive operation; and when the manuscript is finished, it is perhaps laid aside among the stores of some great library, where it may be neglected by students, and must, at any rate, be accessible to very few persons, and subject to be destroyed by numerous accidents. But the admirable invention of printing enables the artist to make a thousand copies from the original manuscript, by having them stamped upon paper, in far less time and with less expense than it would cost to make half a dozen such copies with the pen. From the period of this glorious discovery, knowledge of every kind may be said to have been brought out of the darkness of cloisters and universities, where it was known only to a few scholars, into the broad light of day, where its treasures were accessible to all men.

The Bible itself, in which we find the rules of eternal life, as well as a thousand invaluable lessons for our conduct in this world, was, before the invention of printing, totally inaccessible to all, save the priests of Rome, who found it their interest to discourage the perusal of the Scriptures by any except their own order, and thus screened from discovery those alterations and corruptions, which the inventions of ignorant and designing men had introduced into the beautiful simplicity of the Gospel. But when, by means of printing, the copies of the Bible became so numerous, that every one above the most wretched poverty could, at a cheap price, possess himself of a copy of the blessed rule of life, there was a general appeal from the errors and encroachments of the Church of Rome, to the Divine Word on which they professed to be founded; a treasure formerly concealed from the public, but now placed within the reach of every man, whether of the clergy or laity. The consequence of these inquiries, which printing alone could have rendered practicable, was the rise of the happy Reformation of the Christian Church.

The same noble art made knowledge of a temporal kind as accessible as that which concerned religion. Whatever works of history, science, morality, or entertainment, seemed likely to instruct or amuse the reader, were printed and distributed among the people at large by printers and booksellers, who had a profit by doing so. Thus the possibility of important discoveries being forgotten in the course of years, or of the destruction of useful arts, or elegant literature, by the loss of the records in which they are preserved, was in a great measure removed.

In a word, the printing-press is a contrivance which empowers any one individual to address his countrymen on any topic which he thinks important, and which enables a whole nation to listen to the voice of such individual, however obscure he may be, with the same ease, and greater certainty of understanding what he says, than if a chief of Indians were haranguing the tribe at his council-fire. Nor is the important difference to be forgotten, that the orator can only speak to the persons present, while the author of a book addresses himself, not only to the race now in existence, but to all succeeding generations, while his work shall be held in estimation.

I have thus endeavoured to trace the steps by which a general civilisation is found to take place in nations with more or less rapidity, as laws and institutions, or external circumstances, favourable or otherwise, advance or retard the increase of knowledge, and by the course of which man, endowed with reason, and destined for immortality, gradually improves the condition in which Providence has placed him; while the inferior animals continue to live by means of the same, or nearly the same, instincts of self-preservation, which have directed their species in all its descents since the creation.

I have called your attention at some length to this matter, because you will now have to remark that a material change had gradually and slowly taken place, both in the kingdom of England, and in that of Scotland, when their long quarrels were at length, in appearance, ended by the accession of James the Sixth of Scotland to the English crown, which he held under the title of James the First of that powerful kingdom.

XXXV

The United Kingdom

1603-1612

THE whole island of Great Britain was now united under one king, though it remained in effect two separate kingdoms, governed by their own separate constitutions, and their own distinct codes of laws, and liable again to be separated, as, by the death of King James without issue, the kingdoms might have been claimed by different heirs. For although James had two sons, yet there was a possibility that they might have both died before their father, in which case the sceptres of England and Scotland must have passed once more into different hands. The Hamilton family would, in that case, have succeeded to the kingdom of Scotland, and the next heir of Elizabeth to that of England. Who that heir was, it might have been found difficult to determine.

It was in these circumstances to be apprehended, that James, the sovereign of a poor and barren kingdom, which had for so many ages maintained an almost perpetual war with England, would have met with a prejudiced and unpleasant reception from a nation long accustomed to despise the Scotch for their poverty, and to regard them with enmity on account of their constant hostility to the English blood and name. It might have been supposed also, that a people so proud as the English, and having so many justifiable reasons for their pride, would have regarded with an evil eye the transference of the sceptre from the hand of the Tudors, who had swayed it during five successive reigns, to those of a Stewart, descended from the ancient and determined enemies of the English nation. But it was the wise and gracious pleasure of Providence, that while so many reasons existed to render the accession of James, and, in consequence, the union of the two crowns, obnoxious to the English people, others should occur, which not only balanced, but for a time completely overpowered those objections, as well in the minds of men of sense and education, as in the judgment of the populace, who are usually averse to foreign rulers, for no other reason than that they are such.

Queen Elizabeth, after a long and glorious reign, had, in her latter days, become much more cross and uncertain in her temper than had been the case in her youth, more wilful also, and more inclined to exert her arbitrary power on slight occasions. One peculiar cause of offence given to her people was her obstinate refusal to gratify their anxiety, by making, as the nation earnestly desired, some arrangement for the succession to the throne after her own death. On this subject, indeed, she nursed so much suspicion and jealousy, as gave rise to more than one extraordinary scene. The following is a whimsical instance, among others, of her unwillingness to hear of anything respecting old age and its consequences.

The Bishop of St. David's, preaching in her Majesty's presence, took occasion from his text, which was Psalm xc. v. 12, "So teach us to number our days, that we may apply our hearts unto wisdom," to allude to the Queen's advanced period of life, she being then sixty-three, and to the consequent infirmities attending upon old age; as, for example, when the grinders shall be few in number, and they wax dark who look out at windows—when the daughters of singing shall be abased, and more to the like purpose. With the tone of these admonitions the Queen was so ill satisfied, that she flung open the window of the closet in which she sat, and told the preacher to keep his admonitions to himself, since she plainly saw the greatest clerks (meaning scholars) were not the wisest men. Nor did her displeasure end here. The Bishop was commanded to confine himself to his house for a time, and the Queen, referring to the circumstance some time afterwards, told her courtiers how much the prelate was mistaken in supposing her to be as much decayed as perhaps he might feel himself to be. As for her, she thanked God, neither her stomach nor her strength—her voice for singing, nor her art of fingering instruments, were any whit decayed. And to prove the goodness of her eyes, she produced a little jewel, with an inscription in very small letters, which she offered to Lord Worcester and Sir James Crofts to read. They had too much tact to be sharpsighted on the occasion; she, therefore, read it herself with apparent ease, and laughed at the error of the good Bishop.

The faults of Elizabeth, though arising chiefly from age and ill-temper, were noticed and resented by her subjects, who began openly to show themselves weary of a female reign, forgetting how glorious it had been, and manifested a general desire to have a king to rule over them. With this almost universal feeling, all eyes, even those of Elizabeth's most confidential statesman and counsellor, Sir Robert Cecil, afterwards Earl of Salisbury, were turned to the King of Scotland as next heir to the crown. He was a Protestant prince, which assured him the favour of the Church of England, and of the numerous and strong adherents to the Protestant religion. As such, Cecil entered into a secret correspondence with him, in which he pointed out the line of conduct proper on James's part to secure his interest in England. On the other hand, the English Catholics, on whom Queen Elizabeth's government had imposed many severe penal laws, were equally friendly to the succession of King James, since from that prince, whose mother had been a strict Catholic, they might hope for favour, to the extent at least of some release from the various hardships which the laws of England imposed on them. The Earl of Northumberland conducted a correspondence with James on the part of the Catholics, in which he held high language, and offered to assert the Scottish King's right of succession by force of arms.

These intrigues were kept by James as secret as was in his power. If Elizabeth had discovered either the one or the other, neither the services of Cecil, nor the high birth and power of the great Earl of Northumberland, could have saved them, from experiencing the extremity of her indignation. Cecil, in particular, was at one time on the point of ruin. A post from Scotland delivered into his hands a private packet from the Scottish King, when the secretary was in attendance on Elizabeth. "Open your despatches," said Elizabeth, "and let us hear the news from Scotland." A man of less presence of mind would have been ruined; for if the Queen had seen the least hesitation in her minister's manner, her suspicions would have been instantly awakened, and detection must have followed. But Cecil recollected the

Queen's sensitive aversion to any disagreeable smell, which was strengthened by the belief of the time, that infectious diseases and subtile poisons could be communicated by means of scent alone. The artful secretary availed himself of this, and while he seemed to be cutting the strings which held the packet, he observed it had a singular and unpleasant odour; on which Elizabeth desired it might be taken from her presence, and opened elsewhere with due precaution. Thus Cecil got an opportunity to withdraw from the packet whatever could have betrayed his correspondence with King James. Cecil's policy and inclinations were very generally followed in the English court; indeed, there appeared no heir to the crown, male or female, whose right could be placed in competition with that of James.

It may be added to this general inclination in James's favour, that the defects of his character were of a kind which did not attract much attention while he occupied the throne of Scotland. The delicacy of his situation was then so great, and he was exposed to so many dangers from the dislike of the clergy, the feuds of the nobles, and the tumultuous disposition of the common people, that he dared not indulge in any of those childish freaks of which he was found capable when his motions were more completely at his own disposal. On the contrary, he was compelled to seek out the sagest counsellors, to listen to the wisest advice, and to put a restraint on his own natural disposition for encouraging idle favourites, parasites, and flatterers, as well as to suppress his inward desire to extend the limits of his authority farther than the constitution of the country permitted.

At this period James governed by the advice of such ministers as the Chancellor Maitland, and afterwards of Home, Earl of Dunbar, men of thought and action, of whose steady measures and prudent laws the King naturally obtained the credit. Neither was James himself deficient in a certain degree of sagacity. He possessed all that could be derived from learning alloyed by pedantry, and from a natural shrewdness of wit, which enabled him to play the part of a man of sense, when either acting under the influence of constraint and fear, or where no temptation occurred to induce him to be guilty of some folly. It was by these specious accomplishments that he acquired in his youth the character of an able and wise monarch, although when he was afterwards brought on a more conspicuous stage, and his character better understood, he was found entitled to no better epithet than that conferred on him by an able French politician, who called him, "The wisest fool in Christendom."

Such, however, as King James was, England now received him with more universal acclamation than had attended any of her princes on their ascent to the throne. Multitudes, of every description, hastened to accompany him on his journey through England to the capital city. The wealthy placed their gold at his disposal, the powerful opened their halls for the most magnificent entertainments, the clergy hailed him as the head of the Church, and the poor, who had nothing to offer but their lives, seemed ready to devote them to his service. Some of the Scottish retinue, who were acquainted with James's character, saw and feared the unfavourable effect which such a change of circumstances was likely to work on him. "A plague of these people!" said one of his oldest domestics; "they will spoil a good king."

Another Scot made an equally shrewd answer to an Englishman, who desired to know from him the King's real character. "Did you ever see a jackanapes?" said the Scotchman, meaning a tame monkey; "if you have, you must be aware that if you hold the creature in your hands you can make him bite me, and if I hold him in my hands, I can make him bite you."

Both these sayings were shown to be true in course of time. King James, brought from poverty to wealth, became thoughtless and prodigal, indolent, and addicted to idle pleasures. From hearing the smooth flatteries of the clergy of England, who recognised him as head of the Church, instead of the rude attacks of the Presbyterian ministers of Scotland, who had hardly admitted his claim to be one of its inferior members, he entertained new and more lofty pretensions to divine right. Finally, brought from a country where his personal liberty and the freedom of his government were frequently placed under restraint, and his life sometimes in danger, he was overjoyed to find himself in a condition where his own will was not only unfettered, as far as he himself was concerned, but appeared to be the model by which all loyal subjects were desirous to accommodate theirs; and he seemed readily enough disposed to stretch to its utmost limits the power thus presented to him. Thus, from being a just and equitable monarch, he was inspired with a love of arbitrary power; and from attending, as had been his custom, to state business, he now minded little save hunting and festivals.

In this manner James, though possessing a large stock of pedantic wisdom, came to place himself under the management of a succession of unworthy favourites, and although particularly good-natured, and naturally a lover of justice, was often hurried into actions and measures, which, if they could not be termed absolutely tyrannical, were never-theless illegal and unjust. It is, however, of his Scottish government that we are now to treat, and therefore I am to explain to you, as well as I can, the consequences of the union with England to the people and country of Scotland.

If the English nation were at first delighted to receive King James as their sovereign, the Scottish people were no less enchanted by the prospect of their monarch's ascent to this wealthy and pre-eminent situ-ation. They considered the promotion of their countrymen and prince as an omen of good fortune to their nation; each individual Scotchman expected to secure some part of the good things with which England was supposed to abound, and multitudes hurried to court, to put them-selves in the way of obtaining their share.

James was shocked at the greediness and importunity of his hungry countrymen, and scandalised besides at the poor and miserable appear-ance which many of them made among the rich Englishmen, which brought discredit on the country to which he himself, as well as they, belonged. He sent instructions to the Scottish Privy Council to prevent such intruders from leaving their country, complaining of their manners and appearance, as calculated to bring disgrace upon all the natives of Scotland. A proclamation was accordingly issued at Edinburgh, setting forth that great numbers of men and women of base sort and condition, and without any certain trade, calling, or dependence, repaired from Scotland to court, which was almost filled with them, to the great annoyance of his Majesty, and to the heavy disgrace of the Scottish nation; for these suitors being, in the judgment of all who saw them, but "idle rascals, and poor miserable bodies," their importunity and numbers raised an opinion that there were no persons of good rank, comeliness, or credit in the country which sent forth such a flight of locusts. Further, it was complained that these unseemly supplicants usually alleged that the cause of their repairing to court was to desire payment of old debts due by the King, "which, of all kinds of importu-nity," says the proclamation, with great simplicity, "is the most unpleas-ing to his Majesty." Therefore, general proclamation was directed to be made at all the market crosses in Scotland, that no Scottish person should be permitted to travel to England without leave of the Privy Council; and that vessels transporting individuals, who had not obtained due license, should be liable to confiscation.

But although the King did all that was in his power to prevent these uncouth suitors from repairing to his court, yet there were many other natives of Scotland of a higher description, the sons of men of rank and quality, who, by birth and condition, had the right of attending his court, and approaching his presence, whom he could not prohibit from doing so, without positively disowning all former affections, national feeling, and sympathy or gratitude for past services. The benefits which he conferred on these were ill construed by the English, who seem to have accounted everything as taken from themselves which was bestowed on a Scotchman. The King, though it does not appear that he acted with any unjust purpose, was severely judged, both by his own countrymen and the English. The Scots, who had been his friends in his inferior situation, and, as it might be called, his adversity, naturally expected a share of his bounty, when he was advanced to such high prosperity; while the English, with a jealousy for which much allowance is also to be made, regarded these northern suitors with an evil eye. In short, the Scottish courtiers thought that their claims of ancient services, of allegiance tried under difficult circumstances, of favour due to countrymen, and perhaps even to kindred, which no people carry so far, entitled them to all the advantages which the King might have to bestow; while the English, on the other hand, considered everything given to the Scots as conferred at their expense, and used many rhymes and satirical expressions to that purpose, such as occur in the old song:

> Bonny Scot, all witness can,
> England has made thee a gentleman.
> Thy blue bonnet, when thou came hither,
> Would scarcely keep out the wind or weather;
> But now it is turn'd to a hat and a feather—
> The bonnet is blown the devil knows whither.
> The sword at thy haunch was a huge black blade,
> With a great basket-hilt, of iron made;
> But now a long rapier doth hang by his side,
> And huffingly doth this bonny Scot ride.

Another rhyme, to the same purpose, described a Scottish courtier thus:

> In Scotland he was born and bred,
> And, though a beggar, must be fed.

It is said, that when the Scots complained to the King of this last aspersion, James replied, "Hold your peace, for I will soon make the English as poor as yourselves, and so end that controversy." But as it was not in the power of wit to appease the feud betwixt the nobility and gentry of two proud nations, so lately enemies, all the efforts of the King were unequal to prevent bloody and desperate quarrels between his countrymen and his new subjects, to the great disquiet of the court, and the distress of the good-natured monarch, who, averse to war in all its shapes, and even to the sight of a drawn sword, suffered grievously on such occasions.

There was one of those incidents which assumed a character so formidable, that it threatened the destruction of all the Scots at the court and in the capital, and, in consequence, a breach between the kingdoms so lately and happily brought into alliance. At a public horse-race at Croydon, Philip Herbert, an Englishman of high birth, though, as it fortunately chanced, of no degree of corresponding spirit, received, in a quarrel, a blow in the face by a switch or horse-whip, from one Ramsay, a Scottish gentleman, in attendance on the court. The rashness and violence of Ramsay was construed into a national point of quarrel by the English present, who proposed revenging themselves on the spot by a general attack upon all the Scots on the race-ground. One gentleman, named Pinchbeck, although ill-fitted for such a strife, for he had but the use of two fingers on his right hand, rode furiously through the multitude, with his dagger ready drawn, exhorting all the English to imitate him in an immediate attack on the Scots, exclaiming, "Let us breakfast with those that are here, and dine with the rest in London." But as Herbert did not return the blow, no scuffle or assault actually took place; otherwise, it is probable, a dreadful scene must have ensued. James, with whom Herbert was a particular favourite, rewarded his moderation or timidity by raising him to the rank of Knight, Baron, Viscount, and Earl of Montgomery, all in one day. Ramsay was banished the court for a season; and thus the immediate affront was in some degree alleviated. But the new Earl of Montgomery remained, in the opinion of his countrymen, a dishonoured man; and it is said his mother, the sister of Sir Philip Sydney, wept and tore her hair when she heard of his having endured with patience the insult offered by Ramsay. This is the lady whom, in a beautiful epitaph, Ben Jonson has described as

> Sidney's sister, Pembroke's mother;
> Death, ere thou hast slain another

Wise, and good, and learned as she,
Time shall throw a dart at thee.

Yet the patience of Herbert under the insult was the fortunate prevention of a great national misfortune, for which, if his after conduct had not given tokens of an abject spirit, he might have been praised as a patriot, who had preferred the good of his country to the gratification of his own immediate resentment.

Another offence given by the haughty and irascible temper of a Scotchman, was also likely to have produced disastrous consequences. The Inns of Court are the places of resort and study appointed for those young men who are destined to the profession of the law in England, and they are filled with students, men often of high family and accomplishments, and who, living together in the sort of colleges set apart for their residence, have always kept up the ideas of privilege and distinction, to which their destination to a highly honourable profession, as well as their own birth and condition, entitles them. One of these gentlemen, by name Edward Hawley, appeared at court on a public occasion, and probably intruded farther than his rank authorised; so that Maxwell, a Scotchman, much favoured by James, and an usher of his chamber, not only thrust him back, but actually pulled him out of the presence-chamber by a black ribband, which, like other gallants of the time, Hawley wore at his ear. Hawley, who was a man of spirit, instantly challenged Maxwell to fight; and his second, who carried the challenge, informed him, that if he declined such meeting, Hawley would assault him wherever they should meet, and either kill him or be killed on the spot. James, by his royal interference, was able to solder up this quarrel also. He compelled Maxwell to make an apology to Hawley; and for the more full accommodation of the dispute, accepted of a splendid masque and entertainment offered on the occasion by the students of Gray's Inn Lane, the society to which the injured gentleman belonged.

We may here remark a great change in the manners of the gallants of the time, which had taken place in the progress of civilisation, to which I formerly alluded. The ancient practice of trial by combat, which made a principal part of the feudal law, and which was resorted to in so many cases, had now fallen into disuse. The progress of reason, and the principles of justice, concurred to prove that a combat in the lists might indeed show which of two knights was the best rider and the stoutest swordsman, but that such an encounter could afford no evidence which of the two was innocent or guilty; since it can only be believed in a very ignorant age that Providence is to work a miracle in case of every chance combat, and award success to the party whose virtue best deserves it. The trial by combat, therefore, though it was not actually removed from the statute-book, was in fact only once appealed to after the accession of James, and even then the combat, as a mode of trial unsuited to enlightened times, did not take place.

For the same reason the other sovereigns of Europe discountenanced these challenges and combats, undertaken for pure honour or in revenge of some injury, which it used to be their custom to encourage, and to sanction with their own presence. Such rencounters were now generally looked upon by all sensible persons as an inexcusable waste of gallant men's lives for matters of mere punctilio; and were strictly forbidden, under the highest penalties, by the Kings both of England and France, and, generally speaking, throughout the civilised world. But the royal command could not change the hearts of those to whom it was addressed, nor could the penalties annexed to the breach of the law intimidate men, whom a sense of honour, though a false one, had already induced to hold life cheap. Men fought as many, perhaps even more, single combats than formerly; and although such meetings took place without the publicity and formal show of lists, armour, horses, and the attendance of heralds and judges of the field, yet they were not less bloody than those which had been formerly fought with the observance of every point of chivalry.[1]

According to the more modern practice, combatants met in some solitary place, alone, or each accompanied by a single friend called a

---

[1] "Lady Mary Wortley Montague has said, with equal truth and taste, that the most romantic region of every country is that where the mountains unite themselves with the plains or lowlands. For similar reasons, it may be in like manner said, that the most picturesque period of history is that when the ancient rough and wild manners of a barbarous age are just becoming innovated upon, and contrasted by, the illumination of increased or revived learning, and the instructions of renewed or reformed religion. The reign of James I. of England possessed this advantage in a peculiar degree. Some beams of chivalry, although its planet had been for some time set, continued to animate and gild the horizon; and although probably no one acted precisely on its Quixotic dictates, men and women still talked the chivalrous language of Sir Philip Sydney's Arcadia; and the ceremonial of the tilt-yard was yet exhibited, though it now only flourished as a *Place de Carrousel.*"—*Introduction to the Fortunes of Nigel.* (*Waverly Novels.*)

second, who were supposed to see fair play. The combat was generally fought with the rapier or small sword, a peculiarly deadly weapon, and the combatants, to show they wore no defensive armour under their clothes, threw off their coats and waistcoats, and fought in their shirts. The duty of the seconds, properly interpreted, was only to see fair play; but as these hot-spirited young men felt it difficult to remain cool and inactive when they saw their friends engaged, it was very common for them, though without even the shadow of a quarrel, to fight also; and, in that case, whoever first despatched his antagonist, or rendered him incapable of further resistance, came without hesitation to the assistance of his comrade, and thus the decisive superiority was brought on by odds of numbers, which contradicts all our modern ideas of honour or of gallantry.

Such were the rules of the duel, as these single combats were called. The fashion came from France to England, and was adopted by the Scots and English as the readiest way of settling their national quarrels, which became very numerous.

One of the most noted of these was the bloody and fatal conflict between Sir James Stewart, eldest son of the first Lord Blantyre, a Scottish Knight of the Bath, and Sir George Wharton, an Englishman, eldest son of Lord Wharton, a Knight of the same order. These gentlemen were friends; and, if family report speaks truth, Sir James Stewart was one of the most accomplished young men of his time. A trifling dispute at play led to uncivil expressions on the part of Wharton, to which Stewart answered by a blow. A defiance was exchanged on the spot, and they resolved to fight next day at an appointed place near Waltham. This fatal appointment made, they carried their resentment with a show of friendship, and drank some wine together; after finishing which, Wharton observed to his opponent, "Our next meeting will not part so easily." The fatal rencounter took place; both gentlemen fought with the most determined courage, and both fell with many wounds, and died on the field of battle.

Sometimes the rage and passion of the gallants of the day did not take the fairest, but the shortest, road to revenge; and the courtiers of James I., men of honourable birth and title, were, in some instances, known to attack an enemy by surprise, without regard to the previous appointment of a place of meeting, or any regulation as to the number of the combatants. Nay, it seems as if, on occasions of special provocation, the English did not disdain to use the swords of hired assassins in aid of their revenge, and all punctilios of equality of arms or numbers were set aside as idle ceremonies.

Sir John Ayres, a man of rank and fortune, entertained jealousy of Lord Herbert of Cherbury, celebrated as a soldier and philosopher, from having discovered that his wife, Lady Ayres, wore around her neck the picture of that high-spirited and accomplished nobleman. Incensed by the suspicions thus excited, Sir John watched Lord Herbert, and, meeting him on his return from court, attended by only two servants, he attacked him furiously, backed by four of his followers with drawn weapons, and accompanied by many others, who, though they did not directly unsheath their swords, yet served to lend countenance to the assault. Lord Herbert was thrown down under his horse; his sword, with which he endeavoured to defend himself, was broken in his hand; and the weight of the horse prevented him from rising. One of his lacqueys ran away on seeing his master attacked by such odds; the other stood by him, and released his foot, which was entangled in the stirrup. At this moment Sir John Ayres was standing over him, and in the act of attempting to plunge his sword into his body; but Lord Herbert, catching him by the legs, brought him also to the ground; and, although the young lord had but a fragment of his sword remaining, he struck his unmanly antagonist on the stomach with such force as deprived him of the power to prosecute his bloody purpose; and some of Lord Herbert's friends coming up, the assassin thought it prudent to withdraw, vomiting blood in consequence of the blow he had received.

This scuffle lasted for some time in the streets of London, without any person feeling himself called upon to interfere in behalf of the weaker party; and Sir John Ayres seems to have entertained no shame for the enterprise, but only regret that it had not succeeded. Lord Herbert sent him a challenge as soon as his wounds were in the way of being cured; and the gentleman who bore it, placed the letter on the point of his sword, and in that manner delivered it publicly to the person whom he addressed. Sir John Ayres replied, that the injury he had received from Lord Herbert was of such a nature, that he would not consent to any terms of fair play, but would shoot him from a window with a musket, if he could find an opportunity. Lord Herbert protests, in his Memoirs, that there was no cause given on his part for the jealousy which drove Sir John Ayres to such desperate measures of revenge.

A still more noted case of cruel vengeance, and which served to embitter the general hatred against the Scots, was a crime committed by

Lord Sanquhar, a nobleman of that country, the representative of the ancient family of Creichton. This young lord, in fencing with a man called Turner, a teacher of the science of defence, had the misfortune to be deprived of an eye by the accidental thrust of a foil. The mishap was doubtless both distressing and provoking; but there was no room to blame Turner, by whom no injury had been intended, and who greatly regretted the accident. One or two years after this, Lord Sanquhar being at the court of France, Henry IV., then King, asked him how he had lost his eye. Lord Sanquhar, not wishing to dwell on the subject, answered in general terms, that it was by the thrust of a sword. "Does the man who did the injury still live?" asked the King; and the unhappy question impressed it indelibly upon the heart of the infatuated Lord Sanquhar that his honour required the death of the poor fencing-master. Accordingly, he despatched his page, and another of his followers, who pistolled Turner in his own school. The murderers were taken, and acknowledged they had been employed to do the deed by their lord, whose commands, they said, they had been bred up to hold as indisputable warrants for the execution of whatever he might enjoin. All the culprits being brought to trial and condemned, much interest was made for Lord Sanquhar, who was a young man, it is said, of eminent parts. But to have pardoned him would have argued too gross a partiality in James towards his countrymen and original subjects. He was hanged, therefore, along with his two associates; which Lord Bacon termed the most exemplary piece of justice in any king's reign.

To sum up the account of these acts of violence, they gave occasion to a severe law, called the statute of stabbing. Hitherto, in the mild spirit of English jurisprudence, the crime of a person slaying another without premeditation only amounted to the lesser denomination of murder which the law calls manslaughter, and which had been only punishable by fine and imprisonment. But, to check the use of short swords and poniards, weapons easily concealed, and capable of being suddenly produced, it was provided, that if any one, though without forethought or premeditation, with sword or dagger, attacked and wounded another whose weapon was not drawn, of which wound the party should die within six months after receiving it, the crime should not be accounted homicide, but rise into the higher class of murder, and be as such punished with death accordingly.

XXXVI

Smothering Uniformity

1612-1625

WHILE the quarrels of the English and Scottish nobility disturbed the comfort of James the First's reign, it must be admitted that the monarch applied himself with some diligence to cement as much as possible the union of the two kingdoms, and to impart to each such advantages as they might be found capable of borrowing from the other. The love of power, natural to him as a sovereign, combined with a sincere wish for what would be most advantageous to both countries—for James, when not carried off by his love of idle pleasures, and the influence of unworthy favourites, possessed the power of seeing, and the disposition to advance, the interests of his subjects—alike induced him to accelerate, by every means, the uniting the two separate portions of Britain into one solid and inseparable state, for which nature designed the inhabitants of the same island. He was not negligent in adopting measures to attain so desirable an object, though circumstances deferred the accomplishment of his wishes till the lapse of a century. To explain the nature of his attempt, and the causes of its failure, we must consider the respective condition of England and Scotland as regarded their political institutions.

The long and bloody wars between the houses of York and Lancaster, who, for more than thirty years, contended for the throne of England, had, by slaughter in numerous battles, by repeated proscriptions, public executions, and forfeitures, reduced to a comparatively inconsiderable number, and to a much greater state of disability and weakness, the nobility and great gentry of the kingdom, by whom the crown had been alternately bestowed on one or other of the contending parties. Henry the Seventh, a wise and subtle prince, had, by his success in the decisive battle of Bosworth, attained a secure seat upon the English throne. He availed himself of the weak state of the peers and barons, and the rising power of the cities and boroughs, to undermine and destroy the influence which the feudal system had formerly given to the aristocracy over their vassals; and they submitted to this diminution of their authority, as men who felt that the stormy independence possessed by their ancestors had cost them very dear, and that it was better to live at ease under the King, as a common head of the state, than to possess, each on his own domains, the ruinous power of petty sovereigns, making war upon, and ruining others, and incurring destruction themselves. They therefore relinquished, without much open discontent, most of their oppressive rights of sovereignty over their vassals, and were satisfied to be honoured and respected masters of their own lands, without retaining the power of princes over those who cultivated them. They exacted rents from their tenants instead of service in battle, and attendance in peace, and became peaceful and wealthy, instead of being great and turbulent.

As the nobles sunk in political consideration, the citizens of the towns and seaports, and the smaller gentry and cultivators of the soil, increased in importance as well as in prosperity and happiness. These commoners felt, indeed, and sometimes murmured against, the ascendance acquired by the King, but were conscious, at the same time, that it was the power of the crown which had relieved them from the far more vexatious and frequent exactions of their late feudal lords; and as the burden fell equally on all, they were better contented to live under the sway of one king, who imposed the national burdens on the people at large, than under that of a number of proud lords. Henry VII. availed himself of these favourable dispositions, to raise large taxes, which he partly hoarded up for occasions of emergency, and partly expended on levying bands of soldiers, both foreign and domestic, by whom he carried on such wars as he engaged in, without finding any necessity to call out the feudal array of the kingdom. In this manner he avoided rendering himself dependent on his nobles.

Henry VIII. was a prince of a very different temper, and yet his reign contributed greatly to extend and confirm the power of the English crown. He expended, indeed, lavishly, the treasures of his father; but he replenished them, in a great measure, by the spoils of the Roman Catholic Church, and he confirmed the usurpation of arbitrary authority, by the vigour with which he wielded it. The tyranny which he exercised in his family and court, was unfelt by the citizens and common people, with whom he continued to be rather popular from his splendour, than dreaded for his violence. His power wrested from them, in the shape of compulsory loans and benevolences, large sums of money which he was not entitled to by the grant of Parliament; but though he could not directly compel them to pay such exactions, yet he could exert, as in the case of Alderman Read, the power of sending the refusing party to undergo the dangers and hardships of foreign service, which most wealthy citizens thought still harder than the alternative of paying a sum of money.

The reign of the English Queen Mary was short and inglorious, but she pursued the arbitrary steps of her father, and in no degree relaxed the power which the crown had acquired since the accession of Henry VII. That of Elizabeth tended considerably to increase it. The success of the wise measures which she adopted for maintaining the Protestant religion, and making the power of England respected by foreign states, flattered the vanity, and conciliated the affection, of her subjects. The wisdom and economy with which she distributed the treasures of the state, added to the general disposition of her subjects to place them at her command; and the arbitrary authority which her grandfather acquired by subtlety, which her father maintained by violence, and which her sister preserved by bigotry, was readily conceded to Elizabeth by the love and esteem of her people. It was, moreover, to be considered, that, like the rest of the Tudor family, the Queen nourished high ideas of royal prerogative; and, when thwarted in her wishes by any opposition, not unfrequently called to lively recollection, both by expression and action, whose daughter she was.

In a word, the almost absolute authority of the House of Tudor may be understood from the single circumstance, that although religion is the point on which men do, and ought to think their individual feelings and sentiments especially at liberty, yet, at the arbitrary will of the sovereign, the Church of England was disjoined from that of Rome by Henry the Eighth, was restored to the Roman Catholic faith by Queen Mary, and again declared Protestant by Elizabeth; and on each occasion the change was effected without any commotion or resistance, beyond such temporary tumults as were soon put down by the power of the crown.

Thus, on succeeding to the English throne, James found himself at the head of a nobility who had lost both the habit and power of contesting the pleasure of the sovereign, and of a wealthy body of commons, who, satisfied with being liberated from the power of the aristocracy, were little disposed to resist the exactions of the crown.

His ancient kingdom of Scotland was quite differently situated. The feudal nobility had retained their territorial jurisdictions, and their signorial privileges, in as full extent as their ancestors had possessed them, and therefore had at once the power and the inclination to resist the arbitrary will of the sovereign, as James himself had felt on more occasions than one. Thus, though the body of the Scottish people had not the same protection from just and equal laws, as was the happy lot of the inhabitants of England, and were much less wealthy and independent, yet the spirit of the constitution possessed all the freedom which was inherent in the ancient feudal institutions, and it was impossible for the monarch of Scotland so to influence the parliament of the country, as to accomplish any considerable encroachment on the privileges of the nation.

It was therefore obvious, that besides the numerous reasons of a public nature for uniting South and North Britain under a similar system of government, James saw a strong personal interest for reducing the turbulent nobles and people of Scotland to the same submissive and quiet state in which he found England, but in which it was not his good fortune to leave it. With this view he proposed, that the Legislature of each nation should appoint Commissioners, to consider of the terms on which it might be possible to unite both under the same constitution. With some difficulty on both sides, the Parliament of England was prevailed on to name forty-four Commissioners, while the Scottish Parliament appointed thirty-six, to consider this important subject.

The very first conferences showed how impossible it was to accomplish the desired object, until time should have removed or softened those prejudices, which had existed during the long state of separation and hostility betwixt the two nations. The English

Commissioners demanded, as a preliminary stipulation, that the whole system of English law should be at once extended to Scotland. The Scots rejected the proposal with disdain, justly alleging, that nothing less than absolute conquest by force of arms could authorise the subjection of an independent nation to the customs and laws of a foreign country. The treaty, therefore, was in a great degree shipwrecked at the very commencement—the proposal for the union was suffered to fall asleep, and the King only reaped from his attempt the disadvantage of having excited the suspicions and fears of the Scottish lawyers, who had been threatened with the total destruction of their national system of Jurisprudence. This impression was the deeper, as the profession of the law, which must be influential in every government, was particularly so in Scotland, it being chiefly practised in that kingdom by the sons of the higher class of gentry.

Though in a great measure disappointed in his efforts for effecting a general union and correspondence of laws between the two nations, James remained extremely desirous to obtain at least an ecclesiastical conformity of opinion, by bringing the form and constitution of the Scottish Church as near as possible to that of England. What he attempted and accomplished in this respect, constitutes an important part of the history of his reign, and gave occasion to some of the most remarkable and calamitous events in that of his successor.

I must remind you, my dear child, that the Reformation was effected by very different agency in England, from that which produced a similar change in Scotland. The new plans of Church government adopted in the two nations did not in the least resemble each other, although the doctrines which they teach are so nearly alike, that little distinction can be traced, save what is of a very subtle and metaphysical character. But the outward forms of the two churches are totally different.

You must remember that the Reformation of the Church of England was originally brought about by Henry VIII., whose principal object was to destroy the dependence of the clergy upon the Pope, and transfer to himself, whom he declared Head of the Church in his own regal right, all the authority and influence which had formerly been enjoyed by the Papal See. When, therefore, Henry had destroyed the monastic establishments, and confiscated their possessions, and had reformed such doctrines of the Church as he judged to require amendment, it became his object to preserve the general constitution and hierarchy, that is the gradation of superior and inferior clergy, by whom her functions were administered. The chief difference therefore was, that the patronage exercised by the Pope was, in a great measure, transferred to the crown, and distributed by the hands of the King himself, to whom, therefore, the inferior clergy must naturally be attached by hope of preferment, and the superior orders by gratitude for past favours, and the expectation of further advancement. The order of bishops, in particular, raised to that rank by the crown, and enjoying seats in the House of Lords, must be supposed, on most occasions, willing to espouse the cause, and forward the views of the King, in such debates as might occur in that assembly.

The Reformation in Scotland had taken place by a sudden popular impulse, and the form of Church government adopted by Knox, and the other preachers under whose influence it had been accomplished, was studiously rendered as different as possible from the Roman hierarchy. The Presbyterian system, as I said in a former chapter, was upon the model of the purest republican simplicity; the brethren who served the altar claimed and allowed of no superiority of ranks, and of no influence but what individuals might attach to themselves by superior worth or superior talent. The representatives who formed their church courts, were selected by plurality of votes, and no other Head of the Church, visible or invisible, was acknowledged, save the blessed Founder of the Christian Religion, in whose name the Church courts of Scotland were and still are convoked and dismissed.

Over a body so constituted, the King could have little influence or power; nor did James acquire any by his personal conduct. It was, indeed, partly by the influence of the clergy that he had been in infancy placed upon the throne; but, as their conduct in this was regarded by James, in his secret soul, as an act of rebellion against his mother's authority, he gave the Kirk of Scotland little thanks for what they had done. It must be owned the preachers made no attempt to conciliate his favour; for, although they had no legal call to speak their sentiments upon public and political affairs, they yet entered into them without ceremony, whenever they could show that the interest of the Church gave a specious apology for interference. The Scottish pulpits rang with invectives against the King's ministers, and sometimes against the King himself; and the more hot-headed among the clergy were disposed not only to thwart James's inclinations, and put the worst construction upon his intentions, but even publicly to insult him in their sermons, and favour the insurrections attempted by Stewart, Earl of Bothwell, and others, against his authority. They often entertained him with violent invectives against his mother's memory; and, it is said, that on one occasion, when the King, losing patience, commanded one of these zealots either to speak sense or come down from the pulpit, the preacher replied to this request, which one would have thought a very reasonable one, "I tell thee, man, I will neither speak sense nor come down."

James did not see that these acts of petulance and contumacy arose, in a great measure, from the suspicions which the Scottish clergy justly entertained of his desiring to innovate upon the Presbyterian model; and hastily concluded that their refractory conduct, which was the result of mutual jealousies, was essential to the character of the peculiar form of Church government, and that the spirit of Presbytery was in itself inimical to a monarchical establishment.

As soon, therefore, as the King obtained the high increase of power which arose from his accession to the English throne, he set himself gradually to new-model the Scottish Church, so as to bring it nearer to that of England, and to obtain for the crown some preponderating influence in its councils. But the suspicions of the Presbyterian clergy were constantly alive to their sovereign's intentions. It was in vain he endeavoured to avail himself of the institution of an order of men called Superintendents, to whom the Book of Discipline, drawn up by Knox himself, had assigned a sort of presidency in certain cases, with power of inspecting the merits of the clergy. By re-establishing superior offices among the clergy, James endeavoured to introduce a sort of permanent presidents into the several presbyteries. But the ministers clearly saw his ultimate object. "Busk (dress), busk him as bonnily as you can," cried Mr. John Davidson, "bring him in as fairly as you will, we see the horns of his mitre weel enough;" and the horns of the mitre were, to their apprehension, as odious as the horns of the Pope's tiara, or those of Satan himself. At last the King ventured on a decisive stroke. He named thirteen bishops, and obtained the consent of Parliament for restoring them to the small remains of their dilapidated bishoprics. The other bishoprics, seventeen in number, were converted into temporal lordships.

It cannot be denied that the leaders of the Presbyterian clergy showed the utmost skill and courage in the defence of the immunities of their Church. They were endeared to the people by the purity of their lives, by the depth of learning possessed by some, and the powerful talents exhibited by others; above all, perhaps, by the willingness with which they submitted to deprivation of office, accompanied by poverty, penalties, and banishment, rather than betray the cause which they considered as sacred. The King had in 1605 openly asserted his right to call and to dissolve the General Assemblies of the Church. Several of the clergy, however, in contempt of the monarch, summoned and attended a General Assembly at Aberdeen independent of his authority. This opportunity was taken to chastise the refractory clergymen. Five of their number were punished with banishment. In 1606 the two celebrated preachers named Melville were summoned before the Council, and upbraided by the King with their resistance to his will. They defended themselves with courage, and claimed the right of being tried by the laws of Scotland, a free kingdom, having laws and privileges of its own. But the elder Melville furnished a handle against them by his own imprudence.

In a debate before the Privy Council, concerning a Latin copy of verses, which Andrew Melville had written in derision of the ceremonies of the Church of England, the old man gave way to indecent violence, seized the Archbishop of Canterbury by the lawn sleeves, which he shook, calling them Romish rags, and charged the prelate as a breaker of the Sabbath, the maintainer of an anti-Christian hierarchy, the persecutor of true preachers, the enemy of reformed churches, and proclaimed himself his mortal enemy to the last drop of his blood. This indiscretion and violence afforded a pretext for committing the hot old Presbyterian divine to the Tower; and he was afterwards exiled, and died at Sedan. The younger Melville was confined to Berwick, several other clergymen were banished from their parishes to remote parts, and the Kirk of Scotland was for the time reduced to reluctant submission to the King's will. Thus the order of bishops was once more introduced into the Scottish Church.

James's projects of innovation were not entirely accomplished by the introduction of prelacy. The Church of England, at the Reformation, had retained some particular rites in observance, which had decency at least to recommend them, but which the headlong opposition of the Presbyterians to everything approaching to the Popish ritual induced them to reject with horror. Five of these were introduced into Scotland, by an enactment passed by a parliament held at Perth [1618], and thence distinguished as the Five Articles of Perth. In

modern times, when the mere ceremonial part of divine worship is
supposed to be of little consequence, compared with the temper and
spirit in which we approach the Deity, the Five Articles of Perth seem
to involve matters which might be dispensed or complied with, without being considered as essential to salvation. They were as follows:—
I. It was ordained that the communion should be received in a
kneeling posture, and not sitting, as hitherto practised in the Scottish
churches. II. That, in extreme cases, the communion might be administered in private. III. That baptism also might, when necessary, be
administered in private. IV. That youth, as they grew up, should be
confirmed, as it is termed, by the bishop; being a kind of personal
avowal of the engagements entered into by godfathers and godmothers
at the time of baptism. V. That four days, distinguished by events of the
utmost importance to the Christian religion, should be observed as
holidays. These were—Christmas, on which day our Saviour was born;
Good Friday, when he suffered death; Easter, when he arose from the
dead; and Pentecost, when the Holy Spirit descended on the apostles.

But, notwithstanding the moderate character of these innovations,
the utmost difficulty was found in persuading even those of the Scottish clergy who were most favourable to the King to receive them into
the Church, and they only did so on the assurance that they should not
be required to adopt any additional changes. The main body of the
churchmen, though terrified into sullen acquiescence, were unanimous in opinion that the new regulations indicated a manifest return
towards Popery. The common people held the same opinion; and a
thunderstorm of unusual violence, which took place at the time the
Parliament was sitting in debate upon the adoption of these obnoxious
articles, was considered as a declaration of the wrath of Heaven against
those who were again introducing the rites and festivals of the Roman
Church into the pure and reformed Kirk of Scotland. In short, this
attempt to infuse into the Presbyterian model something of the principles of a moderate prelacy, and to bring it, in a few particulars, into
conformity with that of the sister kingdom, was generally unacceptable
to the Church and to the nation; and it will be hereafter shown, that an
endeavour to extend and heighten the edifice which his father had
commenced, led the way to those acts of violence which cost Charles I.
his throne and life.

XXXVII

The Borders

1603-1625

WE are next to examine the effect which James's accession to the throne of England had upon those lawless parts of his kingdom, the Borders and the Highlands, as well as on the more civilised provinces of Scotland—of which I shall take notice in their order.

The consequences of the union of the crowns were more immediately felt on the Borders, which, from being the extremity of both countries, were now converted into the centre of the kingdom. But it was not easy to see how the restless and violent inhabitants, who had been for so many centuries accustomed to a lawless and military life, were to conduct themselves, when the general peace around left them no enemies either to fight with or plunder.

These Borderers were, as I have elsewhere told you, divided into families, or clans, who followed a leader supposed to be descended from the original father of the tribe. They lived in a great measure by the rapine which they exercised indiscriminately on the English, or their own countrymen, the inhabitants of the more inland districts, or by the protection-money which they exacted for leaving them undisturbed. This kind of plundering was esteemed by them in the highest degree honourable and praiseworthy; and the following, as well as many other curious stories, is an example of this:—

A young gentleman,[1] of a distinguished family belonging to one of these Border tribes, or clans, made, either from the desire of plunder, or from revenge, a raid, or incursion, upon the lands of Sir Gideon Murray of Elibank, afterwards deputy-treasurer of Scotland, and a great favourite of James VI. The Laird of Elibank, having got his people under arms, engaged the invaders, and, encountering them when they were encumbered with spoil, defeated them, and made the leader of the band prisoner. He was brought to the castle of his conqueror, when the lady inquired of her victorious husband, "What he intended to do with his captive?"—"I design," said the fierce baron, "to hang him instantly, dame, as a man taken red-hand in the act of robbery and violence."—"That is not like your wisdom, Sir Gideon," answered his more considerate lady. "If you put to death this young gentleman, you will enter into deadly feud with his numerous and powerful clan. You must therefore do a wiser thing, and, instead of hanging him, we will cause him to marry our youngest daughter, Meg with the meikle mouth, without any tocher" (that is, without any portion). The laird joyfully consented; for this Meg with the large mouth was so ugly, that there was very little chance of her getting a husband in any other circumstances; and, in fact, when the alternative of such a marriage, or death by the gallows, was proposed to the poor prisoner, he was for some time disposed to choose the latter; nor was it without difficulty that he could be persuaded to save his life at the expense of marrying Meg Murray. He did so at last, however; and it is said, that Meg, thus forced upon him, made an excellent and affectionate wife; but the unusual size of mouth was supposed to remain discernible in their descendants for several generations.[2] I mention this anecdote, because it occurred during James the Sixth's reign, and shows, in a striking manner, how little the Borderers had improved in their sense of morality, or distinctions between right and wrong.

A more important, but not more characteristic event, which hap-

---

[1] "William (afterwards Sir William) Scott, eldest son of Walter Scott of Harden, and of his lady, the celebrated Mary Scott, 'the Flower of Yarrow,' of whose way of living it is mentioned that when the last bullock was killed and devoured, it was the lady's custom to place on the table a dish, which, on being uncovered, was found to contain a pair of clean spurs; a hint to the riders that they must shift for their next meal."—Note, *Border Minstrelsy*, New Edit. vol. i. p. 211.

pened not long afterwards, shows, in its progress, the utter lawlessness and contempt of legal authority which prevailed on the Borders in the commencement of this reign, and, in its conclusion, the increased power of the monarch after the Union of the Crowns.

There had been long and deadly feud, on the West Borders, betwixt the two great families of Maxwell and Johnstone. The former house was the most wealthy and powerful family in Dumfriesshire and its vicinity, and had great influence among the families inhabiting the more level part of that county. Their chieftain had the title of Lord Maxwell, and claimed that of Earl of Morton. The Johnstones, on the other hand, were neither equal to the Maxwells in numbers nor in power; but they were a race of uncommon hardihood, much attached to each other and their chieftain, and who, residing in the strong and mountainous district of Annandale, used to sally from thence as from a fortress, and return to its fastnesses after having accomplished their inroads. They were, therefore, able to maintain their ground against the Maxwells, though more numerous than themselves.

So well was this known to be the case, that when, in 1585, the Lord Maxwell was declared to be a rebel, a commission was given to the Laird of Johnstone to pursue and apprehend him. In this, however, Johnstone was unsuccessful. Two bands of hired soldiers, whom the Government had sent to his assistance, were destroyed by the Maxwells; and Lochwood, the chief house of the laird, was taken and wantonly burnt, in order, as the Maxwells expressed it, that Lady Johnstone might have light to put on her hood. Johnstone himself was subsequently defeated and made prisoner. Being a man of a proud and haughty temper, he is said to have died of grief at the disgrace which he incurred; and thus there commenced a long series of mutual injuries between the hostile clans.

Shortly after this catastrophe, Maxwell, being restored to the King's favour, was once more placed in the situation of Warden of the West Borders; and an alliance was made betwixt him and Sir James

---

[2] The union contracted under such singular circumstances gave birth to 1. Sir William Scott the second, who carried on the line of the family of Harden—2. Sir Gideon Scott of High Chester, whose son was created Earl of Tarras on his marriage with Agnes, Countess of Buccleuch, but having no issue, the honours and estate of Buccleuch devolved upon her younger sister Anne, married to the unfortunate Duke of Monmouth —3. Walter Scott of Raeburn, progenitor of our author.—4. John, of whom are descended the Scotts of Wool.

Johnstone, in which they and their two clans agreed to stand by each other against all the world. This agreement being entered into, the clan of Johnstone concluded they had little to apprehend from the justice of the new Lord Warden, so long as they did not plunder any of the name of Maxwell. They accordingly descended into the valley of the Nith, and committed great spoil on the lands belonging to Douglas of Drumlanrig, Creichton Lord Sanquhar, Grierson of Lagg, and Kirkpatrick of Closeburn, all of them independent barons of high birth and great power. The injured parties pursued the depredators with forces hastily assembled, but were defeated with slaughter in their attempt to recover the prey. The despoiled and injured barons next carried their complaints to Maxwell the warden, who alleged his late alliance with Johnstone as a reason why he could not yield them the redress which his office entitled them to expect at his hands. But when, to make up for such risk as he might incur by renewing his enmity with the Johnstones, the barons of Nithsdale offered to bind themselves by a bond of manrent, as it was called, to become the favourers and followers of Lord Maxwell in all his quarrels, excepting against the King, the temptation became too strong to be overcome, and the ambitious warden resolved to sacrifice his newly formed friendship with Johnstone to the desire of extending his authority over so powerful a confederacy.

The secret of this association did not long remain concealed from Johnstone, who saw that his own destruction and the ruin of his clan were the objects aimed at, and hastened to apply to his neighbours in the east and south for assistance. Buccleuch, the relative of Johnstone, and by far his most powerful ally, was then in foreign parts. But the Laird of Elibank, mentioned in the last story, bore the banner of Buccleuch in person, and assembled five hundred men of the clan of Scott, whom our historians term the greatest robbers and fiercest fighters among the Border clans. The Elliots of Liddesdale also assisted Johnstone; and his neighbours on the southern parts, the Grahams of the Debateable Land, from hopes of plunder and ancient enmity to the Maxwells, sent also a considerable number of spears.

Thus prepared for war, Johnstone took the field with activity, while Maxwell, on the other part, hastily assembling his own forces, and those of his new followers, the Nithsdale barons, Drumlanrig, Lagg, Closeburn, the Creichtons, and others, invaded Annandale with the royal banner displayed, and a force of upwards of two thousand men.

Johnstone, unequal in numbers, stood on the defensive, and kept possession of the woods and strong ground; waiting an opportunity of fighting to advantage; while Maxwell, in contempt of him, formed the siege of the castle or tower of Lockerby, the fortress of a Johnstone, who was then in arms with his chief. His wife, a woman of a masculine disposition, the sister or daughter of the laird who had died in Maxwell's prison, defended his place of residence. While Maxwell endeavoured to storm the castle, and while it was bravely defended by its female captain, the chief received information that the Laird of Johnstone was advancing to its relief. He drew off from the siege, marched towards his feudal enemy, and caused it to be published through his little army that he would give a "ten-pound land," that is, land rated in the cess-books at that yearly amount, "to any one who would bring him the head or hand of the Laird of Johnstone." When this was reported to Johnstone, he said he had no ten-pound lands to offer, but that he would bestow a five-merk land upon the man who should bring him the head or hand of Lord Maxwell.

The conflict took place close by the river Dryfe near Lochmaben, and is called the Battle of Dryfe Sands. It was managed by Johnstone with considerable military skill. He showed at first only a handful of horsemen, who made a hasty attack upon Maxwell's army, and then retired in a manner which induced the enemy to consider them as defeated, and led them to pursue in disorder with loud acclamations of victory. The Maxwells and their confederates were thus exposed to a sudden and desperate charge from the main body of the Johnstones and their allies, who fell upon them while their ranks were broken, and compelled them to take to flight. The Maxwells and the confederated barons suffered grievously in the retreat—many were overtaken in the streets of Lockerby, and cut down or slashed in the face by the pursuers; a kind of blow which to this day is called in that country a "Lockerby lick."

Maxwell himself, an elderly man and heavily armed, was borne down from his horse in the beginning of the conflict; and, as he named his name and offered to surrender, his right hand, which he stretched out for mercy, was cut from his body. Thus far history; but family tradition adds the following circumstance: The Lady of Lockerby, who was besieged in her tower as already mentioned, had witnessed from the battlements the approach of the Laird of Johnstone, and as soon as the enemy withdrew from the blockade of the fortress, had sent to the assistance of her chief the few servants who had assisted in the defence. After this she heard the tumult of battle, but as she could not from the tower see the place where it was fought, she remained in an agony of suspense, until, as the noise seemed to pass away in a westerly direction, she could endure the uncertainty no longer, but sallied out from the tower, with only one female attendant, to see how the day had gone. As a measure of precaution, she locked the strong oaken door and the iron grate with which a Border fortress was commonly secured, and knitting the large keys on a thong, took them with her, hanging on her arm.

When the Lady of Lockerby entered on the field of battle, she found all the relics of a bloody fight; the little valley was covered with slain men and horses, and broken armour, besides many wounded, who were incapable of further effort for saving themselves. Amongst others, she saw lying beneath a thorn-tree a tall, gray-haired, noble-looking man, arrayed in bright armour, but bareheaded, and bleeding to death from the loss of his right hand. He asked her for mercy and help with a faltering voice; but the idea of deadly feud in that time and country closed all access to compassion even in the female bosom. She saw before her the only enemy of her clan, and the cause of her father's captivity and death; and raising the ponderous keys which she bore along with her, the Lady of Lockerby is commonly reported to have dashed out the brains of the vanquished Lord Maxwell.

The battle of Dryfe Sands was remarkable as the last great clan battle fought on the Borders, and it led to the renewal of the strife betwixt the Maxwells and Johnstones, with every circumstance of ferocity which could add horror to civil war. The last distinguished act of the tragedy took place thus:—

The son of the slain Lord Maxwell invited Sir James Johnstone to a friendly conference, to which each chieftain engaged to bring one friend only. They met at a place called Auchmanhill, on the 6th August 1608, when the attendant of Lord Maxwell, after falling into bitter and reproachful language with Johnstone of Gunmanlie, who was in attendance on his chief, at length fired his pistol. Sir James Johnstone turning round to see what had happened, Lord Maxwell treacherously shot him through the back with a pistol charged with a brace of poisoned bullets. While the gallant old knight lay dying on the ground, Maxwell rode round him with the view of completing his crime, but Johnstone defended himself with his sword till strength and life failed him.

This final catastrophe of such a succession of bloody acts of revenge took place several years after the union of the crowns, and the consequences, so different from those which ensued on former occasions, show how effectually the King's authority, and the power of enforcing the course of equal justice, had increased in consequence of that desirable event. You may observe, from the incidents mentioned, that in 1585, when Lord Maxwell assaulted and made prisoner the Laird of Johnstone, then the King's warden, and acting in his name, and committed him to the captivity in which he died, James was totally unequal to the task of vindicating his royal authority, and saw himself compelled to receive Maxwell into favour and trust, as if he had done nothing contrary to the laws. Nor was the royal authority more effectual in 1593, when Maxwell, acting as royal warden, and having the King's banner displayed, was in his turn defeated and slain, in so melancholy and cruel a manner, at Dryfe Sands. On the contrary, Sir James Johnstone was not only pardoned, but restored to favour and trust by the King. But there was a striking difference in the consequences of the murder which took place at Auchmanhill in 1608. Lord Maxwell, finding no refuge in the Border country, was obliged to escape to France, where he resided for two or three years; but afterwards venturing to return to Scotland, he was apprehended in the wilds of Caithness, and brought to trial at Edinburgh. James, desirous on this occasion to strike terror, by a salutary warning, into the factious nobility and disorderly Borderers, caused the criminal to be publicly beheaded on 21st May 1613.[1]

Many instances might be added to show that the course of justice on the Border began, after the accession of James to the English throne, to flow with a less interrupted stream, even where men of rank and power were concerned.

The inferior class of freebooters was treated with much less ceremony. Proclamations were made, that none of the inhabitants of either side of the Border (except noblemen and gentlemen of unsuspected character) should retain in their possession armour or weapons, offensive or defensive, or keep any horse above the value of fifty

---

[1] "Thus was finally ended by a salutary example of severity, the 'foul debate' betwixt the Maxwells and Johnstones, in the course of which each family lost two chieftains; one dying of a broken heart, one in the field of battle, one by assassination, and one by the sword of the executioner."—*See Notes to the ballads of "Lord Maxwell's Good Night," and "The Lads of Wamphray," in "The Minstrelsy of the Scottish Border," New Edition.*

shillings. Particular clans, described as broken men, were especially forbid the use of weapons. The celebrated clan of Armstrong had, on the very night in which Queen Elizabeth's death became public, concluding that a time of such misrule as that in which they had hitherto made their harvest was again approaching, and desirous of losing no time, made a fierce incursion into England, extending their ravages as far as Penrith, and done much mischief. But such a consequence had been foreseen and provided against. A strong body of soldiers, both English and Scots, swept along the Border, and severely punished the marauders, blowing up their fortresses with gunpowder, destroying their lands, and driving away their cattle and flocks. Several of the principal leaders were taken and executed at Carlisle. The Armstrongs appear never to have recovered their consequence after this severe chastisement; nor are there many of this celebrated clan now to be found among the landholders of Liddesdale, where they once possessed the whole district.

The Grahams, long the inhabitants of the Debateable Land which was claimed both by England and Scotland, were still more severely dealt with. They were very brave and active Borderers attached to England, for which country, and particularly in Edward VI.'s time, they had often done good service. But they were also very lawless plunderers, and their incursions were as much dreaded by the inhabitants of Cumberland as by those of the Scottish frontier. Thus their conduct was equally the subject of complaint on both sides of the Border; and the poor Grahams, seeing no alternative, were compelled to sign a petition to the King, confessing themselves to be unfit persons to dwell in the country which they now inhabited, and praying that he would provide the means of transporting them elsewhere, where his paternal goodness should assign them the means of subsistence. The whole clan, a very few individuals excepted, were thus deprived of their lands and residences, and transported to the county of Ulster, in Ireland, where they were settled on lands which had been acquired from the conquered Irish. There is a list in existence which shows the rate at which the county of Cumberland was taxed for the exportation of these poor Borderers, as if they had been so many bullocks.

Another efficient mode of getting rid of a warlike and disorderly population, who, though an admirable defence of a country in time of war, must have been great scourges in time of the profound peace to which the Border districts were consigned after the close of the English wars, was the levying a large body of soldiers to serve in foreign countries. The love of military adventure had already carried one legion of Scots to serve the Dutch in their defence against the Spaniards, and they had done great service in the Low Countries, and particularly at the battle of Mechline, in 1578; where, impatient of the heat of the weather, to the astonishment of both friends and enemies, the Scottish auxiliaries flung off their upper garments, and fought like furies in their shirts. The circumstance is pointed out in the plan of the battle, which is to be found in Strada's history, with the explanation, "Here the Scots fought naked."

Buccleuch levied a large additional force from the Border, whose occupation in their native country was gone for ever. These also distinguished themselves in the wars of the Low Countries. It may be supposed that very many of them perished in the field, and the descendants of others still survive in the Netherlands and in Germany.

In addition to the relief afforded by such an outlet for a superfluous military population, whose numbers greatly exceeded what the land could have supplied with food, and who, in fact, had only lived upon plunder, bonds were entered into by the men of substance and family on the Borders, not only obliging themselves to abstain from depredations, but to stand by each other in putting down and preventing such evil doings at the hand of others, and in making common cause against any clan, branch, or surname, who might take offence at any individual for acting in prosecution of this engagement. They engaged also to the King and to each other, not only to seize and deliver to justice such thieves as should take refuge in their grounds, but to discharge from their families or estates all persons, domestics, tenants, or others, who could be suspected of such offences, and to supply their place with honest and peaceable subjects. I am possessed of such a bond, dated in the year 1612, and subscribed by about twenty landholders, chiefly of the name of Scott.

Finally, an unusually severe and keen prosecution of all who were convicted, accused, or even suspected, of offence against the peace of the Border, was set on foot by George Home, Earl of Dunbar, James's able but not very scrupulous minister; and these judicial measures were conducted so severely as to give rise to the proverb of Jeddartt (or Jedburgh) justice, by which it is said a criminal was hanged first and tried afterwards; the truth of which is affirmed by historians as a well-known fact, occurring in numerous instances.

Cruel as these measures were, they tended to remedy a disease which seemed almost desperate. Rent, the very name of which had till that period scarcely been heard on the Border, began to be paid for property, and the proprietors of land turned their thoughts to rural industry, instead of the arts of predatory warfare. But it was more than a century ere the country, so long a harassed and disputed frontier, gained the undisturbed appearance of a civilised land.

Before leaving the subject of the Borders, I ought to explain to you, that as the possession of the strong and important town of Berwick had been long and fiercely disputed between England and Scotland, and as the latter country had never surrendered or abandoned her claim to the place, though it had so long remained an English possession, James, to avoid giving offence to either nation, left the question undecided, and since the union of the Crowns the city is never spoken of as part of England or Scotland, but as the King's Good Town of Berwick-upon-Tweed; and when a law is made for North and South Britain, without special and distinct mention of this ancient town, that law is of no force or avail within its precincts.

XXXVIII

The Western Isles

1603-1625

THE Highlands and Western Islands were in no respect so much affected by the union of the Crowns as the inhabitants of the Borders. The accession of James to the English throne was of little consequence to them, unless in so far as it rendered the King more powerful, and gave him the means of occasionally sending bodies of troops into their fortresses to compel them to order; and this was a measure of unusual rigour, which was but seldom resorted to.

The Highland tribes, therefore, remained in the same state as before, using the same dress, wielding the same arms, divided into the same clans, each governed by its own patriarch, and living in all respects as their ancestors had lived for many centuries before them. Or if there were some marks of softened manners among those Gaelic tribes who resided on the mainland, the inhabitants of the Hebrides or Western Isles, adjacent to the coast of Scotland, are described to us as utterly barbarous. A historian of the period says, "That the Highlanders who dwell on the mainland, though sufficiently wild, show some shade of civilisation; but those in the islands are without laws or morals, and totally destitute of religion and humanity." Some stories of their feuds are indeed preserved, which go far to support this general accusation. I will tell you one or two of them.

The principal possessors of the Hebrides were originally of the name of MacDonald, the whole being under the government of a succession of chiefs, who bore the name of Donald of the Isles, as we have already mentioned, and were possessed of authority almost independent of the Kings of Scotland. But this great family becoming divided into two or three branches, other chiefs settled in some of the islands, and disputed the property of the original proprietors. Thus, the MacLeods, a powerful and numerous clan, who had extensive estates on the mainland, made themselves masters, at a very early period, of a great part of the large island of Skye, seized upon much of the Long Island, as the Isles of Lewis and Harris are called, and fought fiercely with the MacDonalds, and other tribes of the islands. The following is an example of the mode in which these feuds were conducted.

About the end of the sixteenth century a boat, manned by one or two of the MacLeods, landed in Eigg, a small island, peopled by the MacDonalds. They were at first hospitably received; but having been guilty of some incivility to the young women on the island, it was so much resented by the inhabitants, that they tied the MacLeods hand and foot, and putting them on board of their own boat, towed it to sea, and set it adrift, leaving the wretched men, bound as they were, to perish by famine, or by the winds and waves, as chance should determine. But fate so ordered it, that a boat belonging to the Laird of MacLeod fell in with that which had the captives on board, and brought them in safety to the laird's castle of Dunvegan in Skye, where they complained of the injury which they had sustained from the MacDonalds of Eigg. MacLeod, in a great rage, put to sea with his galleys, manned by a large body of his people, which the men of Eigg could not entertain any rational hope of resisting. Learning that their incensed enemy was approaching with superior forces, and deep vows of revenge, the inhabitants, who knew they had no mercy to expect at MacLeod's hands, resolved, as the best chance of safety in their power, to conceal themselves in a large cavern on the seashore.

This place was particularly well calculated for that purpose. The entrance resembles that of a fox-earth, being an opening so small that a man cannot enter save by creeping on hands and knees. A rill of water falls from the top of the rock, and serves, or rather served at the period we speak of, wholly to conceal the aperture. A stranger, even when apprised of the existence of such a cave, would find the greatest difficulty in discovering the entrance. Within, the cavern rises to a great height, and the floor is covered with white dry sand. It is extensive enough to contain a great number of people. The whole inhabitants of Eigg, who, with their wives and families, amounted to nearly two hundred souls, took refuge within its precincts.

MacLeod arrived with his armament, and landed on the island, but could discover no one on whom to wreak his vengeance—all was desert. The MacLeods destroyed the huts of the islanders, and plundered what property they could discover, but the vengeance of the chieftain could not be satisfied with such petty injuries. He knew that the inhabitants must either have fled in their boats, to one of the islands possessed by the MacDonalds, or that they must be concealed somewhere in Eigg. After making a strict but unsuccessful search for two days, MacLeod had appointed the third to leave his anchorage, when, in the gray of the morning, one of the seamen beheld from the deck of his galley the figure of a man on the island. This was a spy whom the MacDonalds, impatient of their confinement in the cavern, had imprudently sent out to see whether MacLeod had retired or no. The poor fellow, when he saw himself discovered, endeavoured, by doubling, after the manner of a hare or fox, to obliterate the track of his footsteps on the snow, and prevent its being discovered where he had re-entered the cavern. But all the arts he could use were fruitless; the invaders again landed, and tracked him to the entrance of the den.

MacLeod then summoned those who were within it, and called upon them to deliver up the individuals who had maltreated his men, to be disposed of at his pleasure. The MacDonalds, still confident in the strength of their fastness, which no assailant could enter but on hands and knees, refused to surrender their clansmen.

MacLeod next commenced a dreadful work of indiscriminate vengeance. He caused his people, by means of a ditch cut above the top of the rock, to turn away the stream of water which fell over the entrance of the cavern. This being done, the MacLeods collected all the combustibles which could be found on the island, particularly turf and quantities of dry heather, piled them up against the aperture, and maintained an immense fire for many hours, until the smoke, penetrating into the inmost recesses of the cavern, stifled to death every creature within. There is no doubt of the truth of this story, dreadful as it is. The cavern is often visited by strangers; and I have myself seen the place where the bones of the murdered MacDonalds still remain, lying as thick on the floor of the cave as in the charnel-house of a church.[1]

The MacLeans, in like manner, a bold and hardy race, who, originally followers of the Lords of the Isles, had assumed independence, seized upon great part both of the isle of Mull and the still more valuable island of Islay, and made war on the MacDonalds with various success. There is a story belonging to this clan, which I may tell you, as giving another striking picture of the manners of the Hebrideans.

The chief of the clan, MacLean of Duart, in the isle of Mull, had a son who received the name of Allan-a-Sop, by which he was distinguished from others of his clan. As his father and mother were not married, Allan was of course illegitimate, and had no inheritance to look for, save that which he might win for himself.

But the beauty of the boy's mother having captivated a man of rank in the clan, called MacLean of Torloisk, he married her, and took her to reside with him at his castle of Torloisk, situated on the shores of the sound, or small strait of the sea, which divides the smaller island of Ulva from that of Mull. Allan-a-Sop paid his mother frequent visits at her new residence, and she was naturally glad to see the poor boy, both from affection, and on account of his personal strength and beauty, which distinguished him above other youths of his age. But she was obliged to confer marks of her attachment on him as privately as she could, for Allan's visits were by no means so acceptable to her husband as to herself. Indeed, Torloisk liked so little to see the lad, that he determined to put some affront on him, which should prevent his returning to the castle for some time. An opportunity for executing his purpose soon occurred.

The lady one morning, looking from the window, saw her son coming wandering down the hill, and hastened to put a girdle cake upon the fire, that he might have hot bread for breakfast. Something called her out of the apartment after making this preparation, and her husband, entering at the same time, saw at once what she had been about, and determined to give the boy such a reception as should disgust him for the future. He snatched the cake from the girdle, thrust it into his step-son's hands, which he forcibly closed on the scalding

---

[1] In the journal of his Voyage to the Hebrides, August 1814, Sir Walter Scott says, "I brought off, in spite of the prejudices of our sailors, a skull from among the numerous specimens of mortality which the cavern afforded."—*See Note, "Lord of the Isles."*

bread, saying, "Here, Allan—here is a cake which your mother has got ready for your breakfast." Allan's hands were severely burnt; and, being a sharp-witted and proud boy, he resented this mark of his step-father's ill-will, and came not again to Torloisk.

At this time the western seas were covered with the vessels of pirates, who, not unlike the Sea-Kings of Denmark at an early period, sometimes settled and made conquests on the islands. Allan-a-Sop was young, strong, and brave to desperation. He entered as a mariner on board of one of these ships, and in process of time obtained the command, first of one galley, then of a small flotilla, with which he sailed round the seas and collected considerable plunder, until his name became both feared and famous. At length he proposed to himself to pay a visit to his mother, whom he had not seen for many years; and setting sail for this purpose, he anchored one morning in the sound of Ulva, and in front of the house of Torloisk. His mother was dead, but his stepfather, to whom he was now as much an object of fear as he had been formerly of aversion, hastened to the shore to receive his formidable stepson, with great affectation of kindness and interest in his prosperity; while Allan-a-Sop, who, though very rough and hasty, does not appear to have been sullen or vindictive, seemed to take his kind reception in good part.

The crafty old man succeeded so well, as he thought, in securing Allan's friendship, and obliterating all recollections of the former affront put on him, that he began to think it possible to employ his stepson in executing his own private revenge upon MacQuarrie of Ulva, with whom, as was usual between such neighbours, he had some feud. With this purpose, he offered what he called the following good advice to his son-in-law: "My dear Allan, you have now wandered over the seas long enough; it is time you should have some footing upon land, a castle to protect yourself in winter, a village and cattle for your men, and a harbour to lay up your galleys. Now, here is the island of Ulva, near at hand, which lies ready for your occupation, and it will cost you no trouble, save that of putting to death the present proprietor, the Laird of MacQuarrie, a useless old carle, who has cumbered the world long enough."

Allan-a-Sop thanked his stepfather for so happy a suggestion, which he declared he would put in execution forthwith. Accordingly, setting sail the next morning, he appeared before MacQuarrie's house an hour before noon. The old chief of Ulva was much alarmed at the

menacing apparition of so many galleys, and his anxiety was not lessened by the news that they were commanded by the redoubted
Allan-a-Sop. Having no effectual means of resistance, MacQuarrie, who
was a man of shrewd sense, saw no alternative save that of receiving
the invaders, whatever might be their purpose, with all outward
demonstrations of joy and satisfaction; the more especially as he recollected having taken some occasional notice of Allan during his early
youth, which he now resolved to make the most of. Accordingly, Mac-
Quarrie caused immediate preparations to be made for a banquet as
splendid as circumstances admitted, hastened down to the shore to
meet the rover, and welcomed him to Ulva with such an appearance of
sincerity, that the pirate found it impossible to pick any quarrel, which
might afford a pretence for executing the violent purpose which he had
been led to meditate.

They feasted together the whole day; and, in the evening, as
Allan-a-Sop was about to retire to his ships, he thanked the laird for his
hospitality, but remarked, with a sigh, that it had cost him very dear.
"How can that be," said MacQuarrie, "when I bestowed this entertainment upon you in free good will?"—"It is true, my friend," replied the
pirate, "but then it has quite disconcerted the purpose for which I
came hither; which was to put you to death, my good friend, and seize
upon your house and island, and so settle myself in the world. It
would have been very convenient for me, this island of Ulva; but your
friendly reception has rendered it impossible for me to execute my
purpose: so that I must be a wanderer on the seas for some time
longer." Whatever MacQuarrie felt at learning he had been so near to
destruction, he took care to show no emotion save surprise, and
replied to his visitor,—"My dear Allan, who was it that put into your
mind so unkind a purpose towards your old friend; for I am sure it
never arose from your own generous nature? It must have been old
Torloisk, who made such an indifferent husband to your mother, and
such an unfriendly stepfather to you when you were a helpless boy;
but now, when he sees you a bold and powerful leader, he desires to
make a quarrel betwixt you and those who were the friends of your
youth. If you consider this matter rightly, Allan, you will see that the
estate and harbour of Torloisk lie to the full as conveniently for you as
those of Ulva, and that, if you are disposed (as is very natural) to make
a settlement by force, it is much better it should be at the expense of

the old churl, who never showed you kindness or countenance, than at that of a friend like me, who always loved and honoured you."

Allan-a-Sop was struck with the justice of this reasoning; and the old offence of his scalded fingers was suddenly recalled to his mind. "It is very true what you say, MacQuarrie," he replied; "and, besides, I have not forgotten what a hot breakfast my stepfather treated me to one morning. Farewell for the present; you shall soon hear news of me from the other side of the sound." Having said thus much, the pirate got on board, and, commanding his men to unmoor the galleys, sailed back to Torloisk, and prepared to land in arms. MacLean hastened to meet him, in expectation to hear of the death of his enemy, MacQuarrie. But Allan greeted him in a very different manner from what he expected. "You hoary old traitor," he said, "you instigated my simple good nature to murder a better man than yourself! But have you forgotten how you scorched my fingers twenty years ago, with a burning cake? The day is come that that breakfast must be paid for." So saying, he dashed out the old man's brains with a battle-axe, took possession of his castle and property, and established there a distinguished branch of the clan of MacLean.

It is told of another of these western chiefs, who is said, upon the whole, to have been a kind and good-natured man, that he was subjected to repeated risk and injury by the treachery of an ungrateful nephew, who attempted to surprise his castle, in order to put his uncle to death, and obtain for himself the command of the tribe. Being detected on the first occasion, and brought before his uncle as a prisoner, the chief dismissed him unharmed; with a warning, however, not to repeat the offence, since, if he did so, he would cause him to be put to a death so fearful that all Scotland should ring with it. The wicked young man persevered, and renewed his attempts against his uncle's castle and life. Falling a second time into the hands of the offended chieftain, the prisoner had reason to term him as good as his word. He was confined in the pit, or dungeon of the castle, a deep dark vault, to which there was no access save through a hole in the roof. He was left without food, till his appetite grew voracious; the more so, as he had reason to apprehend that it was intended to starve him to death. But the vengeance of his uncle was of a more refined character. The stone which covered the aperture in the roof was lifted, and a quantity of salt beef let down to the prisoner, who devoured it eagerly. When he had glutted himself with this food, and expected to be supplied with liquor, to quench the raging thirst which the diet had excited, a cup was slowly lowered down, which, when he eagerly grasped it, he found to be empty! Then they rolled the stone on the opening in the vault, and left the captive to perish by thirst, the most dreadful of all deaths.

Many similar stories could be told you of the wild wars of the islanders; but these may suffice at present to give you some idea of the fierceness of their manners, the low value at which they held human life, the cruel manner in which wrongs were revenged, and the unscrupulous violence by which property was acquired.

The Hebrideans seem to have been accounted by King James a race whom it was impossible to subdue, conciliate, or improve by civilisation; and the only remedy which occurred to him was to settle Lowlanders in the islands, and drive away or extirpate the people by whom they were inhabited. For this purpose, the King authorised an association of many gentlemen in the county of Fife, then the wealthiest and most civilised part of Scotland, who undertook to make a settlement in the isles of Lewis and Harris. These undertakers, as they were called, levied money, assembled soldiers, and manned a fleet, with which they landed on the Lewis, and effected a settlement at Stornoway in that country, as they would have done in establishing a colony on the desert shores of a distant continent.

At this time the property of the Lewis was disputed between the sons of Rora MacLeod, the last lord, who had two families by separate wives. The undertakers, finding the natives thus quarrelling among themselves, had little difficulty in building a small town and fortifying it; and their enterprise in the beginning assumed a promising appearance. But the Lord of Kintail, chief of the numerous and powerful clan of MacKenzie, was little disposed to let this fair island fall into the possession of a company of Lowland adventurers. He had himself some views of obtaining it in the name of Torquil Connaldagh MacLeod, one of the Hebridean claimants, who was closely connected with the family of MacKenzie, and disposed to act as his powerful ally desired. Thus privately encouraged, the islanders united themselves against the undertakers; and, after a war of various fortune, attacked their camp of Stornoway, took it by storm, burnt the fort, slew many of them, and made the rest prisoners. They were not expelled, you may be sure, without bloodshed and massacre. Some of the old persons still alive in the Lewis, talk of a very old woman, living in their youth, who used to say that she had held the light while her countrymen were cutting the throats of the Fife adventurers.

A lady, the wife of one of the principal gentlemen in the expedition, fled from the scene of violence into a wild and pathless desert of rock and morass, called the Forest of Fannig. In this wilderness she became the mother of a child. A Hebridean, who chanced to pass on one of the ponies of the country, saw the mother and infant in the act of perishing with cold, and being struck with the misery of their condition, contrived a strange manner of preserving them. He killed his pony, and opening its belly, and removing the entrails, he put the new-born infant and the helpless mother into the inside of the carcass, to have the advantage of the warmth which this strange and shocking receptacle for some time afforded. In this manner, with or without assistance, he contrived to bear them to some place of security, where the lady remained till she could get back in safety to her own country.

The lady who experienced this remarkable deliverance became afterwards, by a second marriage, the wife of a person of consequence and influence in Edinburgh, a judge, I believe, of the Court of Session. One evening, while she looked out of the window of her house in the Canongate, just as a heavy storm was coming on, she heard a man in the Highland dress say in the Gaelic language, to another with whom he was walking, "This would be a rough night for the Forest of Fannig." The lady's attention was immediately attracted by the name of a place which she had such awful reasons for remembering, and, on looking attentively at the man who spoke, she recognised her preserver. She called him into the house, received him in the most cordial manner, and finding that he was come from the Western Islands on some law business of great importance to his family, she interested her husband in his favour, by whose influence it was speedily and successfully settled; and the Hebridean, loaded with kindness and presents, returned to his native island, with reason to congratulate himself on the humanity which he had shown in so singular a manner.

After the surprise of their fort, and the massacre of the defenders, the Fife gentlemen tired of their undertaking; and the Lord of Kintail had the whole advantage of the dispute, for he contrived to get possession of the Lewis for himself, and transmitted it to his family, with whom it still remains.

It appears, however, that King James did not utterly despair of improving the Hebrides, by means of colonisation. It was supposed that the powerful Marquis of Huntly might have been able to acquire the property, and had wealth enough to pay the crown something for the grant. The whole archipelago was offered to him, with the exception of Skye and Lewis, at the cheap price of ten thousand pounds Scots, or about £800; but the Marquis would not give more than half the sum demanded, for what he justly considered as merely a permission to conquer a sterile region, inhabited by a warlike race.

Such was the ineffectual result of the efforts to introduce some civilisation into these islands. In the next chapter we shall show that the improvement of the Highlanders on the mainland was not much more satisfactory.

XXXIX

The Highlands

1603-1625

THE size and position of the Highlands of Scotland rendered them much less susceptible of improvement than the Border districts, which, far less extensive, and less difficult of access, were now placed between two civilised and peaceful countries, instead of being the frontier of two hostile lands.

The Highlanders, on the contrary, continued the same series of wars among themselves, and incursions upon their Lowland neighbours, which had distinguished them ever since the dawn of their history. Military adventure, in one form or other, was their delight as well as their employment, and all works of industry were considered as unworthy the dignity of a mountaineer. Even the necessary task of raising a scanty crop of barley was assigned to the aged, and to the women and children. The men thought of nothing but hunting and war. I will give you an account of a Highland chieftain, in character and practice not very different from that of Allan-a-Sop, the Hebridean.

The Stewarts, who inhabited the district of Appin, in the West Highlands, were a numerous and warlike clan. Appin is the title of the chief of the clan. The second branch of the family was that of Invernahyle. The founder, a second son of the house of Appin, was called by the uncommon epithet of *Saioleach* or the *Peaceful*. One of his neighbours was the Lord of Dunstaffnage, called Cailen Uaine, or Green Colin, from the green colour which predominated in his tartan. This Green Colin surprised the peaceful Laird of Invernahyle, assassinated him, burnt his house, and destroyed his whole family, excepting an infant at the breast. This infant did not owe its safety to the mercy of Green Colin, but to the activity and presence of mind of its nurse. Finding she could not escape the pursuit of that chief's attendants, the faithful nurse determined to provide for the safety of her foster-child, whose life she knew was aimed at, in the only manner which remained. She therefore hid the infant in a small fissure, or cave, of a rock, and as the only means she had of supplying him with subsistence, hung by a string round his neck a large piece of lard, in the faint hope that instinct might induce the child to employ it as a means of subsistence. The poor woman had only time to get a little way from the place where she had concealed her charge, when she was made prisoner by the pursuers. As she denied any knowledge where the child was, they dismissed her as a person of no consequence, but not until they had kept her two or three days in close confinement, menacing her with death unless she would discover what she had done with the infant.

When she found herself at liberty and unobserved, she went to the hole in which she had concealed her charge, with little hope save of finding such relics as wolves, wild-cats, or birds of prey might have left after feasting upon its flesh, but still with the pious wish to consign the remains of her *dault* or foster-child, to some place of Christian burial. But her joy and surprise were extreme to find the infant still alive and well, having lived during her absence by sucking the lard, which it had reduced to a very small morsel, scarce larger than a hazel nut. The delighted nurse made all haste to escape with her charge to the neighbouring district of Moidart, of which she was a native, being the wife of the smith of the clan of MacDonald, to whom that country belonged. The mother of the infant thus miraculously rescued had also been a daughter of this tribe.

To ensure the safety of her foster-child, the nurse persuaded her husband to bring it up as their own son. The smith, you must remark, of a Highland tribe, was a person of considerable consequence. His skill in forging armour and weapons was usually united with dexterity in using them, and with the strength of body which his profession required. If I recollect right, the smith usually ranked as third officer in the chief's household. The young Donald Stewart, as he grew up, was distinguished for great personal strength. He became skilful in his foster-father's art, and so powerful, that he could, it is said, wield two fore-hammers, one in each hand, for hours together. From this circumstance, he gained the name of *Donuil nan Ord,* that is, Donald of the Hammer, by which he was all his life distinguished.

When he attained the age of twenty-one, Donald's foster-father, the smith, observing that his courage and enterprise equalled his personal strength, thought fit to discover to him the secret of his birth, the injuries which he had received from Green Colin of Dunstaffnage, and the pretensions which he had to the property of Invernahyle, now in the possession of the man who had slain his father, and usurped his inheritance. He concluded his discovery by presenting to his beloved foster-child his own six sons to be his followers and defenders for life and death, and his assistants in the recovery of his patrimony.

Law of every description was unknown in the Highlands. Young Donald proceeded in his enterprise by hostile measures In addition to his six foster-brethren, he got some assistance from his mother's kindred, and levied among the old adherents of his father, and his kinsmen of the house of Appin, such additional force, that he was able to give battle to Green Colin, whom he defeated and slew, regaining at the same time his father's house and estate of Invernahyle. This success had its dangers; for it placed the young chief in feud with all the families of the powerful clan of Campbell, to which the slain Dunstaffnage belonged by alliance at least; for Green Colin and his ancestors had assumed the name, and ranked themselves under the banner, of this formidable clan, although originally they were chieftains of a different and independent race. The feud became more deadly, when, not satisfied with revenging himself on the immediate authors of his early misfortune, Donald made inroads on the Campbells in their own dominions; in evidence of which his historian quotes a verse to this purpose—

> "Donald of the Smithy, the Son of the Hammer,
> Filled the banks of Lochawe with mourning and clamour."

At length the powerful Earl of Argyle resented the repeated injuries which were offered to his clansmen and kindred. The Stewarts of Appin refused to support their kinsman against an enemy so formidable, and insisted that he should seek for peace with the Earl. So that Donald, left to himself, and sensible that he was unable to withstand the force which might be brought against him by this mighty chief, endeavoured to propitiate the Earl's favour by placing himself in his hands.

Stewart went, accordingly, with only a single attendant, towards Inverary, the castle of Argyle, and met with the Earl himself at some distance in the open fields. Donald of the Hammer showed on this occasion that it was not fear which had induced him to this step. Being a man of ready wit, and a poet, which was an accomplishment high in the estimation of the Highlanders, he opened the conference with an extempore verse, which intimated a sort of defiance, rather like the language of a man that cared not what might befall him, than one who craved mercy or asked forgiveness.

> "Son of dark Colin, thou dangerous earl,
> Small is the boon that I crave at thy hand;
> Enough, if in safety from bondage and peril,
> Thou let'st me return to my kindred and land."

The Earl was too generous to avail himself of the advantage which Invernahyle's confidence had afforded him, but he could not abstain from maintaining the conversation thus begun, in a gibing tone. Donuil nan Ord was harsh-featured, and had a custom, allied to his mode of education, and the haughtiness of his character, of throwing back his head, and laughing loudly with his mouth wide open. In ridicule of this peculiarity, in which Donald had indulged repeatedly, Argyle, or one of his attendants, pointed out to his observation a rock in the neighbourhood, which bore a singular resemblance to a human face, with a large mouth much thrown back, and open as if laughing a horse-laugh. "Do you see yonder crag?" said the Earl to Donald of the Hammer: "it is called *Gaire Granda,* or the *Ugly Laugh.*" Donald felt the intended gibe, and as Argyle's lady was a hard-favoured and haughty woman, he replied, without hesitation, in a verse like the following:

> "Ugly the sneer of yon cliff of the hill,
> Nature has stamp'd the grim laugh on the place;
> Would you seek for a grimmer and uglier still,
> You will find it at home in your countess's face."

Argyle took the raillery of Donald in good part, but would not make peace with him, until he agreed to make two *creaghs,* or inroads, one on Moidart, and one on Athole. It seems probable that the purpose of Argyle was to engage his troublesome neighbour in a feud with other clans to whom he bore no goodwill; for whether he of the Hammer fell or was successful, the Earl, in either event, would gain a certain advantage. Donald accepted peace with the Campbells on these terms.

On his return home, Donald communicated to MacDonald of Moidart the engagement he had come under; and that chieftain, his mother's kinsman and ally, concerted that Invernahyle and his band should plunder certain villages in Moidart, the inhabitants of which had offended him, and on whom he desired chastisement should be inflicted. The incursion of Donald the Hammerer punished them to some purpose, and so far he fulfilled his engagement to Argyle, without making an enemy of his own kinsman. With the Athole men, as more distant and unconnected with him, Donald stood on less ceremony, and made more than one successful creagh upon them. His name was now established as one of the most formidable marauders known in the Highlands, and a very bloody action which he sustained against the family of the Grahams of Monteith, made him still more dreaded.

The Earls of Monteith, you must know, had a castle situated upon an island in the lake, or loch, as it is called, of the same name. But though this residence, which occupied almost the whole of the islet upon which its ruins still exist, was a strong and safe place of abode, and adapted accordingly to such perilous times, it had this inconvenience, that the stables, cow-houses, poultry-yard, and other domestic offices, were necessarily separated from the castle, and situated on the mainland, as it would have been impossible to be constantly transporting the animals belonging to the establishment to and fro from the shore to the island. These offices, therefore, were constructed on the banks of the lake, and in some sort defenceless.

It happened upon a time that there was to be a great entertainment in the castle, and a number of the Grahams were assembled. The occasion, it is said, was a marriage in the family. To prepare for this feast, much provision was got ready, and in particular a great deal of poultry had been collected. While the feast was preparing, an unhappy chance brought Donald of the Hammer to the side of the lake, returning at the head of a band of hungry followers, whom he was conducting homewards to the West Highlands, after some of his usual excursions into Stirlingshire. Seeing so much good victuals ready, and being possessed of an excellent appetite, the Western Highlanders neither asked questions, nor waited for an invitation, but devoured all the provisions that had been prepared for the Grahams, and then went on their way rejoicing, through the difficult and dangerous path which leads from the banks of the loch of Monteith, through the mountains, to the side of loch Katrine.

The Grahams were filled with the highest indignation. No one in those fierce times was so contemptible as an individual who would suffer himself to be plundered without exacting satisfaction and revenge, and the loss of their dinner probably aggravated the sense of the insults entertained by the guests. The company who were assembled at the castle of Monteith, headed by the Earl himself, hastily took to their boats, and, disembarking on the northern side of the lake, pursued with all speed the marauders and their leader. They came up with Donald's party in the gorge of a pass, near a rock called Craig-Vad, or the Wolf's Cliff. Here the Grahams called, with loud insults, on the Appin men to stand, and one of them, in allusion to the execution which had been done amongst the poultry, exclaimed in verse—

> "They're brave gallants, these Appin men,
> To twist the throat of cock and hen?"

Donald instantly replied to the reproach—

> "And if we be of Appin's line,
> We'll twist a goose's neck in thine."

So saying, he shot the unlucky scoffer with an arrow. The battle then began, and was continued with much fury till night. The Earl of Monteith and many of his noble kinsmen fell, while Donald, favoured by darkness, escaped with a single attendant. The Grahams obtained, from the cause of the quarrel, the nickname of Gramoch an Garrigh, or Grahams of the Hens: although they certainly lost no honour in the encounter, having fought like game-cocks.

Donald of the Hammer was twice married. His second marriage was highly displeasing to his eldest son, whom he had by his first wife. This young man, whose name was Duncan, seems to have partaken rather of the disposition of his grandfather, Alister *Saoileach,* or the Peaceful, than of the turbulent spirit of his father the Hammerer. He quitted the family mansion in displeasure at his father's second marriage, and went to a farm called Inverfalla, which his father had bestowed upon his nurse in reward for her eminent services. Duncan took up his abode with this valued connection of the family, who was now in the extremity of old age, and amused himself with attempting to improve the cultivation of the farm; a task which not only was considered as below the dignity of a Highland gentleman, but even regarded as the last degree of degradation.

The idea of his son's occupying himself with agricultural operations struck so much shame and anger into the heart of Donald the Hammerer, that his resentment against him became ungovernable. At length, as he walked by his own side of the river, and looked towards Inverfalla, he saw, to his extreme displeasure, a number of men employed in digging and levelling the soil for some intended crop. Soon after, he had the additional mortification to see his son come out and mingle with the workmen, as if giving them directions; and, finally, beheld him take the spade out of an awkward fellow's hand, and dig a little himself to show him how to use it. This last act of degeneracy drove the Hammerer frantic; he seized a curragh, or boat covered with hides, which was near, jumped into it, and pushed across the stream, with the determination of destroying the son who had, in his opinion, brought such unutterable disgrace upon his family. The poor agriculturist seeing his father approach in such haste, and having a shrewd guess of the nature of his parental intentions, fled into the house and hid himself. Donald followed with his drawn weapon; but, deceived by passion and darkness, he plunged his sword into the body of one whom he saw lying on the bed-clothes. Instead of his son, for whom the blow was intended, it lighted on the old foster-mother, to whom he owed his life in infancy and education in youth, and slew her on the spot. After this misfortune, Donald became deeply affected with remorse; and giving up all his estates to his children, he retired to the Abbey of St. Columba, in Iona, passed the remainder of his days as a monk, and died at the age of eighty-seven.

It may easily be believed, that there was little peace and quiet in a country abounding with such men as the Hammerer, who thought the practice of honest industry on the part of a gentleman was an act of degeneracy, for which nothing short of death was an adequate punishment; so that the disorderly state of the Highlands was little short of that of the Isles. Still, however, many of the principal chiefs attended occasionally at the court of Scotland; others were frequently obliged to send their sons to be educated there, who were retained as hostages for the peaceable behaviour of the clan; so that by degrees they came to improve with the increasing civilisation of the times.

The authority also of the great nobles, who held estates in or adjacent to the Highlands, was a means, though a rough one, of making the district over which they exercised their power, submit, in a certain degree, to the occasional influence of the laws. It is true, that the great Earls of Huntly, Argyle, Sutherland, and other nobles did not enforce the Lowland institutions upon their Highland vassals out of mere zeal for their civilisation, but rather because, by taking care to secure the power of the sovereign and the laws on their own side, they could make the infraction of them by the smaller chiefs the pretext for breaking down the independent clans, and making them submit to their own authority.

I will give you an example of the manner in which a noble lady chastised a Highland chief in the reign of James the Sixth. The Head of the House of Gordon, then Marquis of Huntly, was by far the most powerful lord in the northern counties and exercised great influence over the Highland clans who inhabited the mountains of Badenoch, which lay behind his extensive domains. One of the most ancient tribes situated in and near that district is that of MacIntosh, a word which means Child of the Thane, as they boast their descent from Macduff, the celebrated Thane of Fife. This haughty race having fallen at variance with the Gordons, William MacIntosh, their chief, carried his enmity to so great a pitch, as to surprise and burn the castle of Auchindown, belonging to the Gordon family. The Marquis of Huntly vowed the severest vengeance. He moved against the MacIntoshes with his own followers; and he let loose upon the devoted tribe all such neighbouring clans as would do anything, as the old phrase was, for his love or for his fear. MacIntosh, after a short struggle, found himself unequal to sustain the conflict, and saw that he must either behold his clan totally exterminated, or contrive some mode of pacifying Huntly's resentment. The idea of the first alternative was not to be endured, and of the last he saw no chance, save by surrendering himself into the power of the Marquis, and thus personally atoning for the offence which he had committed. To perform this act of generous devotion with as much chance of safety as possible, he chose a time when the Marquis himself was absent, and asking for the lady, whom he judged likely to prove less inexorable than her husband, he presented himself as the unhappy Laird of MacIntosh, who came to deliver himself up to the Gordon, to answer for his burning of Auchindown, and only desired that Huntly would spare his clan. The Marchioness, a stern and haughty woman, had shared deeply in her husband's resentment. She regarded MacIntosh with a keen eye, as the hawk or eagle contemplates the prey within its clutch, and having spoken a word aside to her attendants, replied to the suppliant chief in this manner:—"MacIntosh, you have offended the Gordon so deeply, that Huntly has sworn by his father's soul, that he will never pardon you, till he has brought your neck to the block."—"I will stoop even to that humiliation, to secure the safety of my father's house," said MacIntosh. And as this interview passed in the kitchen of the castle at Bog of Gicht, he undid the collar of his doublet, and kneeling down before the huge block on which, in the rude hospitality of the time, the slain bullocks and sheep were broken up for use, he laid his neck upon it, expecting, doubtless, that the lady would be satisfied with this token of unreserved submission. But the inexorable Marchioness made a sign to the cook, who stepped forward with his hatchet raised, and struck MacIntosh's head from his body.

Another story, and I will change the subject. It is also of the family of Gordon; not that they were by any means more hard-hearted than other Scottish barons, who had feuds with the Highlanders, but because it is the readiest which occurs to my recollection. The Farquharsons of Deeside, a bold and warlike people, inhabiting the dales of Braemar, had taken offence at, and slain, a gentleman of consequence, named Gordon of Brackley. The Marquis of Huntly summoned his forces, to take a bloody vengeance for the death of a Gordon; and that none of the guilty tribe might escape, communicated with the Laird of Grant, a very powerful chief, who was an ally of Huntly, and a relation, I believe, to the slain Baron of Brackley. They agreed, that, on a day appointed, Grant, with his clan in arms, should occupy the upper end of the vale of Dee, and move from thence downwards, while the Gordons should ascend the river from beneath, each party killing, burning, and destroying, without mercy, whatever and whomever they found before them. A terrible massacre was made of the Farquharsons, taken at unawares, and placed betwixt two enemies. Almost all the men and women of the race were slain, and when the day was done, Huntly found himself encumbered with about two hundred orphan children, whose parents had been killed. What became of them you shall presently hear.

About a year after this foray, the Laird of Grant chanced to dine at the Marquis's castle. He was, of course, received with kindness, and entertained with magnificence. After dinner was over, Huntly said to his guest, that he would show him some rare sport. Accordingly, he conducted Grant to a balcony, which, as was frequent in old mansions, overlooked the kitchen, perhaps to permit the lady to give an occasional eye to the operations there. The numerous servants of the Marquis and his visitors had already dined, and Grant beheld the remains of the victuals which had furnished a plentiful meal flung at random into a large trough, like that out of which swine feed. While Grant was wondering what this could mean, the master cook gave a signal with his silver whistle; on which a hatch, like that of a dog kennel, was raised, and there rushed into the kitchen, some shrieking, some shouting, some yelling—not a pack of hounds, which, in number, noise, and tumult, they greatly resembled, but a huge mob of children, half naked, and totally wild in their manners, who threw themselves on the contents of the trough, and fought, struggled, bit, scratched, and clamoured, each to get the largest share. Grant was a man of humanity, and did not see in that degrading scene all the amusement which his noble host had intended to afford him. "In the name of Heaven," he said, "who are these unfortunate creatures that are fed like so many pigs?"—"They are the children of those Farquharsons whom we slew last year on Dee side," answered Huntly. The Laird felt more shocked than it would have been prudent or polite to express. "My Lord," he said, "my sword helped to make these poor children orphans, and it is not fair that your Lordship should be burdened with all the expense of maintaining them. You have supported them for a year and day—allow me now to take them to Castle Grant, and keep them for the same period at my cost. Huntly was tired of the joke of the pig-trough, and willingly consented to have the undisciplined rabble of children taken off his hands. He troubled himself no more about them; and the Laird of Grant, carrying them to his castle, had them dispersed among his clan, and brought up decently, giving them his own name of Grant; but it is said their descendants are still called the Race of the Trough, to distinguish them from the families of the tribe into which they were adopted.

These are instances of the severe authority exercised by the great barons over their Highland neighbours and vassals. Still that authority produced a regard to the laws, which they would not otherwise have received. These mighty lords, though possessed of great power in their jurisdictions, never effected entire independence, as had been done by the old Lords of the Isles, who made peace and war with England, without the consent of the King of Scotland. On the contrary, Argyle, Huntly, Murray, and others, always used at least the pretext of the King's name and authority, and were, from habit and education, less apt to practise wild stretches of arbitrary power than the native chiefs of the Highlands. In proportion, therefore, as the influence of the nobles increased, the country approached more nearly to civilisation.

It must not here be forgotten, that the increase of power acquired by the sovereign, in the person of James VI., was felt severely by one of his great feudal lords, for exercising violence and oppression, even in the most distant extremity of the empire. The Earl of Orkney, descended from a natural son of James V., and of course a cousin-german of the reigning monarch, had indulged himself in extravagant excesses of arbitrary authority amongst the wild recesses of the Orkney and Zetland islands. He had also, it was alleged, shown some token of a wish to assume sovereign power, and had caused his natural son to defend the castle of Kirkwall, by force of arms, against the King's troops. Mr. Littlejohn is now something of a Latin scholar, and he will understand, that this wicked Earl of Orkney's ignorance of that language exposed him to two disgraceful blunders. When he had built the great tower of Scalloway in Zetland, he asked a clergyman for a motto, who supplied him with the following Latin words:—

"Cujus fundamen saxum est, domus illa manebit
Stabilis; et contra, si sit arena, perit."

The Earl was highly pleased with this motto, not understanding that the secret meaning implied, that a house, raised by honourable and virtuous means, was as durable as if founded upon a rock; whereas one like his new castle of Scalloway, constructed by injustice and oppressive means, was like one founded on the faithless sands, and would soon perish. It is now a waste ruin, and bears the defaced inscription as if prophetic of the event.

A worse error was that which occurred in the motto over another castle on the island of Birsa, in Orkney, built by his father and repaired by himself. Here he was pleased to inscribe his father's name and descent thus:—ROBERTUS STUARTUS, FILIUS JACOBI QUINTI, REX

SCOTORUM, HOC EDIFICIUM INSTRUXIT. SIC FUIT, EST, ET, ERIT. It was probably only the meaning of this inscription to intimate, that Earl Robert
was the son of James V., King of Scotland, which was an undeniable
truth; but putting *Rex* in the nominative instead of *Regis,* in the geni-
tive, as the construction required, Earl Patrick seemed to state that his
father had been the King of Scotland, and was gravely charged with
high treason for asserting such a proposition.

If this was rather a severe punishment for false Latin, it must be
allowed that Earl Patrick deserved his condemnation by repeated acts
of the greatest cruelty and oppression on the defenceless inhabitants
of those remote islands. He was held in such terror by them, that one
person who was brought as a witness against him, refused to answer
any question till he had received a solemn assurance that the Earl
would never be permitted to return to Orkney. Being positively
assured of this he gave such a detail of his usurpation and crimes as
made his guilt fully manifest.

For these offences the Earl was tried and executed at Edinburgh;
and his punishment struck such terror among the aristocracy, as
made even those great lords, whose power lay in the most distant
and inaccessible places of Scotland, disposed to be amenable to the
royal authority.

Having thus discussed the changes effected by the union of the
crowns on the Borders, Highlands, and Isles, it remains to notice
the effects produced in the Lowlands, or more civilised parts of
the kingdom.

XL

The Scottish Decline

1603-1625

THE Scottish people were soon made sensible, that if their courtiers and great men made fortunes by King James's favour, the nation at large was not enriched by the union of the crowns. Edinburgh was no longer the residence of a court, whose expenditure, though very moderate, was diffused among her merchants and citizens, and was so far of importance. The sons of the gentry and better classes, whose sole trade had been war and battle, were deprived of employment by the general peace with England, and the nation was likely to feel all the distress arising from an excess of population.

To remedy the last evil, the wars on the Continent afforded a resource peculiarly fitted to the genius of the Scots, who have always had a disposition for visiting foreign parts. The celebrated Thirty Years' War, as it was called, was now raging in Germany, and a large national brigade of Scots was engaged in the service of Gustavus Adolphus, King of Sweden, one of the most successful generals of the age. Their total numbers may be guessed from those of the superior officers, which amounted to thirty-four colonels, and fifty lieutenant-colonels. The similarity of the religion of the Scots with that of the Swedes, and some congenial resemblances betwixt the two nations, as well as the

high fame of Gustavus, made most of the Scots prefer the service of
Sweden; but there were others who went into that of the Emperor of
Austria, of France, of the Italian States,—in short, they were dispersed
as soldiers throughout all Europe. It was not uncommon, when a party
of Scots was mounting a breach, for them to hear some of the defenders call out in the Scottish language, "Come on, gentlemen; this is not
like gallanting it at the Cross of Edinburgh!" and thus learn that they
were opposed to some of their countrymen engaged on the opposite
side. The taste for foreign service was so universal, that young gentlemen of family, who wished to see the world, used to travel on the Continent from place to place, and from province to province, and defray
their expenses by engaging for a few weeks or months in military service in the garrison or guards of the state in which they made their
temporary residence. It is but doing the Scots justice to say, that while
thus acting as mercenary soldiers, they acquired a high character for
courage, military skill, and a faithful adherence to their engagements.
The Scots regiments in the Swedish service were the first troops who
employed platoon firing, by which they contributed greatly to achieve
the victory in the decisive battle of Lutzen.

Besides the many thousand Scottish emigrants who pursued the
trade of war on the Continent, there was another numerous class who
undertook the toilsome and precarious task of travelling merchants, or
to speak plainly, of pedlars, and were employed in conducting the
petty inland commerce, which gave the inhabitants of Germany,
Poland, and the northern parts of Europe in general, opportunities of
purchasing articles of domestic convenience. There were at that time
few towns, and in these towns there were few shops regularly open.
When an inhabitant of the country, of high or low degree, wished to
purchase any article of dress or domestic convenience which he did
not manufacture himself, he was obliged to attend at the next fair, to
which the travelling merchants flocked, in order to expose their goods
to sale. Or if the buyer did not choose to take that trouble, he must
wait till some pedlar, who carried his goods on horseback, in a small
wain, or perhaps in a pack upon his shoulders, made his wandering
journey through the country. It has been made matter of ridicule
against the Scots, that this traffic fell into their hands, as a frugal,
patient, provident, and laborious people, possessing some share of
education, which we shall presently see was now becoming general
among them. But we cannot think that the business which required

such attributes to succeed in it, could be dishonourable to those who pursued it; and we believe that those Scots who, in honest commerce, supplied foreigners with the goods they required, were at least as well employed as those who assisted them in killing each other.[1]

While the Scots thus continued to improve their condition by enterprise abroad, they gradually sank into peaceful habits at home. In the wars of Queen Mary's time, and those of King James's minority, we have the authority of a great lawyer, the first Earl of Haddington, generally known by the name of Tom of the Cowgate, to assure us, that "the whole country was so miserably distracted, not only by the accustomed barbarity of the Highlands and Borders, which was greatly increased, but by the cruel dissensions arising from public factions and private feuds, that men of every rank daily wore steel-jacks, knapscaps or head-pieces, plate-sleeves, and pistols and poniards, being as necessary parts of their apparel as their doublets and breeches." Their disposition was, of course, as warlike as their dress; and the same authority informs us, that whatever was the cause of their assemblies or meetings, fights and affrays were the necessary consequence before they separated; and this not at parliaments, conventions, trystes, and markets only, but likewise in churchyards, churches, and places appointed for the exercise of religion.

This universal state of disorder was not owing to any want of laws against such enormities; on the contrary, the Scottish legislature was more severe than that of England, accounting as murder the killing of any one in a sudden quarrel, without previous malice, which offence the law of England rated under the milder denomination of manslaughter. And this severity was introduced into the law, expressly

---

[1] In the _Fortunes of Nigel,_ King James is introduced as saying,—"It would be as unseemly for a packman, or pedlar, as ye call a travelling-merchant, whilk is a trade to which our native subjects of Scotland are specially addicted, to be blazing his genealogy in the faces of those to whom he sells a bawbee's worth of ribbon, as it would be to him to have a beaver on his head, and a rapier by his side, when the pack was on his shoulders. Na, na—he hings his sword on the cleek, lays his beaver on the shelf, puts his pedigree into his pocket, and gangs as doucely and cannily about his pedling craft as if his blood was nae better than ditch-water; but let our pedlar be transformed, as I have kend it happen mair than aince, into a bein thriving merchant, then ye shall have a transformation, my lads.

In nova fert animus mutatus dicere formas.

Out he pulls his pedigree, on he buckles his sword, gives his beaver a brush, and cooks it in the face of all creation."

to restrain the peculiarly furious temper of the Scottish nation. It was not, therefore, laws which were awanting to restrain violence, but the regular and due execution of such as existed. An ancient Scottish statesman and judge, who was also a poet, has alluded to the means used to save the guilty from deserved punishment. "We are allowed some skill," he says, "in making good laws, but God knows how ill they are kept and enforced; since a man accused of a crime will frequently appear at the bar of the court to which he is summoned, with such a company of armed friends at his back, as if it were his purpose to defy and intimidate both judge and jury." The interest of great men, moreover, obtained often by bribes, interposed between a criminal and justice, and saved by court favour the life which was forfeited to the laws.

James made great reformation in these particulars, as soon as his power, increased by the union of the two kingdoms, gave him the means of doing so. The laws, as we have seen in more cases than one, were enforced with greater severity, and the assistance of powerful friends, nay, the interposition of courtiers and favourites, was less successful in interfering with the course of justice, or obtaining remissions and pardons for condemned criminals. Thus the wholesome terror of justice gradually imposed a restraint on the general violence and disorder which had followed the civil wars of Scotland. Still, however, as the barons held, by means of their hereditary jurisdictions, the exclusive right to try and to punish such crimes as were committed on their own estates; and as they often did not choose to do so, either because the action had been committed by the baron's own direction; or that the malefactor was a strong and active partisan, of whose service the lord might have need; or because the judge and criminal stood in some degree of relationship to each other; in all such cases, the culprit's escape from justice was a necessary consequence. Nevertheless, viewing Scotland generally, the progress of public justice at the commencement of the seventeenth century was much purer, and less liable to interruption than in former ages, and the disorders of the country were fewer in proportion.

The law and its terrors had its effect in preventing the frequency of crime; but it could not have been in the power of mere human laws, and the punishments which they enacted, to eradicate from the national feelings the proneness to violence, and the thirst of revenge, which had been so long a general characteristic of the Scottish people.

The heathenish and accursed custom of deadly feud, or the duty, as it was thought, of exacting blood for blood, and perpetuating a chance quarrel, by handing it down to future generations, could only give place to those pure religious doctrines which teach men to practise, not the revenge, but the forgiveness of injuries, as the only means of acquiring the favour of Heaven.

The Presbyterian preachers, in throwing away the external pomp and ceremonial of religious worship, had inculcated, in its place, the most severe observation of morality. It was objected to them, indeed, that, as in their model of Church government, the Scottish clergy claimed an undue influence over state affairs, so, in their professions of doctrine and practice, they verged towards an ascetic system, in which too much weight was laid on venial transgressions, and the opinions of other Christian churches were treated with too little liberality. But no one who considers their works, and their history, can deny to those respectable men the merit of practising, in the most rigid extent, the strict doctrines of morality which they taught. They despised wealth, shunned even harmless pleasures, and acquired the love of their flocks, by attending to their temporal as well as spiritual wants. They preached what they themselves seriously believed, and they were believed because they spoke with all the earnestness of conviction. They spared neither example nor precept to improve the more ignorant of their hearers, and often endangered their own lives in attempting to put a stop to the feuds and frays which daily occurred in their bounds. It is recorded of a worthy clergyman, whose parish was peculiarly distracted by the brawls of the quarrelsome inhabitants, that he used constantly to wear a stout steel head-piece, which bore an odd appearance contrasted with his clerical dress. The purpose was, that when he saw swords drawn in the street, which was almost daily, he might run between the combatants, and thus separate them, with less risk of being killed by a chance blow. So that his venturous and dauntless humanity was perpetually placing his life in danger.

The clergy of that day were frequently respectable from their birth and connections, often from their learning, and at all times from their character. These qualities enabled them to interfere with effect, even in the feuds of the barons and gentry; and they often brought to milder and more peaceful thoughts, men who would not have listened to any other intercessors. There is no doubt that these good men, and the Christianity which they taught, were the principal means of correcting the furious temper and revengeful habits of the Scottish nation, in whose eyes bloodshed and deadly vengeance had been till then a virtue.

Besides the precepts and examples of religion and morality, the encouragement of general information and knowledge is also an effectual mode of taming and subduing the wild habits of a military and barbarous people. For this also the Lowlands of Scotland were indebted to the Presbyterian ministers.

The Catholic clergy had been especially instrumental in the foundation of three universities in Scotland, namely, those of Glasgow, St. Andrews, and Aberdeen; but these places of education, from the very nature of their institutions were only calculated for the education of students designed for the Church, or of those youths from among the higher classes of the laity, whom their parents desired should receive such information as might qualify them for lawyers and statesmen. The more noble view of the Reformed Church was to extend the blessings of knowledge to the lower, as well as the higher classes of society.

The preachers of the Reformation had appealed to the Scriptures as the rule of their doctrine, and it was their honourable and liberal wish, that the poorest, as well as the richest man, should have an opportunity of judging, by his own perusal of the sacred volume, whether they had interpreted the text truly and faithfully. The invention of printing had made the Scriptures accessible to every one, and the clergy desired that the meanest peasant should be capable of reading them. John Knox, and other leaders had, from the very era of the Reformation, pressed the duty of reserving from the confiscated revenues of the Romish Church the means of providing for the clergy with decency, and of establishing colleges and schools for the education of youth; but their wishes were for a long time disappointed by the avarice of the nobility and gentry, who were determined to retain for their own use the spoils of the Catholic establishment, and by the stormy complexion of the times, in which little was regarded save what belonged to politics and war.

At length the legislature, chiefly by the influence of the clergy, was induced to authorise the noble enactment, which appoints a school to be kept in every parish of Scotland, at a low rate of endowment indeed, but such as enables every poor man within the parish to procure for his children the knowledge of reading and writing; and affords an opportunity for those individuals who show a decided taste for learning, to obtain such progress in classical knowledge as may fit them for college studies. There can be no doubt that the opportunity afforded of procuring instruction thus easily tended, in the course of a generation, greatly to civilise and humanise the character of the Scottish nation; and it is equally certain, that this general access to useful knowledge, has not only given rise to the success of many men of genius, who otherwise would never have aspired above the humble rank in which they were born, but has raised the common people of Scotland in general, in knowledge, sagacity, and intelligence, many degrees above those of most other countries.

The Highlands and Islands did not share the influence of religion and education, which so essentially benefited their Lowland countrymen, owing to their speaking a language different from the rest of Scotland, as well as to the difficulty, or rather at that time the impossibility, of establishing churches or schools in such a remote country, and amongst natives of such wild manners.

To the reign of James VI. it is only necessary to add, that in 1617 he revisited his ancient kingdom of Scotland, from the same instinct, as his Majesty was pleased to express it, which induces salmon, after they have visited the sea, to return to the river in which they have been bred.

He was received with every appearance of affection by his Scottish subjects; and the only occasion of suspicion, doubt, or quarrel, betwixt the King and them, arose from the partiality he evinced to the form and ritual of the Church of England. The true Presbyterians groaned heavily at seeing choristers and singing boys arrayed in white surplices, and at hearing them chant the service of the Church of England; and they were in despair when they saw his Majesty's private chapel adorned with pictures representing scriptural subjects. All this, and everything like an established and prescribed form in prayer, in garb or decoration, was, in their idea, a greater or less approximation to the practices of the Church of Rome. This was, indeed, mere prejudice, but it was a prejudice of little consequence in itself, and James ought to have rather respected than combated feelings connected with much that was both moral and religious, and honoured the right which his Scottish subjects might justly claim to worship God after their own manner, and not according to the rules and ceremonies of a foreign country. His obstinacy on this point was, however, satisfied with carrying through the Articles of Perth, already mentioned, which were finally admitted in the year after his visit to Scotland. He left to his successor the task of endeavouring to accomplish a complete conformity, in ritual and doctrine, between the churches of South and North Britain—and very dear the attempt cost him.

James died at Theobalds on the 27th March 1625, in the fifty-ninth year of his age, and the twenty-second after his accession to the throne of England. He was the least dignified and accomplished of all his family; but, at the same time, the most fortunate.[1] Robert II., the first of the Stewart family, died, it is true, in peace; but Robert III. had sunk under the family losses which he had sustained; James I. was murdered; James II. killed by the bursting of a cannon; James III. (whom James VI. chiefly resembled) was privately slain after the battle of Sauchie-Burn; James IV. fell at Flodden; James V. died of a broken heart; Henry Darnley, the father of James VI. was treacherously murdered; and his mother, Queen Mary, was tyrannically beheaded. He alone, without courage, without sound sagacity, without that feeling of dignity which should restrain a prince from foolish indulgences, became King of the great nation which had for ages threatened to subdue that of which he was born monarch; and the good fortune of

---

[1] "The character of James was rendered a subject of doubt amongst his contemporaries, and bequeathed as a problem to future historians. He was deeply learned, without possessing useful knowledge; sagacious in many individual cases, without having real wisdom; fond of his power, and desirous to maintain and augment it, yet willing to resign the direction of that, and of himself, to the most unworthy favourites; a big and bold assertor of his rights in words, yet one who tamely saw them trampled on in deeds; a lover of negotiations, in which he was always outwitted; and one who feared war, when conquest might have been easy. He was fond of his dignity, while he was perpetually degrading it by undue familiarity; capable of much public labour, yet often neglecting it for the meanest amusement; a wit, though a pedant; and a scholar, though fond of the conversation of the ignorant and the uneducated. Even his timidity of temper was not uniform; and there were moments of his life, and those critical, in which he showed the spirit of his ancestors. He was laborious in trifles, and a trifler where serious labour was required; devout in his sentiments, and yet too often profane in his language; just and beneficent by nature, he yet gave way to the iniquities and oppression of others. He was penurious respecting money which he had to give from his own hands, yet inconsiderately and unboundedly profuse of that which he did not see. In a word, those good qualities which displayed themselves in particular cases and occasions, were not of a nature sufficiently firm and comprehensive to regulate his general conduct; and, showing themselves as they occasionally did, only entitled James to the character bestowed on him by Sully—that he was the wisest fool in Christendom."—*The Fortunes of Nigel*, Chap. v.

the Stewart family, which seems to have existed in his person alone, declined and totally decayed in those of his successors.

James had lost his eldest son, Henry, a youth of extraordinary promise. His second, Charles I., succeeded him in the throne. He left also one daughter, Elizabeth, married to Frederick, the Elector Palatine of the German empire. He was an unfortunate prince, and with a view of obtaining the kingdom of Bohemia, engaged in a ruinous war with the Emperor, by which he lost his hereditary dominions. But the Elector's evil fortune was redeemed in the person of his descendants, from whom sprung the royal family which now possess the British throne, in right of the Princess Elizabeth.

XLI

Jenny Geddes and the Covenanters

1625-1643

CHARLES I., who succeeded his father James, was a prince whose personal qualities were excellent. It was said of him justly, that considered as a private gentleman, there was not a more honourable, virtuous, and religious man in his dominions. He was a kind father, an indulgent master, and even too affectionate a husband, permitting the Queen Henrietta Maria, the beautiful daughter of Henry IV. of France, to influence his government in a degree beyond her sphere. Charles possessed also the personal dignity which his father totally wanted; and there is no just occasion to question that so good a man as we have described him had the intention to rule his people justly and mercifully, in place of enforcing the ancient feudal thraldom. But, on the other hand, he entertained extravagant ideas of the regal power, feelings which, being peculiarly unsuitable to the times in which he lived, occasioned his own total ruin, and, for a time, that of his posterity.

The English people had been now, for a century and more, relieved from the severe yoke of the nobles, and had forgotten how severely it had pressed upon their forefathers. What had galled them in the late reign were the exactions of King James, who, to indulge his prodigal liberality to worthless favourites, had extorted from Parliament large supplies, and having misapplied these, had endeavoured to obtain others in an indirect and illegal manner by granting to individuals, for sums of money, exclusive rights to sell certain commodities, which the monopolist immediately raised to a high rate, and made a large fortune, while the King got little by the bribe which he had received, and the subjects suffered extremely by the price of articles, perhaps necessaries of life, being unduly advanced. Yet James, finding that a spirit of opposition had arisen within the House of Commons, and that pecuniary grants were obtained with difficulty, could not be induced to refrain from such indirect practices to obtain money from the people without the consent of their representatives in Parliament.

It was James's object also to support the royal power in the full authority, which, by gradual encroachments, it had attained during the reign of the Tudors; and he was disposed to talk high of his prerogative, for which he stated himself to be accountable to God alone; whereas it was the just principle of the House of Commons, that the power of the King, like every other power in the constitution, was limited by the laws, and was liable to be legally resisted when it trespassed beyond them. Such were the disputes which James held with his subjects. His timidity prevented him from pushing his claims to extremity, and although courtly divines and ambitious lawyers were ready to have proved, as they pretended, his absolute and indefeasible right to obedience, even in unconstitutional commands, he shrunk from the contest, and left to his son the inheritance of much discontent which his conduct had excited, but which did not immediately break out into a flame.

Charles held the same opinions of his own rights as a monarch, which had been infused into him by his father's instructions, and he was obstinate and persevering where James had been timid and flexible. Arbitrary courts of justice, particularly one termed the Star-chamber, afforded the King the means of punishing those who opposed themselves to the royal will; but the violent exertion of authority only increased the sense of the evil, and a general discontent against the King's person and prerogative began to prevail throughout England.

These menacing appearances were much increased by religious motives. The Church of England had been since the Reformation gradually dividing into two parties, one of which warmly approved of by King James, and yet more keenly patronised by Charles, was peculiarly attached to the rites and ceremonies of the Church, the strict observance of particular forms of worship, and the use of certain pontifical dresses when divine service was performed. A numerous party, called the Puritans, although they complied with the model of the Church of England, considered these peculiar rites and formalities, on which the High Churchmen, as the opposite party began to be called, laid such stress, as remains of Popery, and things therefore to be abolished.

The Archbishop of Canterbury, Dr. Laud, a man of talents and learning, was devotedly attached to the High Church interest, and, countenanced by Charles, he resolved to use all the powers, both of the civil and spiritual courts, to subdue the refractory spirit of the Puritans, and enforce their compliance with the ceremonies which he thought so essential to the well-being of the Church. If men had been left to entertain calm and quiet thoughts on these points, they would in time have discovered, that, having chosen what was esteemed the most suitable rules for the national Church, it would have been more wise and prudent to leave the consciences of the hearers to determine whether they would conform to them, or assemble for worship elsewhere. But prosecutions, fines, pillories, and imprisonments, employed to restrain religious opinions, only make them burn the more fiercely; and those who submitted to such sufferings with patience, rather than renounce the doctrines they had espoused, were counted as martyrs, and followed accordingly. These dissensions in Church and State continued to agitate England from year to year; but it was the disturbances in Scotland which brought them to a crisis.

The King had kept firmly in view his father's favourite project of bringing the Church of Scotland, in point of church government and church ceremonies, to the same model with that of England. But to settle a national church, with a gradation of dignified clergy, required large funds, which Scotland could not afford for such a purpose. In this dilemma the King and his counsellors resolved, by one sweeping act of revocation, to resume to the crown all the tithes and benefices which had been conferred upon laymen at the Reformation, and thus obtain the funds necessary to endow the projected bishoprics.

I must try to explain to you what tithes are. By the law delivered to the Jews, the tithes, that is the tenth part of the yearly produce of the land, whether in animals born on the soil, or in corn, fruit, and vegetable productions, were destined to the support of the priests, who performed the religious service in the Temple of Jerusalem. The same rule was adopted by the Christian Church, and the tithes were levied from the farmer or possessor of the land, for the maintenance of the ecclesiastical establishments. When the Reformation took place, the great nobles and gentry of Scotland got grants of these tithes from the crown, engaging to take upon themselves the support of the clergy, whom they paid at as low a rate as possible. Those nobles and gentry who held such gifts were called titulars of tithes, answering to the English phrase of impropriators. They used the privileges which they had acquired with great rigour. They would not suffer the farmer to lead a sheaf of corn from the field until the tithe had been selected and removed, and in this way exercised their right with far more severity than had been done by the Roman Catholic clergy, who usually accepted a certain reasonable sum of money, as a modification or composition for their claim, and thus left the proprietor of the crop to manage it as he would, instead of actually taking the tithes in kind. But the titulars, as they used their privilege with rigour and to the utmost, were equally tenacious in retaining it.

When assembled in Parliament, or, as it was termed, the Convention of Estates, the Scottish lords who were possessed of grants of tithes determined that, rather than yield to the revocation proposed by the Earl of Nithsdale, who was the royal commissioner, they would massacre him and his adherents in the face of the assembly. This purpose was so decidedly entertained, that Lord Belhaven, an old blind man, placed himself close to the Earl of Dumfries, a supporter of the intended revocation, and keeping hold of his neighbour with one hand, for which he apologised, as being necessary to enable him to support himself, he held in the other the hilt of a dagger concealed in his bosom, that, as soon as the general signal should be given, he might play his part in the tragedy by plunging it into Lord Dumfries's heart. Nithsdale, learning something of this desperate resolution, gave the proposed measure of revocation up for the time, and returned to court.

The King, however, was at length able, by the assistance of a convention of the clergy summoned together by the bishops and by the general clamour of the land-owners, who complained of the rigorous exactions of the titulars, to obtain a partial surrender of the tithes into the power of the crown. The power of levying them in kind was suppressed; the landholder was invested with a right to retain every season's tithe upon paying a modified sum, and to purchase the entire right from the titular (if he had the means to do so) at a rate of purchase restricted to seven years' rent.

These alterations were attended with the greatest advantages to the country in process of time, but they were very offensive to the Scottish nobility, whom they deprived of valuable rights at an inadequate price.

Charles also made an attempt to reverse some of the attainders which had taken place in his father's time, particularly that of Stewart, Earl of Bothwell. Much of this turbulent nobleman's forfeited property had fallen to the lot of the Lord of Buccleuch and Cessford, who were compelled to surrender a part of their spoils. These proceedings, as well as the revocation of the grants of tithes, highly irritated the Scottish nobility, and some wild proposals were held among them for dethroning Charles, and placing the Marquis of Hamilton on the throne.

The only remarkable consequence of this intrigue, was a trial in the long forgotten Court of Chivalry, the last, it may be supposed, that will ever take place. Donald Lord Reay affirmed, that Mr. David Ramsay had used certain treasonable expressions in his, the said Donald's hearing. Both were summoned to appear before the High Constable of England. They appeared accordingly, in great pomp, attended by their friends.

"Lord Reay," says an eye-witness, "was clothed in black velvet, embroidered with silver, carried his sword in a silver embroidered belt, and wore around his neck his badge as a Baronet of Nova Scotia. He was a tall, black, swarthy man, of a portly and stout demeanour." The defender was next ushered in, a fair man, and having a head of ruddy hair so bushy and long, that he was usually termed Ramsay Redhead. He was dressed in scarlet so richly embroidered with gold, that the cloth could scarcely be discerned, but he was totally unarmed. While they fixed their eyes on each other sternly, the charge was read, stating that Ramsay, the defendant, had urged him, Lord Reay, to engage in a conspiracy for dethroning the King, and placing the Marquis of Hamilton upon the throne. He added, that if Ramsay should deny this, he would prove him a villain and a traitor by dint of sword. Ramsay, for answer, called Reay "a liar and a barbarous villain, and protested he should die for it." They had exchanged gloves. After many delays, the court named a day of combat, assigning as the weapons to be used, a spear, a long sword, and a short sword or a dagger. The most minute circumstances were arranged, and provision was even made at what time the parties might have the assistance of armourers and tailors, with hammers, nails, files, scissors, bodkins, needles, and thread. But now, when you are perhaps expecting, with curiosity, a tale of a bloody fight, I have to acquaint you that the King forbade the combat, and the affair was put to sleep. Times were greatly changed since the days when almost every species of accusation might be tried in this manner.

Charles visited his native country of Scotland in 1633, for the purpose of being crowned. He was received by the people at first with great apparent affection; but discontent arose on its being observed, that he omitted no opportunity of pressing upon the bishops, who had hitherto only worn plain black gowns, the use of the more splendid vestments of the English Church. This alteration of habit grievously offended the Presbyterians, who saw in it a further approximation to the Romish ritual; while the nobility, remembering that they had been partly deprived of their tithes, and that their possession of the Church lands was in danger, saw with great pleasure the obnoxious prelates, for whose sake the revocation had been made, incur the odium of the people at large.

It was left for Archbishop Laud to bring all this slumbering discontent into action, by an attempt to introduce into the divine service of the Church of Scotland a Form of Common Prayer and Liturgy similar to that used in England. This, however reasonable an institution in itself, was at variance with the character of Presbyterian worship, in which the clergyman always addressed the Deity in extemporaneous prayer, and in no prescribed, or regular form of words. King James himself, when courting the favour of the Presbyterian party, had called the English service an ill-mumbled mass; forgetting that the objection to the mass applies, not to the prayers, which must be excellent, since they are chiefly extracted from Scripture, but to the worship of the Eucharist, which Protestants think idolatrous, and to the service being in a foreign language. Neither of these objections applies to the English form of prayer; but the expression of the King was not forgotten, and he was reminded of it far more frequently than was agreeable to him.

Upon the whole, this new and most obnoxious change in the form of public worship, throughout Scotland, where the nobility were known to be in a state of great discontent, was very ill-timed. Right or wrong, the people in general were prejudiced against this innovation, in a matter so serious as the form of devotion; and yet, such a change was to be attempted, without any other authority than that of the King and the bishops; while both the Parliament and a General Assembly of the Church of Scotland had a right to be consulted in a matter so important. Nor is it less extraordinary that the Government seems to have been totally unprovided with any sufficient force to overcome the opposition which was most certain to take place.

The rash and fatal experiment was made, 23d July 1637, in the High Church of St. Giles, Edinburgh, where the dean of the city prepared to read the new service before a numerous concourse of persons, none of whom seem to have been favourably disposed to its reception. As the reader of the prayers announced the Collect for the day, an old woman named Jenny Geddes, who kept a green-stall in the High Street, bawled out—"The deil colick in the wame of thee, thou false thief! dost thou say the mass at my lug?" With that she flung at the dean's head the stool upon which she had been sitting, and a wild tumult instantly commenced. The women of lower condition [instigated, it is said, by their superiors] flew at the dean, tore the surplice from his shoulders, and drove him out of the church. The Bishop of Edinburgh mounted the pulpit, but he was also assailed with missiles, and with vehement exclamations of "A Pope! a Pope! Antichrist! pull him down, stone him!" while the windows were broken with stones flung by a disorderly multitude from without. This was not all: the prelates were assaulted in the street, and misused by the mob. The life of the bishop was with difficulty saved by Lord Roxburghe, who carried him home in his carriage, surrounded by his retinue with drawn swords.

This tumult, which has now something ludicrous in its details, was the signal for a general resistance to the reception of the Service-book throughout the whole country. The Privy Council of Scotland were lukewarm, or rather cold, in the cause. They wrote to Charles a detailed account of the tumults, and did not conceal that the opposition to the measure was spreading far and wide.

Charles was inflexible in his purpose, and so greatly incensed, that he showed his displeasure even in trifles. It was the ancient custom, to have a fool, or jester, maintained at court, privileged to break his satirical jests at random. The post was then held by one Archie Armstrong, who, as he saw the Archbishop of Canterbury posting to court, in consequence of the mortifying tidings from Scotland, could not help whispering in the prelate's ear the sly question, "Who's fool now, my lord?" For this jest, poor Archie, having been first severely whipped, was disgraced and dismissed from court, where no fool has again been admitted, at least in an avowed and official capacity.

But Archie was a more accessible object of punishment than the malcontents in Scotland. It was in vain that Charles sent down repeated and severe messages, blaming the Privy Council, the Magistrates, and all who did not punish the rioters, and enforce the reading of the Service-book. The resistance to the measure, which was at first tumultuous, and the work of the lower orders, had now assumed quality and consistency. More than thirty peers, and a very great proportion of the gentry of Scotland, together with the greater part of the royal burghs, had, before the month of December, agreed not merely to oppose the Service-book, but to act together in resisting the further intrusions of Prelacy. They were kept in union and directed by representatives appointed from among themselves, and forming separate Committees, or, as they were termed, Tables or Boards of management.

Under the auspices of these Tables, or Committees, a species of engagement, or declaration, was drawn up, the principal object of which was, the eradication of Prelacy in all its modifications, and the establishment of Presbytery on its purest and most simple basis. This engagement was called the National Covenant, as resembling those covenants which, in the Old Testament, God is said to have made with the people of Israel. The terms of this memorable league professed the Reformed faith, and abjured the rites and doctrines of the Romish Church, with which were classed the newly imposed Liturgy and Canons. This covenant, which had for its object to annul all of prelatic innovation that James's policy, and his son's violence, had been able to introduce into the Presbyterian Church, was sworn to by hundreds, thousands, and hundreds of thousands, of every age and description, vowing, with uplifted hands and weeping eyes, that with the Divine assistance, they would dedicate life and fortune to maintain the object of their solemn engagement.

Undoubtedly, many persons who thus subscribed the National Covenant, did not seriously feel any apprehension that Prelacy would introduce Popery, or that the Book of Common Prayer was in itself a grievance which the people of Scotland did well or wisely to oppose; but they were convinced, that in thus forcing a matter of conscience upon a whole nation, the King disregarded the rights and liberties of his subjects, and foresaw, that if not now withstood, he was most likely to make himself absolute master of their rights and privileges in secular as well as religious affairs. They therefore joined in such measures as procured a general resistance to the arbitrary power so rashly assumed by King Charles.

Meantime, while the King negotiated and procrastinated, Scotland, though still declaring attachment to his person, was nearly in a state of general resistance.

The Covenanters, as they began to be called, held a General Assembly of the Church, at which the Marquis of Hamilton attended as Lord Commissioner for the King. This important meeting was held at Glasgow. There all the measures pointed at by the Covenant were carried fully into effect. Episcopacy was abolished, the existing bishops were deprived of their power, and eight of them excommunicated for divers alleged irregularities.

The Covenanters took arms to support these bold measures. They recalled to Scotland the numerous officers who had been trained in the wars of Germany, and committed the command of the whole to Alexander Lesley, a veteran general of skill and experience, who had possessed the friendship of Gustavus Adolphus. They soon made great progress; for the castles of Edinburgh, Dalkeith, and other national fortresses were treacherously surrendered to, or daringly surprised, by the Covenanters.

King Charles, meantime, was preparing for the invasion of Scotland with a powerful army by land and sea. The fleet was commanded by the Marquis of Hamilton, who, unwilling to commence a civil war, or, as some supposed, not being on this occasion peculiarly zealous in the King's service, made no attempt to prosecute the enterprise. The fleet lay idle in the Firth of Forth, while Charles in person, at the head of an army of twenty-three thousand men, gallantly equipped by the English nobility, seemed as much determined upon the subjugation of his ancient kingdom of Scotland, as ever any of the Edwards or Henrys of England had been. But the Scottish Covenanters showed the same determined spirit of resistance, which, displayed by their ancestors, had frustrated so many invasions, and it was now mingled with much political discretion.

A great degree of military discipline had been introduced into the Scottish levies, considering how short time they had been on foot.

They lay encamped on Dunse Law, a gently sloping hill, very favourable for a military display.[1] Their camp was defended by forty field-pieces, and their army consisted of twenty-four or twenty-five thousand men. The highest Scottish nobles, as Argyle, Rothes, Cassilis, Eglinton, Dalhousie, Lindsay, Loudon, Balcarres, and others, acted as colonels; their captains were gentlemen of high rank and fortune; and the inferior commissions were chiefly bestowed on veteran officers who had served abroad. The utmost order was observed in their camp, whilst the presence of numerous clergymen kept up the general enthusiasm, and seemed to give a religious character to the war.

In this crisis, when a decisive battle was to have been expected, only one very slight action took place, when a few English cavalry, retreating hastily and in disorder, from a still smaller number of Scots, seemed to show that the invaders had not their hearts engaged in the combat. The King was surrounded by many counsellors, who had no interest to encourage the war; and the whole body of English Puritans considered the resistance of Scotland as the triumph of the good cause over Popery and Prelacy. Charles's own courage seems to have failed him, at the idea of encountering a force so well provided, and so enthusiastic, as that of the Covenanters, with a dispirited army acting under divided counsels. A treaty was entered into, though of an insecure character. The King granted a declaration, in which, without confirming the acts of the Assembly of Glasgow, which he would not acknowledge as a lawful one, he agreed that all matters concerning the regulation of church government should be left to a new Convocation of the Church.

Such an agreement could not be lasting. The Covenanting Lords did, indeed, disband their forces, and restore to the King's troops the strong places which they had occupied; but they held themselves ready to take arms, and seize upon them again, on the slightest notice; neither was the King able to introduce any considerable degree of disunion into so formidable a league.

The General Assembly of the Church, convened according to the treaty, failed not to confirm all that had been done by their predecessors at Glasgow; the National Covenant was renewed, and the whole conclusions of the body were in favour of pure and unmingled

---

[1] Dunse Law is a beautiful little hill, close by the town of the same name. It rises in a gradual ascent till it terminates in a plain of nearly thirty acres, and still bears on its broomy top marks of the encampment of the Covenanters.

Presbytery. The Scottish Parliament, on their part, demanded several privileges, necessary, it was said, to freedom of debate, and required that the Estates of the kingdom should be convened at least once every three years. On receiving these demands, Charles thought he beheld a formed scheme for undermining his royal authority, and prepared to renew the war.

His determination involved, however, consequences more important than even the war with Scotland. His private economy had enabled the King to support, from the crown lands and other funds, independent of Parliamentary grants, the ordinary expenses of the state, and he had been able even to sustain the charges of the first army raised to invade Scotland, without having recourse to the House of Commons. But his treasures were now exhausted, and it became indispensable to convoke a Parliament, and obtain from the Commons a grant of money to support the war. The Parliament met, but were too much occupied by their own grievances, to take an immediate interest in the Scottish war, which they only viewed as affording a favourable opportunity for enforcing their own objects. They refused the supplies demanded. The King was obliged to dissolve them, and have recourse to the aid of Ireland, to the Convocation of the Church, to compulsory loans, and other indirect methods of raising money, so that his resources were exhausted by the effort.

On hearing that the King was again collecting his army, and had placed himself at its head, the Parliament of Scotland resolved on reassembling theirs. It was done with such facility, and so speedily, that it was plain they had been, during the short suspension of arms, occupied in preparing for a new rupture. They did not now wait till the King should invade Scotland, but boldly crossed the Tweed, entered England, and advancing to the banks of the Tyne, found Lord Conway posted at Newburn, with six thousand men, having batteries of cannon in his front, and prepared to dispute the passage of the river. On 28th August 1640 the battle of Newburn was fought. The Scots, after silencing the artillery by their superior fire, entered the ford, girdle deep, and made their way across the river. The English fled with a speed and disorder unworthy of their national reputation.

The King, surprised at this defeat, and justly distrusting the faith of many who were in his army and near his person, directed his forces to retreat into Yorkshire, where he had arrived in person; and again, with more serious intentions of abiding by it, commenced a negotiation with his insurgent subjects. At the same time, to appease the growing discontent of the English nation, he resolved again to call a Parliament. There were, no doubt, in the royal camp, many persons to whom the presence of a Scottish army was acceptable, as serving to overawe the more violent royalists; and the Scots were easily induced to protract their stay, when it was proposed to them to receive pay and provisions at the expense of England.

The meeting of that celebrated body called, in English history, the Long Parliament, took place on 3d November 1640. The majority of the members were disaffected with the King's government, on account of his severity in matters of religion, and his tendency to despotism in state affairs. These malcontents formed a strong party, determined to diminish the royal authority, and reduce, if not altogether to destroy, the hierarchy of the Church. The negotiations for peace being transferred from Ripon to London, the presence of the Scottish commissioners was highly acceptable to those statesmen who opposed the King; and the preaching of the clergymen by whom they were accompanied appeared equally instructive to the citizens of London and their wives.

In this favourable situation, and completely successful over the royal will (for Charles I. could not propose to contend at once with the English Parliament and with the Scottish army), the peremptory demands of the Scots were neither light, nor easily gratified. They required that the King should confirm every act of the Scottish Convention of Estates with which he had been at war, recall all the proclamations which he had sent out against them, place the fortresses of Scotland in the hands of such officers as the Convention should approve of, pay all the expenses of the war, and, last and bitterest, they stipulated, that those of the King's counsellors who had advised the late hostilities, should be punished as incendiaries. While the Scots were discussing these severe conditions, they remained in their quarters in England much at their ease, overawing by their presence the King, and those who might be disposed to join him, and affording to the opposition party in the English Parliament an opportunity of obtaining redress for the grievances of which they, in their turn, complained.

The King thus circumstanced was compelled to give way. The oppressive courts in which arbitrary proceedings had taken place were abolished; every species of contrivance by which Charles had endeavoured to levy money without consent of Parliament, a subject on which the people of England were justly jealous, was declared unlawful; and it was provided, that Parliaments should be summoned every three years.

Thus the power of the King was reduced within the boundaries of the constitution: but the Parliament were not satisfied with this general redress of grievances, though including all that had hitherto been openly complained of. A strong party among the members was determined to be satisfied with nothing short of the abolition of Episcopacy in England as well as in Scotland; and many who did not aim at that favourite point, entertained fears, that if the King were left in possession of such powers as the constitution allowed him, he would find means of re-establishing and perpetuating the grievances which, for the time, he had consented to abolish.

Gratified with a donation of three hundred thousand pounds, given under the delicate name of brotherly assistance, the Scottish army at length retired homeward, and left the King and Parliament of England to settle their own affairs. The troops had scarcely returned to Scotland and disbanded, when Charles proposed to himself a visit to his native kingdom. He arrived in Scotland on the 12th of August 1641. There can be little doubt that the purpose of this royal progress was to inquire closely into the causes which had enabled the Scottish nation, usually divided into factions and quarrels, to act with such unanimity, and to try whether it might not be possible for the King to attach to his royal interest and person some of the principal leaders, and thus form a party who might not only prevent his English dominions from being again invaded by an army from Scotland, but might be disposed to serve him, in case he should come to an open rupture with his English Parliament. For this purpose he dispensed dignities and gifts in Scotland with an unsparing hand; made General Lesley Earl of Leven, raised the Lords Loudon and Lindsay to the same rank, and received into his administration several nobles who had been active in the late invasion of England. On most of these persons the King's benefits produced little effect. They considered him only as giving what, if he had dared, he would have withheld. But Charles made a convert to his interest of one nobleman, whose character and actions have rendered him a memorable person in Scottish history.

This was James Graham, Earl of Montrose; a man of high genius, glowing with the ambition which prompts great actions, and conscious of courage and talents which enabled him to aspire to much by small and inadequate means. He was a poet and a scholar, deeply skilled in the art of war, and possessed of a strength of constitution and activity of mind by which he could sustain every hardship, and find a remedy in every reverse of fortune. It was remarked of him by Cardinal du Retz, an unquestionable judge, that he resembled more nearly than any man of his age those great heroes, whose names and history are handed down to us by the Greek and Roman historians. As a qualification to this high praise, it must be added, that Montrose's courage sometimes approached to rashness, and that some of his actions arose more from the dictates of private revenge than became his nobler qualities.

The young Earl had attended the court of Charles when he came home from his travels, but not meeting with the attention which he was conscious of deserving, he withdrew into Scotland, and took a zealous share in forming and forwarding the National Covenant. A man of such talent could not fail to be employed and distinguished. Montrose was sent by the confederated lords of the Covenant to chastise the prelatic town of Aberdeen, and to disperse the Gordons, who were taking arms for the King under the Marquis of Huntly, and succeeded in both commissions. When the army of the Scottish Parliament entered England, he was the first man who forded the Tweed. He passed alone under the fire of the English, to ascertain the depth of the water, and returned to lead over the regiment which he commanded. Notwithstanding these services to the cause of the Covenant, Montrose had the mortification to see that the Earl of Argyle (the ancient feudal enemy of his house) was preferred to him by the heads of the party, and chiefly by the clergy. There was something in the fiery ambition, and unyielding purpose of Montrose, which startled inferior minds; while Argyle, dark, close, and crafty—a man well qualified to affect a complete devotion to the ends of others, when he was, in fact, bent on forwarding his own,—stooped lower to court popularity, and was more successful in gaining it.

The King had long observed that Montrose was dissatisfied with the party to which he had hitherto adhered, and found no difficulty in engaging his services for the future in the royal cause. The noble convert set so actively about inducing others to follow his example, that even during the course of the treaty of Ripon, he had procured the subscription of nineteen noblemen to a bond, engaging themselves to unite in support of Charles. This act of defection being discovered by the Covenanters, Montrose was imprisoned; and the King, on coming to Scotland, had the mortification to find himself deprived of the assistance of this invaluable adherent.

Montrose contrived, however, to communicate with the King from his prison in the castle of Edinburgh, and disclosed so many circumstances respecting the purposes of the Marquis of Hamilton and the Earl of Argyle, that Charles had resolved to arrest them both at one moment, and had assembled soldiers for that purpose. They escaped, however, and retired to their houses, where they could not have been seized but by open violence, and at the risk of a civil war. These noblemen were recalled to court; and to show that the King's confidence in them was unchanged, Argyle was raised to the rank of Marquis. This obscure affair was called the *Incident*; it was never well explained, but at the time excited much suspicion of the King's purposes both in England and in Scotland, and aggravated the disinclination of the English Parliament to leave his royal power on the present unreduced footing.

There can be little doubt that Montrose's disclosures to the King concerned the private correspondence which passed between the Scottish Covenanters and the Opposition party in the Parliament of England, and which Charles might hope to convert into an accusation of high treason against both. But as he did not feel that he possessed a party in Scotland strong enough to contend with the great majority of the nobles of that country, he judged it best to pass over all further notice of the *Incident* for the time, and to leave Scotland under the outward appearance at least of mutual concord. He was formally congratulated on departing a contented King from a contented people—a state of things which did not last long.

It was, indeed, impossible that Scotland should remain long tranquil, while England, with whom she was now so closely connected, was in such dreadful disorder. The King had no sooner returned from Scotland, than the quarrel betwixt him and his Parliament was renewed with more violence than ever. If either party could have reposed confidence in the other's sincerity, the concessions made by the King were such as ought to have gratified the Parliament. But the strongest suspicions were entertained by the prevailing party, that the King considered the grants which he had made, as having been extorted from him by violence, and that he retained the steady purpose of reassuming, in its full extent, the obnoxious and arbitrary power of which he had been deprived for a season, but which he still considered as part of his royal right. They therefore resolved not to quit the ascendency which they had attained until they had deprived the King, for a season at least, of a large portion of his remaining prerogative, although bestowed on him by the constitution, that they might thus prevent his employing it for the recovery of those arbitrary privileges which had been usurped by the throne during the reign of the Tudors.

While the Parliamentary leaders argued thus, the King, on his side, complained that no concession, however large, was found adequate to satisfy the demands of his discontented subjects. "He had already," he urged, "resigned all the points which had been disputed between them, yet they continued as ill satisfied as before." On these grounds the partisans of the crown were alarmed with the idea that it was the purpose of Parliament altogether to abrogate the royal authority, or at least to depose the reigning King.

On the return of Charles to London, the Parliament greeted him with a remonstrance, in which he was upbraided with all the real and supposed errors of his reign. At the same time, a general disposition to tumult showed itself throughout the city. Great mobs of apprentices and citizens, not always of the lowest rank, came in tumult to Westminster, under the pretence of petitioning the Houses of Parliament; and as they passed Whitehall, they insulted, with loud shouts, the guards and servants of the King. The parties soon came to blows, and blood was spilt between them.

Party names, too, were assumed to distinguish the friends of the King from those who favoured the Parliament. The former were chiefly gay young men, who, according to the fashion of the times, wore showy dresses, and cultivated the growth of long hair, which, arranged in ringlets, fell over their shoulders. They were called Cavaliers. In distinction, those who adhered to the Parliament assumed, in their garb and deportment, a seriousness and gravity which rejected all ornament. They wore their hair, in particular, cropped short around the head, and thence gained the name of Roundheads.

But it was the difference in their ideas of religion, or rather of church government, which chiefly widened the division betwixt the two parties. The King had been bred up to consider the preservation of the Church of England and her hierarchy, as a sacred point of his royal duty, since he was recognised by the Constitution as its earthly head and superintendent. The Presbyterian system, on the contrary, was espoused by a large proportion of the Parliament; and they were, for the time, seconded by the other numerous classes of Dissenters, all of whom desired to see the destruction of the Church of England, however unwilling they might be, in their secret mind, that a Presbyterian church government should be set up in its stead. The enemies of the English hierarchy greatly predominating within the Houses of Parliament, the lords spiritual, or bishops, were finally expelled from their seats in the House of Lords, and their removal was celebrated as a triumph by the London citizens.

While matters were in this state, the King committed a great imprudence. Having conceived that he had acquired from Montrose's discovery, or otherwise, certain information that five of the leading members of the House of Commons had been guilty of holding such intimate communication with the Scots when in arms, as might authorise a charge of high treason against them, he formed the highly rash and culpable intention of going to the House of Commons in person, with an armed train of attendants, and causing the accused members to be arrested. By this ill-advised measure, Charles doubtless expected to strike terror into the opposite party; but it proved altogether ineffectual. The five members had received private information of the blow to be aimed at them, and had fled into the City, where they found numbers willing to conceal, or defend them. The King, by his visit to the House of Commons, only showed that he could stoop to act almost in the capacity of a common constable, or catchpole; and that he disregarded the respect due to the representatives of the British people, in meditating such an arrest of their members in the presence of that body.

After this very rash step on the part of the King, every chance of reconciliation seemed at an end. The Commons rejected all amicable proposals, unless the King would surrender to them, for a time at least, the command of the militia or armed force of the kingdom; and that would have been equivalent to laying his crown at their feet. The King refused to surrender the command of the militia even for an instant; and both parties prepared to take up arms. Charles left London, where the power of the Parliament was predominant, assembled what friends he could gather at Nottingham, and hoisted the royal standard there, as the signal of civil war, on 25th August 1642.

The hostilities which ensued, over almost all England, were of a singular character. Long accustomed to peace, the English had but little knowledge of the art of war. The friends of the contending parties assembled their followers, and marched against each other, without much idea of taking strong positions, or availing themselves of able manoeuvres, but with the simple and downright purpose of meeting, fighting with, and defeating those who were in arms on the other side. These battles were contested with great manhood and gallantry, but with little military skill or discipline. It was no uncommon thing for one wing or division of the contending armies, when they found themselves victorious over the body opposed to them, to amuse themselves with chasing the vanquished party for leagues off the field of battle, where the victory was in the meanwhile lost for want of their support. This repeatedly happened through the precipitation of the King's cavalry; a fine body of men, consisting of the flower of the English nobility and gentry; but as ungovernable as they were valorous, and usually commanded by Prince Rupert, the King's nephew, a young man of fiery courage, not gifted with prudence corresponding to his bravery and activity.

In these unhappy civil contentions, the ancient nobility and gentry of England were chiefly disposed to the service of the King; and the farmers and cultivators of the soil followed them as their natural leaders. The cause of the Parliament was supported by London, with all its wealth and its numbers, and by the other large towns, seaports, and manufacturing districts, throughout the country. At the commencement of the war, the Parliament, being in possession of most of the fortified places in England, with the magazines of arms and ammunition which they contained, having also numbers of men prepared to obey their summons, and with power to raise large sums of money to pay them, seemed to possess great advantages over the party of Charles. But the gallantry of the King's followers was able to restore the balance, and proposals were made for peace on equal terms, which, had all parties been as sincere in seeking it, as the good and wise of each side certainly were, might then have been satisfactorily concluded.

A treaty was set on foot at Oxford in the winter and spring of 1643, and the Scottish Parliament sent to England a committee of the persons employed as conservators of the peace between the kingdoms, to negotiate, if possible, a pacification between the King and his Parliament, honourable for the crown, satisfactory for the liberty of the subject, and secure for both. But the King listened to the warmer and more passionate counsellors, who pointed out to him that the Scots would, to a certainty, do their utmost to root out Prelacy in any system of accommodation which they might assist in framing; and that having,

in fact, been the first who had set the example of a successful resistance
to the crown, they could not now be expected to act as friends to the
King in any negotiation in which his prerogative was concerned. The
result was, that the Scottish Commissioners, finding themselves treated
with coldness by the King, and with menace and scorn by the more
vehement of his followers, left Oxford still more displeased with the
Royal cause than they were when they had come thither.

XLII

Civil War

1643-1644

IN 1643, when the advance of spring permitted the resumption of hostilities, it was found that the state of the King's party was decidedly superior to that of the Parliament, and it was generally believed that the event of the war would be decided in the Royal favour, could the co-operation of the Scots be obtained. The King privately made great offers to the Scottish nation, to induce them to declare in his favour, or at least remain neuter in the struggle. He called upon them to remember that he had gratified all their wishes, without exception, and reminded them that the late peace between England and Scotland provided, that neither country should declare war against the other without due provocation, and the consent of Parliament. But the members of the Scottish Convention of Estates were sensible, that if they should assist the King to conquer the English Parliament, for imitating their own example of insurrection, it would be naturally followed by their undergoing punishment themselves for the lesson which they had taught the English. They feared for the Presbyterian system,—some of them, no doubt, feared for themselves,—and all turned a deaf ear to the King's proposals.

On the other hand a deputation from Parliament pressed upon the Scottish Convention another clause in the treaty of peace made in

1641, namely, that the Parliament of either country should send aid to each other to repel invasion or suppress internal disturbances. In compliance with this article, the English Commissioners desired the assistance of a body of Scottish auxiliaries. The country being at this time filled with disbanded officers and soldiers who were eager for employment, the opportunity and the invitation were extremely tempting to them, for they remembered the free quarters and good pay which they had enjoyed while in England. Nevertheless, the leading members of the Convention of Estates were aware, that to embrace the party of the Parliament of England, and despatch to their assistance a large body of auxiliary forces, selected, as they must be, from their best levies, would necessarily expose their authority in Scotland to considerable danger; for the King's friends who had joined in the bond with Montrose were men of power and influence, and, having the will, only waited for the opportunity, to act in his behalf; and might raise, perhaps, a formidable insurrection in Scotland itself, when relieved from the superiority of force which at present was so great on the side of the Convention. But the English Commissioners held out a bait which the Convention found it impossible to resist.

From the success which the ruling party had experienced in establishing the Church of Scotland on a Presbyterian model, and from the great influence which the clergy had acquired in the councils of the nation by the late course of events, both the clergy and laity of that persuasion had been induced to cherish the ambitious desire of totally destroying the hierarchy of the Church of England, and of introducing into that kingdom a form of church government on the Presbyterian model. To accomplish this favourite object, the leading Presbyterians in Scotland were willing to run every risk, and to make every exertion.

The Commissioners of England were most ready to join with this idea, so far as concerned the destruction of Prelacy; but they knew that the English Parliament party were greatly divided among themselves on the propriety of substituting the Presbyterian system in its place. The whole body of Sectarians, or Independents, were totally opposed to the introduction of any national church government whatever, and were averse to that of Presbytery in particular, the Scottish clergy having, in their opinion, shown themselves disposed to be as absolute and intolerant in their church judicatories as the bishops had been while in power. But, with a crafty policy, the Commissioners conducted the negotiation in such a manner as to give the Scottish Convention reason to believe, that they would accomplish their favourite desire of seeing the system which they so much admired, acknowledged, and adopted in England, while, in fact, they bound their constituents, the English Parliament, to nothing specific on the subject.

The Commissioners proposed to join with the Scottish nation in a new edition of the Covenant, which had before proved such a happy bond of union among the Scots themselves. In this new bond of religious association, which was called the Solemn League and Covenant, it was provided, that the church government of Scotland should be supported and maintained on its present footing; but with regard to England, the agreement was expressed with studied ambiguity—the religious system of England, it was provided, should be reformed "according to the word of God, and the example of the best reformed churches." The Scots, usually more cautious in their transactions, never allowed themselves to doubt for a moment, that the rule and example to be adopted under this clause must necessarily be that of Presbytery, and under this conviction both the nobles and the clergy hastened with raptures, and even with tears of joy, to subscribe the proposed League. But several of the English Commissioners enjoyed in secret the reserved power of interpreting the clause otherwise, and of explaining the phrase in a sense applicable to their own ideas of emancipation from church government of every kind.

The Solemn League and Covenant was sworn to in Scotland with general acclamation, and was received and adopted by the English Parliament with the same applause, all discussion of the dubious article being cautiously avoided. The Scots proceeded, with eager haste, to send to the assistance of the Parliament of England a well-disciplined army of upwards of twenty thousand men, under the command of Alexander Lesley, Earl of Leven. An officer of character, named Baillie, was Leven's lieutenant, and David Lesley, a man of greater military talents than either, was his major-general. Their presence contributed greatly to a decisive victory which the Parliament forces gained at Marston Moor; and, indeed, as was to be expected from their numbers and discipline, quickly served to give that party the preponderance in the field.

But while the Scottish auxiliaries were actively serving the common cause of the Parliament in England, the courageous and romantic enterprise of the Earl of Montrose, advanced by the King to the dignity of Marquis, broke out in a train of success, which threatened to throw Scotland itself into the hands of the King and his friends. This nobleman's bold genius, when the royalist party in Scotland seemed totally crushed and dispersed, devised the means of assembling them together, and of menacing the Convention of Estates with the destruction of their power at home, even at the moment when they hoped to establish the Presbyterian Church in both kingdoms, by the success of the army which they had despatched into England.

After obtaining his liberation from imprisonment, Montrose had repaired to England, and suggested to the King a plan of operations to be executed by a body of Irish, to be despatched by the Earl of Antrim from the county of Ulster, and landed in the West Highlands. With these he proposed to unite a force collected from the Highland clans, who were disinclined to the Presbyterian government, great enemies to the Marquis of Argyle, and attached to the Royal cause, because they regarded the King as a chieftain whose clan was in rebellion against him, and who, therefore, deserved the support of every faithful mountaineer. The promise of pay, to which they had never been accustomed, and the certainty of booty, would, as Montrose judiciously calculated, readily bring many chieftains and clans to the Royal Standard. The powerful family of the Gordons, in Aberdeenshire, who, besides enjoying almost princely authority over the numerous gentlemen of their family, had extensive influence among the mountain tribes in their neighbourhood, or, in the Scottish phrase, "could command a great Highland following," might also be reckoned upon with certainty; as they had been repeatedly in arms for the King, had not been put down without a stout resistance, and were still warmly disposed towards the Royal cause. The support of many of the nobility and gentry in the north, might also be regarded as probable, should Montrose be able to collect a considerable force. The Episcopal establishment, so odious to the lords and barons of the southern and western parts of Scotland, was popular in the north. The northern barons were displeased with the extreme strictness of the Presbyterian clergy, and dissatisfied with the power they had often assumed of interfering with the domestic arrangements of families, under pretext of maintaining moral discipline. Finally, there were in all parts of Scotland active and daring men disappointed of obtaining employment or preferment under the existing government, and therefore willing to join in any enterprise, however desperate, which promised a change.

All this was known to the Convention of Estates; but they had not fully estimated the magnitude of the danger. Montrose's personal talents were, to a certain extent, admitted, but ordinary men were incapable of estimating such a character as his; and he was generally esteemed a vain, though able young man, whose remarkable ambition was capable of urging him into rash and impracticable undertakings. The great power of the Marquis of Argyle was relied upon as a sufficient safeguard against any attempt on the West Highlands, and his numerous, brave, and powerful clan had long kept all the other tribes of that country in a species of awe, if not of subjection.

But the character of the Highlanders was estimated according to a sort of calculation, which time had rendered very erroneous. In the former days of Scotland, when the Lowlands were inhabited by men as brave, and much better armed and disciplined than the mountaineers, the latter had indeed often shown themselves alert as light troops, unwearied in predatory excursions; but had been generally, from their tumultuary charge, liable to defeat, either from a steady body of spearmen, who received their onset with lowered lances, or from an attack of the feudal chivalry of the Lowlands, completely armed and well mounted. At Harlaw, Corrichie, Glenlivat, and on many other occasions, the irregular forces of the Highlands had been defeated by an inferior number of their Lowland opponents.

These recollections might lead the governors of Scotland, during the civil war, to hold a Highland army in low estimation. But, if such was their opinion, it was adopted without considering that half a century of uninterrupted peace had rendered the Lowlander much less warlike, while the Highlander, who always went armed, was familiar with the use of the weapons which he constantly wore, and had a greater love for fighting than the Lowland peasant, who, called from the peaceful occupations of the farm, and only prepared by a few days' drill, was less able to encounter the unwonted dangers of a field of battle. The burghers, who made a formidable part of the array of the Scottish army in former times, were now still more unwarlike than the peasant, being not only without skill in arms, and little accustomed to danger, but deficient also in the personal habits of exercise which the rustic had preserved. This great and essential difference between the Highlander and Lowlander of modern days could scarcely be estimated in the middle of the seventeenth century, the causes by which it was brought about being gradual, and attracting little attention.

Montrose's first plan was to collect a body of royalist horse on the frontiers of England, to burst at once into the centre of Scotland at their head, and force his way to Stirling, where a body of cavaliers had promised to assemble and unite with him. The expedition was disconcerted by a sort of mutiny among the English horse who had joined him; in consequence of which, Montrose disbanded his handful of followers, and exhorted them to make their way to the King, or to the nearest body of men in arms for the royal cause, while he himself adopted a new and more desperate plan. He took with him only two friends, and disguised himself as the groom of one of them, whom he followed, ill mounted and worse dressed, and leading a spare horse. They called themselves gentlemen belonging to Leven's army; for, of course, if Montrose had been discovered by the Covenanting party, a rigorous captivity was the least he might expect. At one time he seemed on the point of being detected. A straggling soldier passed his two companions, and coming up to Montrose, saluted him respectfully by his name and title. Montrose tried to persuade him that he was mistaken; but the man persisted, though with the utmost respect and humility of deportment. "Do I not know my noble Lord of Montrose?" he said; "But go your way and God be with you." The circumstance alarmed Montrose and his companions; but the poor fellow was faithful, and never betrayed his old leader.

In this disguise he reached the verge of the Highlands, and lay concealed in the house of his relation, Graham of Inchbraco, and afterwards, for still greater safety, in an obscure hut on the Highland frontier, while he despatched spies in every direction, to bring him intelligence of the state of the Royalist party. Bad news came from all quarters. The Marquis of Huntly had taken arms hastily and imprudently, and had been defeated and compelled to fly; while Gordon of Haddow, the most active and gallant gentleman of the name, was made prisoner, and, to strike terror into the rest of the clan, was publicly executed by order of the Scottish Parliament.

Montrose's spirit was not to be broken even by this disappointment; and, while anxiously awaiting further intelligence, an indistinct rumour reached him that a body of soldiers from Ireland had landed in the West Highlands, and were wandering in the mountains, followed and watched by Argyle with a strong party of his clan. Shortly after, he learned, by a messenger despatched on purpose, that this was the promised body of auxiliaries sent to him from Ulster by the Earl of

Antrim. Their commander was Alaster MacDonald, a Scoto-Irishman, I believe, of the Antrim family. He was called Coll Kittoch, or Colkitto, from his being left-handed; a very brave and daring man, but vain and opinionative, and wholly ignorant of regular warfare. Montrose sent orders to him to march with all speed into the district of Athole, and despatched emissaries to raise the gentlemen of that country in arms, as they were generally well affected to the King's cause. He himself set out to join this little band, attired in an ordinary Highland garb, and accompanied only by Inchbraco as his guide. The Irish were surprised and disappointed to see their expected general appear so poorly dressed and attended; nor had Montrose greater reason to congratulate himself on the appearance of his army. The force which was assembled did not exceed fifteen hundred Irish, instead of the thousands promised, and these were but indifferently armed and appointed, while only a few Highlanders from Badenoch were yet come to the appointed rendezvous.

These active mountain warriors, however, few as they were, had, a day or two before, come to blows with the Covenanters. MacPherson of Cluny, chief of his name, had sent out a party of men, under MacPherson of Invereshie, to look out for Montrose, who was anxiously expected in the Highlands. They beheld the approach of a detached body of horse, which they concluded was the escort of their expected general. But when they drew nearer, the MacPhersons found it to be several troops of the cavalry of the Covenanters, commanded by Colonel Herries, and quartered in Glencairn, for the purpose of keeping the Highlanders in check. While the horsemen were advancing in formidable superiority of numbers, Invereshie, who was drawing up his Highlanders for action, observed one of them in the act of stooping; and as he lifted his stick to strike him for such conduct in the face of the enemy, the Highlander arose, and proved to be MacPherson of Dalifour, one of the boldest men of the clan. Much surprised, Invereshie demanded how he, of all men, could think of stooping before an enemy. "I was only fastening a spur on the heel of my brogue," said Dalifour, with perfect composure. "A spur! and for what purpose, at such a time and place as this?" asked Invereshie. "I intend to have a good horse before the day is over," answered the clansman with the same coolness. Dalifour kept his word; for the Lowland horse, disconcerted by a smart fire, and the broken nature of the ground, being worsted in the first onset, he got possession of a charger, on which he followed the pursuit, and brought in two prisoners.

The report of this skirmish gave a good specimen to Montrose of the mettle of the mountaineers, while the subsequent appearance of the Atholemen, eight hundred strong, and the enthusiastic shouts with which they received their general, soon gave confidence to the light-hearted Irishmen. Montrose instantly commenced his march upon Strathern, and crossed the Tay. He had scarce done so, when he discovered on the hill of Buchanty a body of about four hundred men, who, he had the satisfaction to learn by his scouts, were commanded by two of his own particular friends, Lord Kilpont and Sir John Drummond. They had taken arms, on hearing that a body of Irish were traversing the country; and learning that they were there under Montrose's command, for the King's service, they immediately placed themselves and their followers under his orders.

Montrose received these succours in good time, for while Argyle pursued him with a large body of his adherents, who had followed the track of the Irish, Lord Elcho, the Earl of Tullibardine, and Lord Drummond, had collected an army of Lowlanders to protect the city of Perth, and to fight Montrose, in case he should descend from the hills. Montrose was aware that such an enterprise as he had undertaken could only be supported by an excess of activity and decision. He therefore advanced upon the forces of Elcho, whom he found, on the 1st September 1644, drawn up in good order in a large plain called Tippermuir, within three miles of Perth. They were nearly double Montrose's army in number, and much encouraged by numerous ministers, who exhorted them to fight valiantly, and promised them certain victory. They had cannon also, and cavalry, whereas Montrose had no artillery, and only three horses, in his army. After a skirmish with the cavalry of his opponents, who were beaten off, Montrose charged with the Highlanders, under a heavy fire from his Irish musketeers. They burst into the ranks of the enemy with irresistible fury, and compelled them to fly. Once broken, the superiority of numbers became useless, as the means of supporting a main body by reserves was not then known or practised. The Covenanters fled in the utmost terror and confusion, but the light-footed Highlanders did great execution in the pursuit. Many honest burghers, distressed by the extraordinary speed which they were compelled to exert, broke their wind, and died in consequence. Montrose sustained little or no loss.

The town of Perth surrendered, and for this act a long string of reasons were given, which are rather amusingly stated in a letter from the ministers of that town; but we have only space to mention a few of them. First, it is alleged, that out of Elcho's defeated army only about twelve of the Fifeshire men offered themselves to the magistrates in defence of the town, unarmed, and most of them were pot-valiant from liquor. Secondly, it is affirmed, that the citizens had concealed themselves in cellars and vaults, where they lay panting in vain endeavours to recover the breath which they had wasted in their retreat, scarcely finding words enough to tell the provost "That their hearts were away, and that they would fight no more though they should be killed." Thirdly, the letter states, that if the citizens had had the inclination to stand out, they had no means of resistance, most of them having flung away their weapons in their flight. Finally, the courage of the defenders was overpowered by the sight of the enemy, drawn up like so many hellhounds before the gates of the town, their hands deeply dyed in the blood recently shed, and demanding, with hideous cries, to be led to further slaughter. The magistrates perhaps deserve no blame, if they capitulated in such circumstances, to avoid the horrors of a storm. But their conduct shows, at the same time, how much the people of the Lowlands had degenerated in point of military courage.

Perth consequently opened its gates to the victor. But Argyle, whose northern army had been augmented by a considerable body of cavalry, was now approaching with a force, against which Montrose could not pretend to defend an open town. He abandoned Perth, therefore, and marched into Angus-shire, hoping he might find adherents in that county. Accordingly, he was there joined by the old Earl of Airlie and two of his sons, who never forsook him in success or disaster.

This accession of strength was counterbalanced by a shocking event. There was a Highland gentleman in Montrose's camp, named James Stewart of Ardvoirlich, whose birth had been attended with some peculiar circumstances, which, though they lead me from my present subject, I cannot refrain from noticing. While his mother was pregnant there came to the house of Ardvoirlich a band of outlaws, called Children of the Mist, Macgregors, some say, others call them Macdonalds of Ardnamurchan. They demanded food, and the lady caused bread and cheese to be placed on the table, and went into the kitchen to order a better meal to be made ready, such being the unvarying process of Highland hospitality. When the poor lady returned, she saw upon the table, with its mouth stuffed full of food, the bloody head of her brother, Drummond of Drummondernoch, whom the outlaws had met and murdered in the wood. The unhappy woman shrieked, ran wildly into the forest, where, notwithstanding strict search, she could not be found for many weeks. At length she was secured, but in a state of insanity, which doubtless was partly communicated to the infant which was born shortly after. The lad, however, grew up. He was an uncertain and dangerous character, but distinguished for his muscular strength, which was so great, that he could, in grasping the hand of another person, force the blood from under the nails. This man was much favoured by the Lord Kilpont, whose accession to the King's party we lately mentioned; indeed, he was admitted to share that young nobleman's tent and bed. It appears that Ardvoirlich had disapproved of the step which his friend had taken in joining Montrose, and that he had solicited the young lord to join him in deserting from the royal army, and, it is even said, in murdering the general. Lord Kilpont rejected these proposals with disdain; when, either offended at his expressions, or fearful of being exposed in his treacherous purpose, Ardvoirlich stabbed his confiding friend mortally with his dagger. He then killed the sentinel who kept guard on the tent, and escaped to the camp of Argyle, where he received preferment. Montrose was awaked by the tumult which this melancholy event excited in the camp, and rushing into the crowd of soldiers, had the unhappiness to see the bleeding corpse of his noble friend thus basely and treacherously murdered. The death of this young nobleman was a great loss to the royal cause.

Montrose, so much inferior in numbers to his enemies, could not well form any fixed plan of operations. He resolved to make up for this, by moving with the most extraordinary celerity from one part of the country to another, so as to strike severe blows where they were least expected, and take the chance of awakening the drooping spirit of the Royalists. He therefore marched suddenly on Aberdeen, to endeavour to arouse the Gordons to arms, and defeat any body of Covenanters which might overawe the King's friends in that country. His army was now, however, greatly reduced in numbers; for the Highlanders, who had no idea of serving for a whole campaign, had most of them returned home to their own districts, to lodge their booty in safety, and get in their harvest. It was, on all occasions, the greatest inconvenience attending a Highland army, that after a battle, whether they won the day or lost it, they were certain to leave their standard in great numbers, and held it their undoubted right to do so; insomuch, that a victory thinned their ranks as much as a defeat is apt to do those of other armies. It is true, that they could be gathered again with equal celerity; but this humour, of deserting at their pleasure, was a principal reason why the brilliant victories of Montrose were productive of few decided results.[1]

On reaching Aberdeen, Montrose hastened to take possession of the bridge of Dee, the principal approach to that town, and having made good this important point, he found himself in front of an army commanded by Lord Burleigh. He had the mortification also to find, that part of a large body of horse in the Covenanting army were Gordons, who had been compelled to take arms in that cause by Lord Lewis Gordon, the third son of the Marquis of Huntly, a wild and wilful young man, whose politics differed from those of his father, and upon whom he had once committed a considerable robbery.

Finding himself greatly inferior in horse, of which he had not fifty, Montrose intermingled with his cavalry some of his musketeers, who, for breath and speed, could keep up with the movements of such horse as he possessed. The Gordons, not perhaps very favourable to the side on which they ranked, made an ineffectual attack upon the horse of Montrose, which was repelled. And when the mingled musketeers and cavalry in their turn advanced on them, Lord Lewis's men fled, in spite of his own personal exertions; and Montrose, we are informed, found it possible to move his handful of cavalry to the other wing of his army,

---

[1] "Even so lately as during the rebellion of 1745-6, when the young Chevalier Charles Edward, by way of making an example, caused a soldier to be shot for desertion, the Highlanders who composed his army were affected as much by indignation as by fear. They could not conceive any principle of justice upon which a man's life could be taken, for merely going home when it did not suit him to remain longer with the army. Such had been the uniform practice of their fathers. When a battle was over, the campaign was, in their opinion, ended; if it was lost, they sought safety in their mountains—if won, they returned there to secure their booty. At other times they had their cattle to look after, and their harvests to sow or reap, without which their families would have perished for want. This circumstance serves to show, even if history had not made us acquainted with the same fact, that the Highlanders had never been accustomed to make war with the view of permanent conquest, but only with the hope of deriving temporary advantage, or deciding some immediate quarrel."—*Legend of Montrose,* chap. xv.

and to encounter and defeat the horse of the Covenanters on both flanks successively, with the same wearied party of riders. The terror struck into his opponents by the novelty of mixing musketeers with cavalry, contributed not a little to this extraordinary success. While this was passing, the two bodies of infantry cannonaded each other, for Montrose had in the field the guns which he took at Tibbermuir. The Covenanters had the superiority in this part of the action, but it did not daunt the Royalists. The gaiety of an Irishman, whose leg was shot off by a cannon-ball, so that it hung only by a bit of skin, gave spirit to all around him.—"Go on," he cried, "this bodes me promotion; as I am now disabled for the foot service, I am certain my lord the Marquis will make me a trooper." Montrose left the courage of his men no time to subside—he led them daringly up to the enemy's teeth, and succeeded in a desperate charge, routing the Covenanters, and pursuing them into the town and through the streets. Stormed as it was by such a tumultuary army, Aberdeen and its inhabitants suffered greatly. Many were killed in the streets; and the cruelty of the Irish in particular was so great, that they compelled the wretched citizens to strip themselves of their clothes before they killed them, to prevent their being soiled with blood! The women durst not lament their husbands or their fathers slaughtered in their presence, nor inter the dead which remained unburied in the streets until the Irish departed. Montrose necessarily gave way to acts of pillage and cruelty, which he could not prevent, because he was unprovided with money to pay his half-barbarous soldiery. Yet the town of Aberdeen had two reasons for expecting better treatment:—First, that it had always inclined to the King's party; and, secondly, that Montrose himself had, when acting for the Covenanters, been the agent in oppressing for its loyalty the very city which his troops were now plundering on the opposite score.

Argyle always continued following Montrose with a superior army, but, it would appear, not with a very anxious desire to overtake him. With a degree of activity that seemed incredible, Montrose marched up the Spey, hoping still to raise the Gordons. But that clan too strongly resented his former conduct towards them, as General for the Covenant, besides being sore with recollections of their recent check at the bridge of Dee; and, on all these accounts, declined to join him. On the other hand, the men of Moray, who were very zealous against Montrose, appeared on the northern bank of the Spey to oppose his passage. Thus hemmed in on all sides, and headed back like an animal of chase from the course he intended to pursue, Montrose and his little army showed an extremity of courage. They hid their cannon in a bog, destroyed what they had of heavy baggage, entered Badenoch, where the Clan Chattan had shown themselves uniformly friendly, and descended from thence apon Athole, and so on to Angusshire. After several long and rapid marches, Montrose returned into Strathbogie, recrossing the great chain of the Grampians; and, clinging still to the hope of being able to raise the gentlemen of the name of Gordon, who were naturally disposed to join the royal standard, again repaired to Aberdeenshire.

Here this bold leader narrowly escaped a great danger. His army was considerably dispersed, and he himself lying at the castle of Fyvie, when he found himself at once threatened, and nearly surrounded, by Argyle and Lothian, at the head of very superior forces. A part of the enemy had already occupied the approach to Montrose's position by means of ditches and enclosures, through which they had insinuated themselves, and his own men were beginning to look out of countenance, when Montrose, disguising his apprehensions, called to a gay and gallant young Irish officer, as if he had been imposing a trifling piece of duty,—"What are you doing, O'Kean? can you not chase these troublesome rascals out of the ditches and enclosures?" O'Kean obeyed the command in the spirit in which it was given; and, driving the enemy before him, got possession of some of their gunpowder, which was much needed in Montrose's army. The remark of the Irishman on this occasion, who heavily complained of the neglect of the enemy in omitting to leave a supply of ball, corresponding to the powder, showed the confidence with which Montrose had been able to inspire his men.

The Earl of Lothian, on the other side, came with five troops of horse upon Montrose's handful of cavalry, amounting scarcely to fifty men. But Montrose had, on the present occasion, as at the bridge of Dee, sustained his troopers by mingling them with musketry. So that Lothian's men, receiving an unexpected and galling fire, wheeled about, and could not again be brought to advance. Many hours were spent in skirmishing, with advantage on Montrose's part, and loss on that of Argyle, until at length the former thought it most advisable to retreat from Fyvie to Strathbogie.

On the road he was deserted by many Lowland gentlemen who had joined him, and who saw his victories were followed with no better results than toilsome marches among wilds, where it was nearly impossible to provide subsistence for man or horse, and which the approach of winter was about to render still more desolate. They left his army, therefore, promising to return in summer; and of all his Lowland adherents, the old Earl of Airlie and his sons alone remained. They had paid dearly for their attachment to the Royal cause, Argyle having plundered their estates, and burnt their principal mansion, the "Bonnie house of Airlie," situated on the river Isla, the memory of which conflagration is still preserved in Scottish song.

But the same circumstances which wearied out the patience of Montrose's Lowland followers, rendered it impossible for Argyle to keep the field; and he sent his army into winter quarters, in full confidence that his enemy was cooped up for the season in the narrow and unprovided country of Athole and its neighbourhood, where he might be suffered to exist with little inconvenience to the rest of Scotland, till spring should enable the Covenanters to attack him with a superior force. In the meantime, the Marquis of Argyle returned to his own domains.

XLIII

Montrose

1644-1645

IT was about the middle of December that Argyle was residing at his castle of Inverary, in the most perfect confidence that the enemy could not approach him; for he used to say, he would not for a hundred thousand crowns that any one knew the passes from the eastward into the country of the Campbells. While the powerful Marquis was enjoying the fancied security of his feudal dominions, he was astounded with the intelligence that Montrose, with an army of Highlanders, wading through drifts of snow, scaling precipices, and traversing the mountain-paths, known to none save the solitary shepherd or huntsman, had forced an entry into Argyleshire, which he was laying waste with all the vindictive severity of deadly feud. There was neither time nor presence of mind for defence. The able-bodied men were slaughtered, the cattle driven off, the houses burnt; and the invaders had divided themselves into three bands, to make the devastation more complete. Alarmed by this fierce and unexpected invasion, Argyle embarked on board a fishing-boat, and left his friends and followers to their fate. Montrose continued the work of revenge for nearly a month, and then concluding he had destroyed the influence which Argyle, by the extent of his power, and the supposed strength of his country, had possessed over the minds of the Highlanders, he withdrew towards Inverness, with the purpose of organising a general gathering of the clans. But he had scarce made this movement, when he learned that his rival, Argyle, had returned into the Western Highlands with some Lowland forces; that he had called around him his numerous clan, burning to revenge the wrongs which they had sustained, and was lying with a strong force near the old castle of Inverlochy, situated at the western extremity of the chain of lakes through which the Caledonian Canal is now conducted.

The news at once altered Montrose's plans.

He returned upon Argyle by a succession of the most difficult mountain-passes covered with snow; and the vanguard of the Campbells saw themselves suddenly engaged with that of their implacable enemy. Both parties lay all night on their arms; but, by break of day, Argyle betook himself to his galley, and rowing off shore, remained a spectator of the combat, when, by all the rules of duty and gratitude, he ought to have been at the head of his devoted followers. His unfortunate clansmen supported the honour of the name with the greatest courage, and many of the most distinguished fell on the field of battle. Montrose gained a complete victory, which greatly extended his influence over the Highlands and in proportion diminished that of his discomfited rival.

Having collected what force he could, Montrose now marched triumphantly to the north-east; and in the present successful posture of his affairs at length engaged the Gordons to join him with a good body of cavalry, commanded by their young chief, Lord Gordon. The Convention of Estates were now most seriously alarmed. While Montrose had roamed through the Highlands, retreating before a superior enemy, and every moment apparently on the point of being overwhelmed, his progress was regarded as a distant danger. But he was now threatening the low country, and the ruling party were not so confident of their strength there as to set so bold an adventurer at defiance. They called from the army in England General Baillie, an officer of skill and character, and Sir John Urry, or, as the English called him, Hurry, a brave and good partisan, but a mere soldier of fortune, who had changed sides more than once during the civil war.

These generals commanded a body of veteran troops, with which they manoeuvred to exclude Montrose from the southern districts, and prevent his crossing the Tay, or Forth. At the same time the mandate of the Marquis of Huntly, or the intrigues of Lord Lewis Gordon, again recalled most of the Gordons from Montrose's standard, and his cavalry was reduced to one hundred and fifty. He was compelled once more to retire to the mountains, but desirous to dignify his retreat by some distinguished action, he resolved to punish the town of Dundee for their steady adherence to the cause of the Covenant. Accordingly, suddenly appearing before it with a chosen body selected for the service, he stormed the place on three points at once. The Highlanders and Irish, with incredible fury, broke open the gates, and forced an entrance. They were dispersing in quest of liquor and plunder, when at the very moment that Montrose threatened to set the town on fire, he received intelligence, that Baillie and Urry, with four thousand men, were within a mile of the place. The crisis required all the activity of Montrose; and probably no other authority than his would have been able to withdraw the men from their revelling and plundering to get his army into order, and to effect a retreat to the mountains, which he safely accomplished in the face of his numerous enemies, and with a degree of skill which established his military character as firmly as any of his victories.

Montrose was well seconded in this difficulty, by the hardihood and resolution of his men, who are said to have marched about sixty miles, and to have passed three days and two nights in manoeuvring and fighting, without either food or refreshment. In this manner that leader repeatedly baffled the numerous forces and able generals who were employed against him. The great check upon his enterprise was the restlessness of the Highlanders, and the caprice of the gentlemen who formed his cavalry, who all went and came at their own pleasure.

I have told you that the Gordons had been withdrawn from Montrose's standard, contrary to their own inclinations, by the command of Huntly, or the address of Lord Lewis Gordon. By employing his followers in enterprises in which the plunder was certain and the danger small, this young nobleman collected under his standard all those who were reluctant to share the toilsome marches, military hardships, and bloody fights to which they were led under that of Montrose. Hence a rhyme, not yet forgotten in Aberdeenshire,

> "If you with Lord Lewis go,
> You'll get reif and prey enough;
> If you with Montrose go,
> You'll get grief and wae enough."

But the Lord Gordon, Lewis's elder brother, continuing attached in the warmest manner to Montrose, was despatched by him to bring back the gentlemen of his warlike family, and his influence soon assembled considerable forces. General Baillie, learning this, detached Urry, his colleague, with a force which he thought sufficient to destroy Lord Gordon, while he himself proposed to engage the attention of Montrose till that point was gained.

But Montrose, penetrating the intention of the Covenanting generals, eluded Baillie's attempts to bring him to action, and traversed the mountains of the north like a whirlwind, to support Lord Gordon and crush Urry. He accomplished his first object; the second appeared more difficult. Urry had been joined by the Covenanters of the shire of Moray, with the Earls of Seaforth, Sutherland, and others who maintained the same cause, and had thus collected an army more numerous than that of Montrose, even when united to Lord Gordon.

Montrose prepared, nevertheless, to give battle at the village of Aulderne, and drew up his men in an unusual manner, to conceal his inequality of force. The village, which is situated on an eminence, with high ground behind, was surrounded by enclosures on each side and in front. He stationed on the right of the hamlet Alexander MacDonald, called Colkitto, with four hundred Irishmen and Highlanders, commanding them to maintain a defensive combat only, and giving them strict orders not to sally from some strong sheepfolds and enclosures, which afforded the advantages of a fortified position. As he wished to draw the attention of the enemy towards that point, he gave this wing charge of the royal standard, which was usually displayed where he commanded in person. On the left side of the village of Aulderne, he drew up the principal part of his force, he himself commanding the infantry, and Lord Gordon the cavalry. His two wings being thus formed, Montrose had in reality no centre force whatever; but a few resolute men were posted in front of the village, and his cannon being placed in the same line made it appear as if the houses covered a body of infantry.

Urry, deceived by these dispositions, attacked with a preponderating force the position of MacDonald on the right. Colkitto beat the assailants back with the Irish musketeers, and the bows and arrows of the Highlanders, who still used these ancient missile weapons. But when the enemy, renewing their attack, taunted MacDonald with cowardice for remaining under shelter of the sheepfolds, that leader, whose bravery greatly excelled his discretion, sallied forth from his fastness, contrary to Montrose's positive command, to show he was not averse to fight on equal ground. The superiority of numbers, and particularly of cavalry, which was instantly opposed to him, soon threw his men into great disorder, and they could with difficulty be rallied by the desperate exertions of Colkitto, who strove to make amends for his error, by displaying the utmost personal valour.

A trusty officer was despatched to Montrose to let him know the state of affairs. The messenger found him on the point of joining battle, and whispered in his ear that Colkitto was defeated. This only determined Montrose to pursue with the greater audacity the plan of battle which he had adopted. "What are we doing?" he called out to Lord Gordon; "MacDonald has been victorious on the right, and if we do not make haste, he will carry off all the honours of the day." Lord Gordon instantly charged with the gentlemen of his name, and beat the Covenanters' horse off the field; but the foot, though deserted by the horse, stood firm for some time, for they were veteran troops. At length they were routed on every point, and compelled to fly with great loss.

Montrose failed not instantly to lead succours to the relief of his right wing, which was in great peril. Colkitto had got his men again secured in the enclosures; he himself, having been all along the last to retreat, was now defending the entrance sword in hand, and with a target on his left arm. The pikemen pressed him so hard as to fix their spears in his target, while he repeatedly freed himself of them by cutting the heads from the shafts, in threes and fours at a time, by the unerring sweep of his broadsword.

While Colkitto and his followers were thus hard pressed, Montrose and his victorious troops appeared, and the face of affairs was suddenly changed. Urry's horse fled, but the foot, which were the strength of his army, fought bravely, and fell in the ranks which they occupied. Two thousand men, about a third of Urry's army, were slain in the battle of Aulderne, and, completely disabled by the overthrow, that commander was compelled once more to unite his scattered forces with those of Baillie.

After some marching and counter-marching, the armies again found themselves in the neighbourhood of each other, near to the village of Alford.

Montrose occupied a strong position on a hill, and it was said that the cautious Baillie would have avoided the encounter, had it not been that, having crossed the river Don, in the belief that Montrose was in full retreat, he only discovered his purpose of giving battle when it was too late to decline it. The number of infantry was about two thousand in each army. But Baillie had more than double his opponent's number of cavalry. Montrose's, indeed, were gentlemen, and therefore in the day of battle were more to be relied on than mere hirelings. The Gordons dispersed the Covenanting horse, on the first shock; and the musketeers, throwing down their muskets, and mingling in the tumult with their swords drawn, prevented the scattered cavalry from rallying. But as Lord Gordon threw himself, for the second time, into the heat of the fight, he fell from his horse, mortally wounded by a shot from one of the fugitives. This accident, which gave the greatest distress to Montrose, suspended the exertions of the cavalry, who, chiefly friends, kinsmen, and vassals of the deceased, flocked around him to lament the general loss. But the veterans of Montrose, charging in separate columns of six and ten men deep, along a line of three men only, broke the battle array of the Covenanters on various points, and utterly destroyed the remnant of Baillie's array, though they defended themselves bravely. This battle was fought 2d July 1645.

These repeated victories gave such lustre to Montrose's arms, that he was now joined by the Highland clans in great numbers, and by many of the Lowland anti-Covenanters, who had before held back, from doubt of his success in so unequal a contest.

On the other hand, the Convention of Estates, supported by the Counsels of Argyle, who was bold in council though timid in battle, persevered in raising new troops, notwithstanding their repeated misfortunes and defeats. It seemed, indeed, as if Heaven had at this disastrous period an especial controversy with the kingdom of Scotland. To the efforts necessary to keep up and supply their auxiliary army in England, was added the desolation occasioned by a destructive civil war, maintained in the north with the utmost fury, and conducted on both sides with deplorable devastation. To these evils, as if not sufficient to exhaust the resources of a poor country, were now added those of a wide-wasting plague, or pestilence, which raged through all the kingdom, but especially in Edinburgh, the metropolis. The Convention of Estates were driven from the capital by this dreadful infliction, and retreated to Perth, where they assembled a large force under General Baillie, while they ordered a new levy of ten thousand men generally throughout the kingdom. While Lanark, Cassilis, Eglinton, and other lords of the western shires, went to their respective counties to expedite the measure, Montrose, with his usual activity, descended from the mountains at the head of an army, augmented in numbers, and flushed with success.

He first approached the shores of the Forth, by occupying the shire of Kinross. And here I cannot help mentioning the destruction of a noble castle belonging to the House of Argyle. Its majestic ruins are situated on an eminence occupying a narrow glen of the Ochil chain of hills. In former days, it was called, from the character of its situation perhaps, the castle of Gloom; and the names of the parish, and the stream by which its banks are washed, had also an ominous sound. The castle of Gloom was situated on the brook of Grief or Gryfe, and in the parish of Doulour or Dollar. In the sixteenth century the Earl of Argyle, the owner of this noble fortress, obtained an act of Parliament for changing its name to Castle Campbell. The feudal hatred of Montrose, and of the clans composing the strength of his army, the vindictive resentment also of the Ogilvies, for the destruction of "the Bonnie House of Airlie," and that of the Stirlingshire cavaliers for that of Menstrie, doomed this magnificent pile to flames and ruin. The destruction of many a meaner habitation by the same unscrupulous and unsparing spirit of vengeance has been long forgotten, but the majestic remains of Castle Campbell still excite a sigh in those that view them, over the miseries of civil war.

After similar acts of ravage, not to be justified, though not unprovoked, Montrose marched westward along the northern margin of the Forth, insulting Perth, where the army of the Covenanters remained in their intrenchments, and even menacing the castle of Stirling, which, well garrisoned and strongly situated, defied his means of attack. About six miles above Stirling, Montrose crossed the Forth, by the deep and precarious ford which the river presents before its junction with the Teith. Having attained the southern bank, he directed his course westward, with the purpose of dispersing the levies which the western lords were collecting, and doubtless with the view of plundering the country, which had attached itself chiefly to the Covenant. Montrose had, however, scarcely reached Kilsyth, when he received the news that Baillie's army, departing from Perth, had also crossed the Forth, at the bridge of Stirling, and was close at hand. With his usual alacrity, Montrose prepared for battle, which

Baillie, had he been left to his own judgment, would have avoided;
for that skilful though unfortunate general knew by experience the
talents of Montrose, and that the character of his troops was
admirably qualified for a day of combat; he also considered that an
army so composed might be tired out by cautious operations, and
entertained the rational hope that the Highlanders and Lowland Cavaliers would alike desert their leader in the course of a protracted and
indecisive warfare. But Baillie was no longer the sole commander of
the Covenanting army. A Committee of the Estates, consisting of
Argyle, Lanark, and Crawford-Lindsay, had been nominated to attend
his army, and control his motions; and these, especially the Earl of
Lindsay, insisted that the veteran general should risk the last regular
army which the Covenanters possessed in Scotland, in the perils of a
decisive battle. They marched against Montrose, accordingly, at break
of day on the 15th August 1645.

When Montrose beheld them advance, he exclaimed that it was
what he had most earnestly desired. He caused his men to strip to their
shirts, in token of their resolution to fight to the death. Meantime the
Covenanters approached. Their vanguard attacked an advanced post of
Montrose, which occupied a strong position among cottages and
enclosures. They were beaten off with loss. A thousand Highlanders,
with their natural impetuosity, rushed without orders to pursue the
fugitives, and to assault the troops who were advancing to support
them. Two regiments of horse, against whom this mountain torrent
directed its fury, became disordered and fell back. Montrose saw the
decisive moment, and ordered first a troop of horse, under command
of Lord Airlie, and afterwards his whole army, to attack the enemy, who
had not yet got into line, their rear-guard and centre coming up too
slowly to the support of their vanguard. The hideous shout with which
the Highlanders charged, their wild appearance, and the extraordinary
speed with which they advanced, nearly naked, with broadsword in
hand, struck a panic into their opponents, who dispersed without any
spirited effort to get into line of battle, or maintain their ground. The
Covenanters were beaten off the field, and pursued with indiscriminate
slaughter for more than ten miles. Four or five thousand men were
slain in the field and in the flight; and the force of the Convention was
for the time entirely broken.

Montrose was now master, for the moment, of the kingdom of
Scotland. Edinburgh surrendered; Glasgow paid a heavy contribution;

the noblemen and other individuals of distinction who had been imprisoned as Royalists in Edinburgh, and elsewhere throughout the kingdom, were set at liberty; and so many persons of quality now declared for Montrose, either from attachment to the Royal cause, which they had hitherto concealed, or from the probability of its being ultimately successful, that he felt himself in force sufficient to call a Parliament at Glasgow in the King's name.

Still, however, the success of this heroic leader had only given him possession of the open country; all the strong fortresses were still in possession of the Covenanters; and it would have required a length of time, and the services of an army regularly disciplined and supplied with heavy artillery, to have reduced the castles of Edinburgh, Stirling, Dumbarton and other places of great strength. But if Montrose had possessed the forces necessary for such a work, he had neither leisure nor inclination to undertake it. From the beginning of his extraordinary, and hitherto successful career, he had secretly entertained the dazzling hope of leading a victorious army into England, and replacing King Charles in possession of his disputed authority. It was a daring scheme, and liable to many hazards; yet if the King's affairs in England had remained in any tolerable condition, especially if there had been any considerable army of Royalists in the north of England to join or co-operate with Montrose, there is no calculating what the talents and genius of such an enterprising leader might have ultimately done in support of the Royal cause.

But Charles, as I will presently tell you more particularly, had suffered so many and such fatal losses, that it may be justly doubted whether the assistance of Montrose, unless at the head of much larger forces than he could be expected to gather, would have afforded any material assistance against the numerous and well-disciplined army of the Parliament. The result of a contest which was never tried can only be guessed at. Montrose's own hopes and confidence were as lofty as his ambition; and he did not permit himself to doubt the predictions of those who assured him, that he was doomed to support the tottering throne, and reinstate in safety the falling monarch.

Impressed with such proud anticipations, he wrote to the King, urging him to advance to the northern border, and form a junction, with his victorious army, and concluding his request with the words which Joab, the lieutenant of King David, is recorded in Scripture to have used to the King of Israel,—"I have fought against Rabbah, and have taken the city of waters. Now therefore gather the rest of the people together, and encamp against the city, and take it; lest I take the city, and it be called after my name."[1]

While Montrose was thus urging King Charles, by the brilliant prospects which he held out, to throw himself on his protection, his own army mouldered away and dispersed, even in a greater degree than had been the case after his less distinguished successes. The Highland clans went home to get in their harvest, and place their spoil in safety. It was needless and useless to refuse them leave, for they were determined to take it. The north country gentlemen also, wearied of the toils of the campaign, left his army in numbers; so that when Montrose received, by the hands of Sir Robert Spottiswood, the King's commission under the Great Seal, naming him captain-general and lieutenant-governor of Scotland, he commanded a force scarcely more effective than when he was wandering through Athole and Badenoch. The King's orders, however, and his own indomitable spirit of enterprise, determined his march towards the Borders.

About fifty years before, these districts would have supplied him, even upon the lighting of their beacons, with ten thousand cavalry, as fond of fighting and plunder as any Highlander in his army. But that period, as I have told you, had passed away. The inhabitants of the Border-land had become peaceful, and the chiefs and lords, whose influence might still have called them out to arms, were hostile to the Crown, or, at best, lukewarm in its cause. The Earl of Buccleuch, and his friends of the name of Scott, who had never forgotten the offence given by the revocation of James's donations to their chief, were violent Covenanters, and had sent a strong clan-regiment with the Earl of Leven and the Scottish auxiliaries. Traquair, Roxburghe, and Hume, all entertained, or affected, regard to the King, but made no effectual effort in raising men. The once formidable name of Douglas, and the exertions of the Earl of Annandale, could only assemble some few troops of horse, whom the historian, Bishop Guthrie, describes as truthless trained bands. Montrose expected to meet a body of more regular cavalry, who were to be despatched from England; but the King's continued misfortunes prevented him from making such a diversion.

Meanwhile the Scottish army in England received an account of the despair to which the battle of Kilsyth had reduced the Convention of

---

[1] 2 Samuel, xii. 27, 28

Estates, and learned that several of its most distinguished members were already exiles, having fled to Berwick and other strong places on the Border, which were garrisoned by the Parliamentary forces. The importance of the crisis was felt, and David Lesley was despatched, at the head of five or six thousand men, chiefly cavalry, and the flower of the Scottish auxiliary army, with the charge of checking the triumphs of Montrose.

Lesley crossed the Border at Berwick, and proceeded on his march towards the metropolis, as if it had been his view to get between Montrose and the Highlands, and to prevent his again receiving assistance from his faithful mountaineers. But that sagacious general's intentions were of a more decisive character; for, learning that Montrose, with his little army lay quartered in profound security near Selkirk, he suddenly altered his march, left the Edinburgh road when he came to Edge-bucklingbrae, above Musselburgh, crossed the country to Middleton, and then turning southward, descended the vale of the Gala to Melrose, in which place, and the adjacent hamlets, he quartered his army for the night.

Montrose's infantry, meanwhile, lay encamped on an elevated ascent, called Philiphaugh,[2] on the left bank of the Ettrick, while his cavalry, with their distinguished general in person, were quartered in the town of Selkirk; a considerable stream being thus interposed betwixt the two parts of his army, which should have been so stationed as to be ready to support each other on a sudden alarm. But Montrose had no information of the vicinity of Lesley, though the Covenanters had passed the night within four miles of his camp. This indicates that he must have been very ill served by his own patrols, and that his cause must have been unpopular in that part of the country, since a single

---

[2] "The river Ettrick, immediately after its junction with the Yarrow, and previous to its falling into the Tweed, makes a large sweep to the southward, and winds almost beneath the lofty banks on which the town of Selkirk stands: having upon the northern side a large and level plain, extending in an easterly direction, from a hill covered with natural copse-wood, called the Harehead-wood, to the high ground which forms the banks of the Tweed, near Sunderland Hall. This plain is called Philiphaugh,* it is about a mile and a half in length, and a quarter of a mile broad; and being defended, to the northward, by the hills which separate Tweed from Yarrow, by the river Ettrick in front, and by the high grounds, already mentioned on each flank, it forms, at once, a convenient and a secure field of encampment."

* "The Scottish language is rich in words expressive of local situation. The single word *haugh* conveys to a Scotsman almost all that I have endeavoured to explain in the text by circumlocutory description."—*Minstrels of the Scottish Border,* vol. ii. pp. 170–171.

horseman, at the expense of half an hour's gallop, might have put him fully on his guard.

On the morning of the 13th September 1645 Lesley, under cover of a thick mist, approached Montrose's camp, and had the merit, by his dexterity and vigilance, of surprising him whom his enemies had never before found unprepared. The Covenanting general divided his troops into two divisions, and attacked both flanks of the enemy at the same time. Those on the left made but a tumultuary and imperfect resistance; the right wing, supported by a wood, fought in a manner worthy of their general's fame. Montrose himself, roused by the firing and noise of the action, hastily assembled his cavalry, crossed the Ettrick, and made a desperate attempt to recover the victory, omitting nothing which courage or skill could achieve, to rally his followers. But when at length left with only thirty horse, he was compelled to fly, and retreating up the Yarrow, crossed into the vale of Tweed, and reached Peebles, where some of his followers joined him.

The defeated army suffered severely. The prisoners taken by the Covenanters were massacred without mercy, and in cold blood. They were shot in the courtyard of Newark Castle, upon Yarrow, and their bodies hastily interred at a place, called, from that circumstance, Slain-men's-lee. The ground being, about twenty years since, opened for the foundation of a schoolhouse, the bones and skulls, which were dug up in great quantities, plainly showed the truth of the country tradition. Many cavaliers, both officers and others, men of birth and character, the companions of Montrose's many triumphs, fell into the hands of the victors, and were, as we shall afterwards see, put to an ignominious death. The prisoners, both of high and low degree, would have been more numerous but for the neighbourhood of the Harehead-wood, into which the fugitives escaped. Such were the immediate consequences of this battle; concerning which the country people often quote the following lines:—

> "At Philiphaugh the fray began;
> At Harehead-wood it ended.
> The Scots out owre the Grahams they ran,
> Sae merrily they bended."[1]

---

[1] For more particulars regarding the battle of Philiphaugh, see this ballad, with Introduction and Notes, in the *Border Minstrelsy*, vol. ii. pp. 166–182.

Montrose, after this disastrous action, retreated again into the Highlands, where he once more assembled an army of mountaineers. But his motions ceased to be of the consequence which they had acquired before he had experienced defeat. General Middleton, a man of military talents, but a soldier of fortune, was despatched against him by the Convention of Estates, which was eager to recover the same power in the Highlands which David Lesley's victory had re-established throughout the Lowlands.

While Montrose was thus engaged in an obscure mountain warfare, the King having already surrendered himself to the Scottish auxiliaries, in total despair of the ultimate success, and anxious for the safety of his adventurous general, sent orders to him to dissolve his army, and to provide for his personal security by leaving the kingdom. Montrose would not obey the first order, concluding it had been extorted from the monarch. To a second, and more peremptory injunction he yielded obedience, and disbanding his army, embarked in a brig bound for Bergen in Norway, with a few adherents, who were too obnoxious to the Covenanters to permit of their remaining in Scotland. Lest their little vessel should be searched by an English ship of war, Montrose wore the disguise of a domestic, and passed for the servant of his chaplain and biographer, Dr. George Wishart. You may remember that he wore a similar disguise on entering Scotland, in order to commence his undertaking.

This and the preceding chapter give an account of the brief, but brilliant period of Montrose's success. A future one will contain the melancholy conclusion of his exertions and of his life.

XLIV

The Covenanters and Cromwell

1645-1647

I MUST now tell you the fate of the unfortunate cavaliers who had been made prisoners at Philiphaugh. The barbarous treatment of the common soldiers you are already aquatinted with.

Argyle, the leader of the Convention of Estates, had to resent the devastation of his country, and the destruction of his castles; and his desire of vengeance was so common to the age, that it would have been accounted neglect of his duty to his slain kinsmen and plundered clan, if he had let slip the favourable opportunity of exacting blood for blood. Other noblemen of the Convention had similar motives; and, besides, they had all been greatly alarmed at Montrose's success; and nothing makes men more pitiless than the recollection of recent fears. It ought partly to have assuaged these vindictive feelings, that Montrose's ravages, although they were sufficiently wasting, were less encouraged by the officers than arising from the uncontrollable license of an unpaid soldiery. The prisoners had always been treated with honour and humanity, and frequently dismissed on parole. So that, if the fate of Montrose's companions had depended on the Convention alone, it is possible, that almost all might have been set at liberty upon moderate conditions. But unfortunately the Presbyterian clergy thought proper to interfere strenuously between the prisoners and the mercy which they might otherwise have experienced.

And here it must be owned, that the Presbyterian ministers of that period were in some respects a different kind of men from their predecessors, in the reign of James VI. Malice cannot, indeed, accuse them of abusing the power which they had acquired since their success in 1640, for the purpose of increasing either their own individual revenues, or those of the Church; nor had the system of strict morality, by which they were distinguished, been in any degree slackened. They remained in triumph, as they had been in suffering, honourably poor and rigidly moral. But yet though inaccessible to the temptations of avarice or worldly pleasure, the Presbyterian clergy of this period cannot be said to have been superior to ambition and the desire of power; and as they were naturally apt to think that the advancement of religion was best secured by the influence of the Church to which they belonged, they were disposed to extend that influence by the strictest exertion of domestic discipline. Inquiry into the conduct of individuals was carried on by the Church-courts with indecent eagerness; and faults or follies, much fitter for private censure and admonition, were brought forward in the face of the public congregation. The hearers were charged every Sabbath-day, that each individual should communicate to the Kirk Session (a court composed of the clergyman and certain selected laymen of the parish) whatever matter of scandal or offence against religion and morality should come to their ears; and thus an inquisitorial power was exercised by one-half of the parish over the other. This was well meant, but had bad consequences. Every idle story being made the subject of anxious investigation, the private happiness of families was disturbed, and discord and suspicion were sown where mutual confidence is most necessary.

This love of exercising authority in families was naturally connected with a desire to maintain that high influence in the state which the Presbyterian church had acquired since the downfall of Prelacy. The Scottish clergy had of late become used to consider their peculiar form of church government, which unquestionably has many excellences, as something almost essential as religion itself; and it was but one step farther, to censure every one who manifested a design to destroy the system, or limit the power, of the Presbyterian discipline, as an enemy to religion of every kind, nay, even to the Deity himself. Such opinions were particularly strong amongst those of the clergy

who attended the armies in the field, seconded them by encouragement from the pulpits, or aided them by actually assuming arms
themselves. The ardour of such men grew naturally more enthusiastic
in proportion to the opposition they met with, and the dangers they
encountered. The sights and sentiments which attend civil conflict,
are of a kind to reconcile the human heart, however generous and
humane by nature, to severe language and cruel actions. Accordingly,
we cannot be surprised to find that some of the clergy forgot that a
malignant, for so they called a Royalist, was still a countryman and
fellow Christian, born under the same government, speaking the same
language, and hoping to be saved by the power of the same creed,
with themselves; or that they directed against such Cavaliers and Episcopalians those texts of Scripture, in which the Jews were, by especial
commission, commanded to extirpate the heathen inhabitants of the
Promised Land.

One of these preachers enlarged on such a topic after Lesley's victory, and chose his text from the 15th chapter of 1st Samuel, where the
prophet rebukes Saul for sparing the King of the Amalekites, and for
having saved some part of the flocks and herds of that people, which
Heaven had devoted to utter destruction,—"What meaneth then this
bleating of the sheep in mine ears?" In his sermon, he said that Heaven
demanded the blood of the prisoners taken at Philiphaugh, as devoted
by the Divine command to destruction; nor could the sins of the
people be otherwise atoned for, or the wrath of Heaven averted from
the land. It is probable, that the preacher was himself satisfied with the
doctrine which he promulgated; for it is wonderful how people's judgment is blinded by their passions, and how apt we are to find plausible
and even satisfactory reasons, for doing what our interest, or that of the
party we have embraced, strongly recommends.

The Parliament, consisting entirely of Covenanters, instigated by
the importunity of the clergy, condemned eight of the most distinguished cavaliers to execution. Four were appointed to suffer at St.
Andrews, that their blood might be an atonement, as the phrase went,
for the number of men (said to exceed five thousand) whom the
county of Fife had lost during Montrose's wars. Lord Ogilvy was the
first of these; but that young nobleman escaped from prison and death
in his sister's clothes. Colonel Nathaniel Gordon, one of the bravest
men and best soldiers in Europe, and six other cavaliers of the first distinction, were actually executed.

We may particularly distinguish the fate of Sir Robert Spottiswood, who, when the wars broke out, was Secretary Lord President of the Court of Session, and accounted a judge of great talent and learning. He had never borne arms; but the crime of having brought to Montrose his commission as Captain-General of Scotland, and of having accepted the office of secretary, which the Parliament had formerly conferred on Lanark, was thought quite worthy of death, without any further act of treason against the Estates. When on the scaffold, he vindicated his conduct with the dignity of a judge, and the talents of a lawyer. He was rudely enjoined to silence by the Provost of St. Andrews, who had formerly been a servant of his father's, when prelate of that city. The victim submitted to this indignity with calmness, and betook himself to his private devotions. He was even in this task interrupted by the Presbyterian minister in attendance, who demanded of him whether he desired the benefit of his prayers, and those of the assembled people. Sir Robert replied, that he earnestly demanded the prayers of the people, but rejected those of the preacher; for that, in his opinion, God had expressed his displeasure against Scotland, by sending a lying spirit into the mouth of the prophets,—a far greater curse, he said, than those of sword, fire, and pestilence. An old servant of his family took care of Spottiswood's body, and buried it privately. It is said that this faithful domestic, passing through the market-place a day or two afterwards, and seeing the scaffold on which his master had suffered still unremoved, and stained with his blood, was so greatly affected, that he sank down in a swoon, and died as they were lifting him over his own threshold. Such are the terrible scenes which civil discord gives occasion to; and, my dear child, you will judge very wrong if you suppose them peculiar to one side or other of the contending parties in the present case. You will learn hereafter, that the same disposition to abuse power, which is common, I fear, to all who possess it in an unlimited degree, was exercised with cruel retaliation by the Episcopalian party over the Presbyterians, when their hour of authority returned.

We must now turn our thoughts to England, the stage on which the most important scenes were acting, to which these in Scotland can only be termed very subordinate. And here I may remark, that, greatly to the honour of the English nation,—owing, perhaps, to the natural generosity and good-humour of the people, or to the superior influence of civilisation,—the civil war in that country, though contested with the utmost fury in the open field, was not marked by anything approaching to the violent atrocities of the Irish, or the fierce and ruthless devastation exercised by the Scottish combatants. The days of deadly feud had been long past, if the English ever followed that savage custom, and the spirit of malice and hatred which it fostered had no existence in that country. The English parties contended manfully in battle, but, unless in the storming of towns, when all the evil passions are afloat, they seem seldom to have been guilty of cruelty or wasteful ravage. They combated like men who have quarrelled on some special point, but, having had no ill-will against each other before, are resolved to fight it out fairly, without bearing malice. On the contrary, the cause of Prelacy or Presbytery, King or Parliament, was often what was least in the thoughts of the Scottish barons, who made such phrases indeed the pretext for the war, but in fact looked forward to indulging, at the expense of some rival family, the treasured vengeance of a hundred years.

But though the English spirit did not introduce into their civil war the savage aspect of the Scottish feuds, they were not free from the religious dissensions, which formed another curse of the age. I have already said, that the party which opposed itself to the King and the Church of England was, with the followers of the Parliament, and the Parliament itself, divided into two factions, that of the Presbyterians and that of the Independents. I have also generally mentioned the points on which these two parties differed. I must now notice them more particularly.

The Presbyterian establishment, as I have often stated, differs from that of the Church of England, in the same manner as a republic, all the members of which are on a footing of equality, differs from a monarchical constitution. In the Kirk of Scotland all the ministers are on an equality; in the Church of England there is a gradation of ranks, ascending from the lowest order of clergymen to the rank of bishop. But each system is alike founded upon the institution of a body of men, qualified by studies of a peculiar nature to become preachers of the Gospel, and obliged to show they are so qualified, by undergoing trials and examinations of their learning and capacity, before they can take holy orders, that is to say, become clergymen. Both Churches also agree in secluding from ordinary professions and avocations the persons engaged in the ministry, and in considering them as a class of men set apart for teaching religious duties and solemnising religious rites. It is also the rule alike of Episcopalians and Presbyterians that the National Church, as existing in its courts and judicatories, has power to censure, suspend from their functions, and depose from their clerical character and clerical charge such of its members as, either by immoral and wicked conduct, or by preaching and teaching doctrines inconsistent with the public creed, shall render themselves unfit to execute the trust reposed in them. And further, both these national churches maintain, that such courts and judicatories have power over their lay hearers, and those who live in communion with them, to rebuke transgressors of every kind, and to admonish them to repentance; and if such admonish them to repentance; and if such admonitions are neglected, to expel them from the congregation by the sentence of excommunication.

Thus far most Christian churches agree; and thus far the claims and rights of a national church are highly favourable to the existence of a regular government; since reason, as well as the general usage of the religious world, sanctions the establishment of the clergy as a body of men separated from the general class of society, that they may set an example of regularity of life by the purity of their morals. Thus set apart from the rest of the community, they are supported at the expense of the state, in order that the reverence due to them may not be lessened by their being compelled, for the sake of subsistence, to mingle in the ordinary business of life, and share the cares and solicitudes incidental to those who must labour for their daily bread.

How far the civil magistrate can be wisely entrusted with the power of enforcing spiritual censures, or seconding the efforts of the Church to obtain general conformity, by inflicting the penalties of fines, imprisonment, bodily punishment, and death itself, upon those who differ in doctrinal points from the established religion, is a very different question. It is no doubt true, that wild sects have sometimes started up, whose tenets have involved direct danger to the state. But such offenders ought to be punished, not as offenders against the Church, but as transgressors against the laws of the kingdom. While their opinions remain merely speculative, the persons entertaining them may deserve expulsion from the national Church, with which indeed they could consistently desire no communion; but while they do not carry these erroneous tenets into execution, by any treasonable act, it does not appear the province of the civil magistrate to punish them for opinions only. And if the zeal of such sectaries should drive them into action, they deserve punishment, not for holding unchristian doctrines, but for transgressing the civil laws of the realm. This distinction was little understood in the days we write of, and neither the English nor the Scottish Church can be vindicated from the charge of attempting to force men's consciences, by criminal persecutions for acts of non-conformity, though not accompanied by any civil trespass.

Experience and increasing knowledge have taught the present generation that such severities have always increased the evil they were intended to cure; and that mild admonition, patient instruction, and a good example, may gain many a convert to the established churches, whom persecution and violence would have only confirmed in his peculiar opinions. You have read the fable of the traveller, who wrapped his cloak the faster about him when the storm blew loud, but threw it aside in the serene beams of the sunshine. It applies to the subject I have been speaking of, as much as to the advantages of gentleness and mild persuasion in social life.

I return to the distinction between the Independents and Presbyterians during the civil wars of the reign of Charles I. The latter, as you already know, stood strongly out for a national church and an established clergy, with full powers to bind and loose, and maintained by the support of the civil government. Such a church had been fully established in Scotland, and it was the ardent wish of its professors that the English should adopt the same system. Indeed, it was in the hope of attaining this grand object that the consent of the Scottish Convention of Estates was given to sending an auxiliary army to assist the Parliament of England; and they had never suffered themselves to doubt that the adoption of the Presbyterian discipline in that country was secured by the terms of the Solemn League and Covenant. But the Independents had, from the beginning, entertained the secret resolution of opposing the establishment of a national church of any kind in England.

The opinions of these sectaries stood thus on matters of church government. Every one, they said, had a right to read the Scriptures, and draw such conclusions respecting the doctrines which are there inculcated as his own private judgment should hold most conformable to them. They went farther, and argued, that every man who felt himself called upon to communicate to others the conclusions which he had derived from reading the Bible, and meditating on its contents, had a right, and a call from Heaven, to preach and teach the peculiar belief which he had thus adopted. It was no matter how obscure had been the individual's condition in life, or how limited the course of his education; he was equally entitled, in their opinion, to act as a minister, as if he had studied with success for twenty years, and taken orders from a bishop, or from a presbytery. If such a gifted preacher could prevail on six persons to admit his doctrines, these six persons, according to the doctrine of the Independents, made a Christian congregation; and, as far as religious instruction was concerned, the orator became their spiritual head and teacher. Be his hearers many or few, they were thenceforward his sheep, and he their spiritual shepherd. But to all the rest of the world, except his own congregation, the Independents held, that every preacher remained an ordinary layman, having no claim on the state for revenue or subsistence. If he could persuade his congregation to contribute to his support, he was the more fortunate. If not, he lived by his ordinary calling of a baker, a tailor, or a shoemaker, and consoled himself that he resembled St. Paul, who wrought with his hands for his livelihood.

Of the congregations or sects thus formed, there were in England hundreds, perhaps thousands, most of them disagreeing from each other in doctrine, and only united by the common opinion peculiar to them all as Independents, that each private Christian had a right to teach or to listen to whatever doctrines he thought fit; that there ought to exist no church courts of any kind; that the character of a preacher was only to be recognised by those disciples who chose to be taught by him; and that, in any more extensive point of view, there ought not to exist any body of priests or clergymen by profession, any church government, or church judicatories, or any other mode of enforcing religious doctrine, save by teaching it from the pulpit, and admonishing the sinner, or, if necessary, expelling him from the congregation. This last, indeed, could be no great infliction, where there were so many churches ready to receive him, or where, if he pleased, he might set up a church for himself.

The Sectaries, as the Independents were termed, entertained, as may be supposed, very wild doctrines. Men of an enthusiastic spirit, and sometimes a crazed imagination, as opinionative as they were ignorant, and many of them as ignorant as the lowest vulgar, broached an endless variety of heresies, some of them scandalous, some even blasphemous; others, except on account of the serious subject they referred to, extremely ludicrous.

But the preachers and hearers of these strange doctrines were not confined to the vulgar and ignorant. Too much learning made some men mad. Sir Henry Vane, one of the subtlest politicians in England, and Milton, one of the greatest poets ever born, caught the spirit of the times and became Independents. But above all, Oliver Cromwell, destined to rise to the supreme power in England, was of that form of religion.

This remarkable person was of honourable descent, but, inheriting a small fortune, had practised at one time the occupation of a brewer. After a course of gaiety and profligacy during early youth, he caught a strong taint of the enthusiasm of the times, and made himself conspicuous by his aversion to Prelacy, and his zealous opposition to the arbitrary measures of the King. He became a member of Parliament, but, as he spoke indifferently, made no figure in that body, being only prominent for his obstinacy and uncompromising zeal. When, however, the Parliament raised their army, the military talents of Cromwell made him early distinguished. It was remarked that he was uniformly successful in every contest in which he was personally engaged, and that he was the first officer who could train and bring to the field a body of cavalry capable of meeting the shock of the Cavaliers, whose high birth, lofty courage, and chivalrous bravery, made them formidable opponents of the Parliamentary forces. His regiment of Ironsides, as they were called, from the cuirasses which the men wore, were carefully exercised, and accustomed to strict military discipline, while their courage was exalted by the enthusiasm which their commander contrived to inspire. He preached to them himself, prayed for them and with them, and attended with an air of edification to any who chose to preach or pray in return. The attention of these military fanatics was so fixed upon the mysteries of the next world, that death was no terror to them; and the fiery valour of the Cavaliers was encountered and repelled by men who fought for their own ideas of religion as determinedly as their enemies did for honour and loyalty. The spirit of the Independent sectaries spread generally through the army, and the Parliament possessed no troops so excellent as those who followed these doctrines.

The great difference betwixt the Presbyterians and Independents consisted, as I have told you, in the desire of the former to establish their form of religion and church government as the national church establishment of England, and of course to compel a general acquiescence in their articles of faith. For this, a convention of the most learned and able divines was assembled at Westminster, who settled the religious creed of the intended church according the utmost rigour of the Presbyterian creed. This assumption of exclusive power over the conscience alarmed the Independents, and in the dispute which ensued, the consciousness of their own interest with the army gave the sectaries new courage and new pretensions.

At first the Independents had been contented to let the Presbyterians of England, a numerous and wealthy body, take the lead in public measures. But as their own numbers increased, and their leaders became formidable from their interest with the army, they resisted the intention which the Presbyterians showed of establishing their own faith in England as well as Scotland. Sir Henry Vane persuaded them to temporise a little longer, since to oppose Presbytery was to disgust the Scottish auxiliaries, enamoured as they were of their national system. "We cannot yet dispense with the assistance of the Scots," he said; "the sons of Zeruiah are still too many for us." But the progress of the war, while it totally ruined the King's party, gradually diminished the strength of the Presbyterians, and increased that of the Independents. The Earls of Essex and Manchester, generals chosen from the former party, had sustained many losses, which were attributed to incapacity; and they were accused of having let slip advantages, from which it was supposed they had no wish to drive the King to extremity. People began to murmur against the various high offices in the army and state being exclusively occupied by members of Parliament, chiefly Presbyterians; and the protracted length of the civil hostilities was imputed to the desire of such persons to hold in their possession as long as possible the authority which the war placed in their hands.

The Parliament felt that their popularity was in danger of being lost, and looked about for means of recovering it. While their minds were thus troubled, Cromwell suggested a very artful proposal. To recover the confidence of the nation, the members of Parliament, he said, ought to resign all situations of trust or power which they possessed, and confine themselves exclusively to the discharge of their legislative duty. The Parliament fell into the snare. They enacted what was called the self-denying ordinance; by which, in order to show their disinterested patriotism, the members laid down all their offices, civil and military, and rendered themselves incapable of resuming them. This act of self-deprivation proved in the event a death-blow to the power of the Presbyterians; the places which were thus simply resigned being instantly filled up by the ablest men in the Independent party.

Two members of Parliament, however, were allowed to retain command. The one was Sir Thomas Fairfax, a Presbyterian, whose military talents had been highly distinguished during the war, but who was much under the guidance of Oliver Cromwell. The other was Cromwell himself, who had the title of lieutenant-general only, but in fact enjoyed, through his influence over the soldiers, and even over Fairfax himself, all the advantage of supreme command.

The success of Cromwell in this grand measure led to remodelling the army after his own plan, in which he took care their numbers should be recruited, their discipline improved, and, above all, their ranks filled up with Independents. The influence of these changes was soon felt in the progress of the war. The troops of the King sustained various checks, and at length a total defeat in the battle of Naseby, from the effect of which the affairs of Charles could never recover. Loss after loss succeeded; the strong places which the Royalists possessed were taken one after another; and the King's cause was totally ruined. The successes of Montrose had excited a gleam of hope, which disappeared after his defeat at Philiphaugh. Finally, King Charles was shut up in the city of Oxford, which had adhered to his cause with the most devoted loyalty; the last army which he had in the field was destroyed; and he had no alternative save to remain in Oxford till he should be taken prisoner, to surrender himself to his enemies, or to escape abroad.

In circumstances so desperate, it was difficult to make a choice. A frank surrender to the Parliament, or an escape abroad, would have perhaps been the most advisable conduct. But the Parliament and their own Independent army were now on the brink of quarrelling. The establishment of the Presbyterian Church was resolved upon, though only for a time and in a limited form, and both parties were alike dissatisfied; the zealous Presbyterians, because it gave the church courts too little power; the Independents, because it invested them with any control, however slight, over persons of a different communion. Amidst the disputes of his opponents, the King hoped to find his way back to the throne.

For this purpose, and to place himself in a situation, as he hoped, from whence to negotiate with safety, Charles determined to surrender himself to that Scottish army which had been sent into England, under the Earl of Leven, as auxiliaries of the English Parliament. The King concluded that he might expect personal protection, if not assistance, from an army composed of his own countrymen. Besides, the Scottish army had lately been on indifferent terms with the English. The Independent troops who now equalled, or even excelled·them in discipline, and were actuated by an enthusiasm which the Scots did not possess, looked with an evil eye on an army composed of foreigners and Presbyterians. The English in general, as soon as their assistance was no longer necessary, began to regard their Scottish brethren as an incumbrance; and the Parliament, while they supplied the Independent forces liberally with money and provisions, neglected the Scots in both these essentials, whose honour and interest were affected in proportion. A perfect acquaintance with the discontent of the Scottish army induced Charles to throw himself upon their protection in his misfortunes.

He left Oxford in disguise, on 27th April 1646, having only two attendants. Nine days after his departure, he surprised the old Earl of Leven and the Scottish camp, who were then forming the siege of Newark, by delivering himself into their hands. The Scots received the unfortunate monarch with great outward respect, but guarded his person with vigilance. They immediately broke up the siege, and marched with great speed to the north, carrying the person of the King along with them, and observing the strictest discipline on their retreat. When their army arrived at Newcastle, a strong town which they themselves had taken, and where they had a garrison, they halted to await the progress of negotiations at this singular crisis.

Upon surrendering himself to the Scottish army, King Charles had despatched a message to the Parliament, expressing his having done so, desiring that they would send him such articles of pacification as they should agree upon, and offering to surrender Oxford, Newark, and whatever other garrisons or strong places he might still possess, and order the troops he had on foot to lay down their arms. The places were surrendered accordingly, honourable terms being allowed; and the army of Montrose in the Highlands, and such other forces as the Royalists still maintained throughout England, were disbanded, as I have already told you, by the King's command.

The Parliament showed great moderation, and the civil war seemed to be ended. The articles of pacification which they offered were not more rigorous than the desperate condition of the King must have taught him to expect. But questions of religion interfered to prevent the conclusion of the treaty.

In proportion as the great majority of the Parliament were attached to the Presbyterian forms, Charles was devoted to the system of Episcopacy. He deemed himself bound by his coronation oath to support the Church of England, and he would not purchase his own restoration to the throne by consenting to its being set aside. Here, therefore, the negotiation betwixt the King and his Parliament was broken off; but another was opened between the English Parliament and the Scottish army, concerning the disposal of the King's person.

If Charles could have brought his mind to consent to the acceptance of the Solemn League and Covenant, it is probable that he would have gained all Scotland to his side. This, however, would have been granting to the Scots what he had refused to the Parliament; for the support of Presbytery was the essential object of the Scottish invasion. On the other hand, it could hardly be expected that the Scottish Convention of Estates should resign the very point on which it had begun and continued the war. The Church of Scotland sent forth a solemn warning, that all engagement with the King was unlawful. The question, therefore, was, what should be done with the person of Charles.

The generous course would have been, to have suffered the King to leave the Scottish army as freely as he came there. In that case he might have embarked at Tynemouth, and found refuge in foreign countries. And even if the Scots had determined that the exigencies of the times, and the necessity of preserving the peace betwixt England and Scotland, together with their engagements with the Parliament of England, demanded that they should surrender the person of their King to that body, the honour of Scotland was intimately concerned in so conducting the transaction that there should be no room for alleging that any selfish advantage was stipulated by the Scots as a consequence of giving him up. I am almost ashamed to write that this honourable consideration had no weight.

The Scottish army had a long arrear of pay due to them from the English Parliament, which the latter had refused, or at least delayed, to make forthcoming. A treaty for the settlement of these arrears had been set on foot; and it had been agreed that the Scottish forces should retreat into their own country, upon payment of two hundred thousand pounds, which was one-half of the debt finally admitted. Now, it is true that these two treaties, concerning the delivery of the King's person to England, and the payment by Parliament of their pecuniary arrears to Scotland, were kept separate, for the sake of decency; but it is certain, that they not only coincided in point of time, but bore upon and influenced each other. No man of candour will pretend to believe that the Parliament of England would ever have paid this considerable sum, unless to facilitate their obtaining possession of the King's person; and this sordid and base transaction, though the work exclusively of a mercenary army, stamped the whole nation of Scotland with infamy. In foreign countries they were upbraided with the shame of having made their unfortunate and confiding sovereign a hostage, whose liberty or surrender was to depend on their obtaining payment of a paltry sum of arrears; and the English nation reproached them with their greed and treachery, in the popular rhyme—

> "Traitor Scot
> Sold his King for a groat."

The Scottish army surrendered the person of Charles to the Commissioners for the English Parliament, on receiving security for their arrears of pay, and immediately evacuated Newcastle and marched for their own country. I am sorry to conclude the chapter with this mercenary and dishonourable transaction; but the limits of the work requires me to bring it thus to a close.

XLV

Regicide

1647-1649

OUR last chapter concluded with the dishonorable transaction by which the Scottish army surrendered Charles I. into the hands of the Parliament of England, on receiving security for a sum of arrears due to them by that body.

The Commissioners of Parliament, thus possessed of the King's person, conducted him as a state prisoner to Holmby House, in Northamptonshire, which had been assigned as his temporary residence; but from which a power different from theirs was soon about to withdraw him.

The Independents, as I have said, highly resented as a tyranny over their consciences the establishment of Presbytery, however temporary, or however mitigated, in the form of a national church; and were no less displeased that the army, whose ranks were chiefly filled with these military saints, as they called themselves, who were principally of the Independent persuasion, was, in the event of peace, which seemed close at hand, threatened either to be sent to Ireland or disbanded. The discontent among the English soldiery became general; they saw that the use made of the victories, which their valour had mainly contributed to gain, would be to reduce and disarm them, and send out of the kingdom such regiments as might be suffered to retain their arms and military character. And besides the loss of pay, profession, and importance, the sectaries had every reason to apprehend the imposition of the Presbyterian yoke, as they termed the discipline of that church. These mutinous dispositions were secretly encouraged by Cromwell, Ireton, and Fleetwood, officers of high rank and influence, to whom the Parliament had entrusted the charge of pacifying them. At length the army assumed the ominous appearance of a separate body in the state, whose affairs were managed by a council of superior officers, with assistance from a committee of persons, called Agitators, being two privates chosen from each company. These bold and unscrupulous men determined to gain possession of the person of the King, and to withdraw him from the power of the Parliament.

In pursuance of this resolution, Joyce, originally a tailor, now a cornet, and a furious agitator for the cause of the army, on the 4th of June 1647, appeared suddenly at midnight before Holmby House. The troops employed by the Commissioners to guard the King's person, being infected, it may be supposed, with the general feeling of the army, offered no resistance. Joyce, with little ceremony, intruded himself, armed with his pistols, into the King's sleeping apartment, and informed his Majesty that he must please to attend him. "Where is your commission?" said the unfortunate King. "Yonder it is," answered the rude soldier, pointing to his troop of fifty horse, which, by the early dawning, was seen drawn up in the courtyard of the place.—"It is written in legible characters," replied Charles; and without further remonstrance he prepared to attend the escort.

The King was conducted to Newmarket, and from thence to the palace of Hampton Court; and though in the hands of a body which had no lawful authority or responsible character, he was at first treated with more respect, and even kindness, than he had experienced either from the Scottish army, or from the English Commissioners. The officers distrusted, perhaps, the security of their own power, for they offered a pacification on easy terms. They asked an equal national representation, freely chosen; stipulated that the two Houses of Parliament should enjoy the command of the militia for fourteen years; and even agreed that the order of Bishops should be re-established, but without any temporal power or coercive jurisdiction. So far the terms were more moderate than, from such men and in such a moment, the King could have expected. But on one point the council of officers were rigidly determined; they insisted that seven of the adherents of Charles, chosen from those who had, with wisdom or with valour, best supported the sinking cause of Royalty, should be declared incapable of pardon. Charles was equally resolute in resisting this point; his conscience had suffered too deeply on the occasion of Strafford's execution, to which he had yielded in the beginning of these troubles, to permit him ever to be tempted again to abandon a friend.

In the meantime the Parliament was preparing to exert its authority in opposing and checking the unconstitutional power assumed by the army; and the city of London, chiefly composed of Presbyterians, showed a general disposition to stand by the Houses of Legislature. But when that formidable army drew near to London, both Parliament and citizens became intimidated; and the former expelled from their seats the leading Presbyterian members, and suffered the Independents to dictate to the dispirited remainder what measures they judged necessary. Prudence would, at this moment, have strongly recommended to Charles an instant agreement with the army. But the Presbyterians of England had not resigned hopes; and the whole kingdom of Scotland, incensed at the triumph of the sectaries, and the contumely offered to the Solemn League and Covenant, which had been stigmatised, in the House of Commons, as an almanac out of date, their commissioners made, in private, liberal offers to restore the King by force of arms. In listening to these proposals, Charles flattered himself that he should be able to hold the balance betwixt the Presbyterians and Independents; but he mistook the spirit of the latter party, from whom this private negotiation did not long remain a secret, and who were highly incensed by the discovery.

The Presbyterians had undertaken the war with professions of profound respect towards the King's person and dignity. They had always protested that they made war against the evil counsellors of the King, but not against his person; and their ordinances, while they were directed against the Malignants, as they termed the Royalists, ran in the King's own name, as well as in that of the two Houses of Parliament, by whose sole authority they were sent forth. The Independents, on the contrary, boldly declared themselves at war with *the Man Charles*, as the abuser of the regal power and the oppressor of the saints. Cromwell himself avouched such doctrines in open Parliament. He said it was childish to talk of there being no war with the King's person, when Charles appeared in armour, and at the head of his troops in open battle; and that he himself was so far from feeling any scruple on the subject, that he would fire his pistol at the King as readily as at any of his adherents, should he meet him in the fight.

After the discovery of the King's treaty with the Scottish Commissioners, Cromwell, admitting Charles's power of understanding and reasoning, denounced him as a man of the deepest dissimulation, who had broken faith, by professing an entire reliance on the wisdom of the Parliament, while, by a separate negotiation with the Scottish Commissioners, he was endeavoring to rekindle the flames of civil war between the sister kingdoms. After speaking to this purpose, Cromwell required, and by the now irresistible interest of the Independents he obtained, a declaration from the House, that the Parliament would receive no further applications from Charles, and make no addresses to him in future.

The unfortunate King, while in the power of this uncompromising faction, by whom his authority seemed to be suspended, if not abolished, ought to have been aware, that if he was to succeed in any accommodation with them at all, it could only be by accepting, without delay or hesitation, such terms as they were disposed to allow him. If he could have succeeded in gratifying their principal officers by promises of wealth, rank, and distinction, which were liberally tendered to them,[1] it is probable that their influence might have induced their followers to acquiesce in his restoration, especially if it afforded the means of disconcerting the plans of the Presbyterians. But Charles ought, at the same time, to have reflected, that any appearance of procrastination on his part must give rise to suspicions of his sincerity on the part of the military leaders; and that the Independents, having once adopted an idea that he was trifling with or deceiving them, had none of that sanctimonious respect for his title, or person, that could prevent his experiencing the utmost rigour.

The Independents and their military council, accordingly, distrusting the sincerity of Charles, and feeling every day the increase of their own power, began to think of establishing it on an entirely different basis from that of monarchy. They withdrew from the King the solemn marks of respect with which he had been hitherto indulged, treated

---

[1] "To Cromwell be offered the garter, a peerage, and the command of the army; and to Ireton the lieutenancy of Ireland. Nor did he think that they could reasonably, from their birth or former situation, entertain more ambitious views."—Russell's *Modern Europe.*

him with neglect and incivility, deprived him of his chaplains, confined his person more closely, doubled the guards upon him, and permitted none to have access to him, but such as possessed their confidence.

Alarmed at these ominous severities, Charles now resolved to escape by flight, and left Hampton Court accordingly. Unhappily, either misled by his attendant or by his own indiscretion, he took refuge in the Isle of Wight, where the governor of Carisbrook Castle [Colonel Hammond] was the friend of Cromwell, and a fierce Independent. Here the unfortunate monarch only fell into a captivity more solitary, more severe, and more comfortless, than any which he had yet experienced. He himself from his window pointed out to Sir Philip Warwick an old gray-headed domestic on the street, who brought in wood to the fire, and observed to him, that the conversation of that menial was the best that he bad been suffered to enjoy for months. There is even reason to think his life was aimed at, and that the King was privately encouraged to make an effort to escape from a window in the castle, while a person was placed in readiness to shoot him in the attempt.

The council of war renounced all further communication with Charles; the Parliament, now under the Independent influence, sent down Commissioners to treat, but with preliminary conditions harder than any yet offered to him. Two resources remained to him—the services of the disbanded loyalists, whom his faithful adherents might again summon to arms—but they were dispersed, disarmed, and heart-broken; or the assistance of the Scots—but they were distant and disunited. Yet Charles resolved to try his fortunes on this perilous cast, rather than treat with the Parliament, influenced as it was by the army.

The presence of two Scottish Commissioners who had accompanied those of the Parliament to Carisbrook, enabled Charles to execute a secret treaty with them, by which he agreed to confirm the Solemn League and Covenant, establish Presbytery, at least for a season, and concur in the extirpation of the sectaries. These articles, if they had been granted while Charles was at Newcastle, would have been sufficient to have prevented the surrender of his person by the Scottish army; but it was the King's unfortunate lot, on this, as on all former occasions, to delay his concessions until they came too late, and were liable to be considered insincere.

When this treaty (which was called the Engagement, because the Commissioners engaged to restore the King by force of arms) was presented to the Scottish Parliament, it was approved by the more moderate part of the Presbyterians, who were led by the Duke of Hamilton, together with his brother the Earl of Lanark, the Lord Chancellor Loudon, and the Earl of Lauderdale; this last being destined to make a remarkable figure in the next reign. But the majority of the Presbyterian clergy, supported by the more zealous among their hearers, declared that the concessions of the King were totally insufficient to engage Scotland in a new war, as affording no adequate cause for a quarrel with England. This party was headed by the Marquis of Argyle.

I may here mention respecting this nobleman, that after Montrose's army was disbanded, he had taken severe vengeance on the MacDonalds, and other clans who had assisted in the desolation of Argyleshire. Having the aid of David Lesley, with a body of regular troops, he reduced successively some forts into which Alaster MacDonald (Colkitto) had thrown garrisons, and uniformly put the prisoners to the sword. The MacDougals were almost exterminated in one indiscriminate slaughter, and the Lamonts were put to death in another act of massacre. Sir James Turner, an officer who served under Lesley, lays the blame of these inhumanities on a hard-hearted clergyman called Neaves. David Lesley was disgusted at it, and when, after some such sanguinary execution, he saw his chaplain with his shoes stained with blood, he asked him reproachfully, "Have you enough of it now, Master John?"

These atrocities, by whomever committed, must have been perpetrated in revenge of the suffering of Argyle and his clan; and to these must be added the death of old Colkitto, the father of Alaster MacDonald, likewise so called, who, being taken in one of these Highland forts, was tried by a jury convened by authority of George Campbell, the Sheriff Substitute of Argyle, from whose sentence we are told very few escaped, and was executed of course.

All these grounds of offence having been given to the Royalists, in a corner of the country where revenge was considered as a duty and a virtue, it is not extraordinary that Argyle should have objected most earnestly to the Engagement, which was an enterprise in which the King's interest was to be defended, with more slender precautions against the influence of the Malignants, or pure Royalists, than seemed consistent with the safety of those who had been most violent against them. Many of the best officers of the late army declined to serve with the new levies, until the Church of Scotland should approve the cause of quarrel. The Parliament, however, moved by compassion for their native monarch, and willing to obliterate the disgrace which attached to the surrender of the King at Newcastle, appointed an army to be levied, to act in his behalf. The kingdom was thus thrown into the utmost confusion between the various factions of the Engagers and their opponents. The civil magistrates, obeying the commands of the Parliament, ordered the subjects to assume arms under pain of temporal punishment; while the clergy, from the pulpit, denounced the vengeance of Heaven against those who obeyed the summons.

The Engagers prevailed so far as to raise a tumultuary and ill-disciplined army of about fifteen thousand men, which was commanded by the Duke of Hamilton. This ill-fated nobleman deserved the praise of being a moderate man during all the previous struggles; and, though loving his King, seems uniformly to have endeavoured to reconcile his administration with the rights and even the prejudices of his countrymen. But he had little decision of character, and less military skill. While the Scotch were preparing their succours slowly and with hesitation, the English cavaliers, impatient at the danger and captivity of the King, took arms. But their insurrections were so ill connected with each other, that they were crushed successively, save in two cases, where the insurgents made themselves masters of Colchester and Pembroke, in which towns they were instantly besieged.

Hamilton ought to have advanced with all speed to raise the siege of these places; but instead of this he loitered away more than forty days in Lancashire, until Cromwell came upon him near Warrington, where head and heart seem alike to have failed the unfortunate Duke. Without even an attempt at resistance, he abandoned his enterprise, and made a disorderly retreat, leaving his artillery and baggage. Baillie, with the infantry, being deserted by his general, surrendered to the enemy at Uttoxeter; and Hamilton himself, with the cavalry, took the same deplorable course. None escaped save a resolute body of men under the Earl of Callender, who broke through the enemy, and forced their way back to their own country.

The news of this disaster flew to Scotland. The refractory clergy took the merit of having prophesied the downfall of the Engagers, and stirred up the more zealous Presbyterians to take possession of the government. Argyle drew to arms in the Highlands, whilst the western peasantry assembling, and headed by their divines, repaired to Edinburgh. This insurrection, called the Whigamores' Raid, from the word was *whig, whig,* that is, *get on, get on,* which is used by the western peasants in driving their horses,—a name destined to become the distinction of a powerful party in British history.

The Earl of Lanark was at the head of some troops on the side of the Engagement, but, afraid of provoking the English, in whose hands his brother Hamilton was a prisoner, he made no material opposition to the Whigamores. Argyle became once more the head of the government. It was during this revolution that Cromwell advanced to the Borders, when, instead of finding any enemies to fight with, he was received by the victorious Whigamores as a friend and brother. Their horror at an army of sectaries had been entirely overpowered by their far more violent repugnance to unite with Cavaliers and Malignants in behalf of the King. Cromwell, on that occasion, held much intimate correspondence with Argyle, which made it generally believed that the Marquis, in their private conferences, acquiesced in the violent measures which were to be adopted by the successful general against the captive King, whose fate was now decided upon. The unfortunate Marquis always denied this, nor was the charge ever supported by any tangible evidence.

During these military and political transactions, Charles had been engaged in a new treaty with the English Parliament which was conducted at Newport in the Isle of Wight. It was set on foot in consequence of Cromwell's absence with his army, which restored the Parliament to some freedom of debate, and the Presbyterian members to a portion of their influence. If anything could have saved that unfortunate Prince, it might have been by accomplishing an agreement with the House of Commons, while Hamilton's army was yet entire, and before the insurrections of the Royalists had been entirely suppressed. But he delayed closing the treaty until the army returned, flushed with victory over the English Cavaliers and Scottish Engagers, and denouncing vengeance on the head of the King, whom they accused of being the sole author of the civil war, and liable to punishment as such. This became the language of the whole party. The pulpits rang with the exhortations of the military preachers, demanding that the King should be given over, as a public enemy, to a public trial.

It was in vain that Charles had at length, with lingering reluctance, yielded every request which the Parliament could demand of him. It was equally in vain that the Parliament had publicly declared that the concessions made by the King were sufficient to form the basis of a satisfactory peace. The army, stirred up by their ambitious officers and fanatic preachers, were resolved that Charles should be put to an open and ignominious death; and a sufficient force of soldiery was stationed in and around London to make resistance impossible, either on the part of the Presbyterians or the Royalists.

In order to secure a majority in the House of Commons, Colonel Pride, a man who had been a brewer, drew up his regiment at the doors of the House of Parliament, and in the streets adjacent, and secured the persons of upwards of forty members, who being supposed favourable to reconciliation with the King, were arrested and thrown into prison; above one hundred more were next day excluded. This act of violence was called Pride's Purge. At the same time the House of Lords was shut up. The remainder of the House of Commons, who alone were permitted to sit and vote, were all of the Independent party, and ready to do whatever should be required by the soldiers. This remnant of a Parliament, under the influence of the swords of their own soldiers, proceeded to nominate what was called a High Court of Justice for the trial of King Charles, charged with treason, as they termed it, against the people of England. The Court consisted of one hundred and thirty-three persons, chosen from the army, the Parliament, and from such of the citizens of London as were well affected to the proposed change of government from a kingdom to a commonwealth. Many of the judges nominated refused, notwithstanding, to act upon such a commission. Meantime, the great body of the English people beheld these strange preparations with grief and terror. The Scots, broken by the defeat of Hamilton and the success of the Whigamores' Raid, had no means of giving assistance.

Those who drove this procedure forward were of different classes, urged by different motives.

The higher officers of the army, Cromwell, Ireton, and others, seeing they could not retain their influence by concluding a treaty with Charles, had resolved to dethrone and put him to death, in order to establish a military government in their own persons. These men had a distinct aim, and they in some degree attained it. There were others among the Independent party, who thought they had offended the King so far beyond forgiveness, that his deposition and death were necessary for their own safety. The motives of these persons are also within the grasp of common apprehension.

But there were also among the Independent members of Parliament men of a nobler character. There were statesmen who had bewildered themselves with meditating upon theoretical schemes, till they had fancied the possibility of erecting a system of republican government on the foundation of the ancient monarchy of England. Such men, imposed on by a splendid dream of unattainable freedom, imagined that the violence put upon the Parliament by the soldiery, and the death of the King, when it should take place, were but necessary steps to the establishment of this visionary fabric of perfect liberty, like the pulling down of an old edifice to make room for a new building. After this fanciful class of politicians, came enthusiasts of another and coarser description, influenced by the wild harangues of their crack-brained preachers, who saw in Charles not only the head of the enemies with whom they had been contending for four years with various fortune, but also a wicked King of Amalekites, delivered up to them to be hewn in pieces in the name of Heaven. Such were the various motives which urged the actors in this extraordinary scene.

The pretext by which they coloured these proceedings was, that the King had levied war against his people, to extend over them an unlawful authority. If this had been true in point of fact, it was no ground of charge against Charles in point of law; for the constitution of England declares that the King can do no wrong, that is, cannot be made responsible for any wrong which he does. The vengeance of the laws, when such wrong is committed, is most justly directed against those wicked ministers by whom the culpable measure is contrived, and the agents by whom it is executed. The constitution of England wisely rests on the principle, that if the counsellors and instruments of a prince's pleasure are kept under wholesome terror of the laws, there is no risk of the monarch, in his own unassisted person, transgressing the limits of his authority.

But in fact the King had not taken arms against the Parliament to gain any *new* and extraordinary extent of power. It is no doubt true, that the Parliament, when summoned together, had many just grievances to complain of; but these were not, in general, innovations of Charles, but such exertions of power as had been customary in the four last reigns, when the crown of England had been freed from the restraint of the barons, without being sufficiently subjected to the control of the House of Commons, representing the people at large. They were, however, very bad precedents; and, since the King had shown a desire to follow them, the Parliament were most justly called upon to

resist the repetition of old encroachments upon their liberty. But before
the war broke out, the King had relinquished in favour of the Commons all they had demanded. The ultimate cause of quarrel was, which
party should have the command of the militia or public force of the
kingdom. This was a constitutional part of the King's prerogative; for
the executive power cannot be said to exist unless united with the
power of the sword. Violence on each side heightened the general want
of confidence. The Parliament, as has been before stated, garrisoned,
and held out the town of Hull against Charles; and the King infringed
the privileges of the Commons, by coming with an armed train to
arrest five of their members during the sitting of Parliament. So that the
war must be justly imputed to a train of long-protracted quarrels, in
which neither party could be termed wholly right, and still less entirely
wrong, but which created so much jealousy on both sides as could
scarcely terminate otherwise than in civil war.

The High Court of Justice, nevertheless, was opened, and the King
was brought to the bar on 19th January 1649. The soldiers, who
crowded the avenues, were taught to cry out for justice upon the royal
prisoner. When a bystander, affected by the contrast betwixt the King's
present and former condition, could not refrain from saying aloud,
"God save your Majesty," he was struck and beaten by the guards
around him—"A rude chastisement," said the King, "for so slight an
offence." Charles behaved throughout the whole of the trying scene
with the utmost dignity. He bore, without complaining, the reproaches
of murderer and tyrant, which were showered on him by the riotous
soldiery; and when a ruffian spit in his face, the captive monarch wiped
it off with his handkerchief, and only said, "Poor creatures! for half a
crown they would do the same to their father."

When the deed of accusation, stated to be in the name of the people
of England, was read, a voice from one of the galleries exclaimed, "not
the tenth part of them!" Again, as the names of the judges were called
over, when that of General Fairfax occurred, the same voice replied, "He
has more sense than to be here." Upon the officer who commanded the
guard ordering the musketeers to fire into the gallery from which the
interruption came, the speaker was discovered to be Lady Fairfax, wife
of Sir Thomas, the general of the forces, and a daughter of the noble
house of Vere, who in this manner declared her resentment at the extraordinary scene.

The King, when placed at the bar, looked around on the awful preparations for trial, on the bench, crowded with avowed enemies, and displaying, what was still more painful, the faces of one or two ungrateful friends, without losing his steady composure. When the public accuser began to speak, he touched him with his staff, and sternly admonished him to forbear. He afterwards displayed both talent and boldness in his own defence. He disowned the authority of the novel and incompetent court before which he was placed; reminded those who sat as his judges that he was their lawful King, answerable indeed to God for the use of his power, but declared by the constitution incapable of doing wrong. Even if the authority of the people were sufficient to place him before the bar, he denied that such authority had been obtained. The act of violence, he justly stated, was the deed, not of the English nation, but of a few daring men, who had violated, by military force, the freedom of the House of Commons, and altogether destroyed and abolished the House of Peers. He declared that he spoke not for himself, but for the sake of the laws and liberties of England.

Though repeatedly interrupted by Bradshaw, a lawyer, president of the pretended High Court of Justice, Charles pronounced his defence in a manly, yet temperate manner. Being then three times called on to answer to the charge, he as often declined the jurisdiction of the court. Sentence of death was then pronounced, to be executed in front of the royal palace, lately his own.

On the 30th January 1649 Charles I. was brought forth through one of the windows in front of the banqueting house at Whitehall, upon a large scaffold hung with black, and closely surrounded with guards. Two executioners in masks attended (one wearing a long gray beard), beside a block and cushion. Juxon, a bishop of the Church of England, assisted the King's devotions. As Charles laid his head on the block, he addressed to the bishop, emphatically, the word *remember*[1] and then gave the signal for the fatal stroke. One executioner struck

---

[1] "It being remarked that the King, the moment before he stretched out his neck to the executioner, had said to Juxon, with a very earnest accent, the single word REMEMBER! great mysteries were supposed to be concealed under that expression; and the generals vehemently insisted with the prelate that he should inform them of the King's meaning. Juxon told them, that the King, having frequently charged him to inculcate on his son the forgiveness of the murderers, had taken this opportunity, in the last moment of his life, when his commands, he supposed, would be regarded as sacred and inviolable, to reiterate that desire; and that his mild spirit thus terminated its present course by an act of benevolence towards his greatest enemies."—HUME.

the head from the shoulders at a single blow; the other held it up, and proclaimed it the head of a traitor. The soldiers shouted in triumph, but the multitude generally burst out into tears and lamentations.

This tragic spectacle was far from accomplishing the purpose intended by those who had designed it. On the contrary, the King's serene and religious behaviour at his trial and execution excited the sympathy and sorrow of many who had been his enemies when in power; the injustice and brutality, which he bore with so much dignity, overpowered the remembrance of the errors of which be had been guilty; and the almost universal sense of the iniquity of his sentence, was a principal cause of the subsequent restoration of his family to the throne.

XLVI

Scotland's Own

1649-1654

THE death of Charles I. was nowhere more deeply resented than in his native country of Scotland; and the national pride of the Scots was the more hurt, that they could not but be conscious that the surrender of his person by their army at Newcastle was the event which contributed immediately to place him in the hands of his enemies.

The government, since the Whigamores' Raid, had continued in the hands of Argyle and the more rigid Presbyterians; but even they, no friends to the House of Stewart, were bound by the Covenant, which was their rule in all things, to acknowledge the hereditary descent of their ancient Kings, and call to the throne Charles, the eldest son of the deceased monarch, provided he would consent to unite with his subjects in taking the Solemn League and Covenant, for the support of Presbytery, and the putting down of all other forms of religion. The Scottish Parliament met, and resolved accordingly to proclaim Charles II. their lawful sovereign; but, at the same time, not to admit him to the actual power as such, until he should give security for the religion, unity, and peace of the kingdoms. Commissioners were sent to wait upon Charles, who had retired to the Continent, in order to offer him the throne of Scotland on these terms.

The young Prince had already around him counsellors of a different character. The celebrated Marquis of Montrose, and other Scottish nobles, few in number, but animated by their leader's courage and zeal, advised him to reject the proposal of the Presbyterians to recall him to the regal dignity on such conditions, and offered their swords and lives to place him on the throne by force of arms.

It appears that Charles II., who never had any deep sense of integrity, was willing to treat with both of these parties at one and the same time; and that he granted a commission to the Marquis to attempt a descent on Scotland, taking the chance of what might be accomplished by his far-famed fortune and dauntless enterprise, while he kept a negotiation afloat with the Presbyterian commissioners, in case of Montrose's failure.

That intrepid but rash enthusiast embarked at Hamburgh, with some arms and treasure, supplied by the northern courts of Europe. His fame drew around him a few of the emigrant Royalists, chiefly Scottish, and be recruited about six hundred German mercenaries. His first descent was on the Orkney islands, where he forced to arms a few hundreds of unwarlike fishermen. He next disembarked on the mainland; but the natives fled from him, remembering the former excesses of his army. Strachan, an officer under Lesley, came upon the Marquis by surprise, near a pass called Invercharron, on the confines of Ross-shire. The Orkney men made but little resistance; the Germans retired to a wood, and there surrendered; the few Scottish companions of Montrose fought bravely, but in vain. Many gallant cavaliers were made prisoners. Montrose, when the day was irretrievably lost, threw off his cloak bearing the star, and afterwards changed clothes with an ordinary Highland kern, that he might endeavour to effect his escape, and swam across the river Kyle. Exhausted with fatigue and hunger, he was at length taken by a Ross-shire chief, MacLeod of Assint, who happened to be out with a party of his men in arms. The Marquis discovered himself to this man, thinking himself secure of favour, since Assint had been once his own follower. But, tempted by a reward of four hundred bolls of meal, this wretched chief delivered his old commander into the unfriendly hands of David Lesley.[1]

The Covenanters, when he who had so often made them tremble

---

[1] Assint was afterwards tried at Edinburgh, for his treachery, but by means of bribery and the corrupt influence of the times, he escaped punishment.—WISHART.

was at length delivered into their hands, celebrated their victory with all the exultation of mean, timid, and sullen spirits, suddenly released from apprehension of imminent danger. Montrose was dragged in a sort of triumph from town to town, in the mean garb in which he had disguised himself for flight. To the honour of the town of Dundee, which, you will recollect, had been partly plundered and partly burnt by Montrose's forces, during his eventful progress in 1645, the citizens of that town were the first who supplied their fallen foe with clothes befitting his rank, with money, and with necessaries. The Marquis himself must have felt this as a severe rebuke for the wasteful mode in which he had carried on his warfare; and it was a still more piercing reproach to the unworthy victors, who now triumphed over a heroic enemy in the same manner as they would have done over a detected felon.

While Montrose was confined in the house of the Laird of Grange, in Fifeshire, he had almost made his escape through the bold stratagem of the Laird's wife, a descendant of the house of Somerville. This lady's address had drenched the guards with liquor; and the Marquis, disguised in female attire, with which she had furnished him, had already passed the sleeping sentinels, when he was challenged and stopped by a half-drunken soldier, who had been rambling about without any duty or purpose. The alarm being given, he was again secured, and the lady's plot was of no avail. She escaped punishment only by her husband's connection with the ruling party.

Before Montrose reached Edinburgh, he had been condemned by the Parliament to the death of a traitor. The sentence was pronounced, without further trial, upon an act of attainder passed whilst he was plundering Argyle in the winter of 1644; and it was studiously aggravated by every species of infamy.

The Marquis was, according to the special order of Parliament, met at the gates by the magistrates, attended by the common hangman, who was clad for the time in his own livery. He was appointed, as the most infamous mode of execution, to be hanged on a gibbet thirty feet high, his head to be fixed on the tolbooth or prison of Edinburgh, his body to be quartered, and his limbs to be placed over the gates of the principal towns of Scotland. According to the sentence, he was conducted to jail on a cart, whereon was fixed a high bench, on which he was placed, bound and bareheaded, the horse led by the executioner, wearing his bonnet, and the noble prisoner exposed to the scorn of the

people, who were expected to hoot and revile him. But the rabble, who
came out with the rudest purposes, relented when they saw the dignity
of his bearing; and silence, accompanied by the sighs and tears of the
crowd, attended the progress, which his enemies had designed should
excite other emotions. The only observation he made was, that "the
ceremonial of his entrance had been somewhat fatiguing and tedious."

He was next brought before the Parliament to hear the terms of his
sentence, where he appeared with the same manly indifference. He
gazed around on his assembled enemies with as much composure as
the most unconcerned spectator; heard Loudon, the chancellor,
upbraid him, in a long and violent declamation, with the breach of
both the first and second Covenant; with his cruel wars at the head of
the savage Irish and Highlandmen; and with the murders, treasons,
and conflagrations, which they had occasioned. When the chancellor
had finished, Montrose with difficulty obtained permission to reply.

He told the Parliament, with his usual boldness, that if he
appeared before them uncovered, and addressed them with respect, it
was only because the King had acknowledged their assembly, by entering into a treaty with them. He admitted he had taken the first, or
National Covenant, and had acted upon it so long as it was confined to
its proper purposes, but had dissented from and opposed those who
had used it as a pretext for assailing the Royal authority. "The second,
or Solemn League and Covenant," he said, "he had never taken, and
was therefore in no respect bound by it. He had made war by the King's
express commission; and although it was impossible, in the course of
hostilities, absolutely to prevent acts of military violence, he had always
disowned and punished such irregularities. He had never," he said,
"spilt the blood of a prisoner, even in retaliation of the cold-blooded
murder of his officers and friends—nay, he had spared the lives of
thousands in the very shock of battle. His last undertaking," he continued, "was carried on at the express command of Charles II., whom
they had proclaimed their sovereign, and with whom they were treat-
ing as such. Therefore, he desired to be used by them as a man and a
Christian, to whom many of them had been indebted for life and property, when the fate of war had placed both in his power. He required
them, in conclusion, to proceed with him according to the laws of
nature and nations, but especially according to those of Scotland, as
they themselves would expect to be judged when they stood at the bar
of Almighty God."

The sentence already mentioned was then read to the undaunted prisoner, on which he observed, he was more honoured in having his head set on the prison, for the cause in which he died, than he would have been had they decreed a golden statue to be erected to him in the market-place, or in having his picture in the King's bedchamber. As to the distribution of his limbs, he said he wished he had flesh enough to send some to each city of Europe, in memory of the cause in which he died. He spent the night in reducing these ideas into poetry.[1]

Early on the morning of the next day he was awakened by the drums and trumpets calling out the guards, by orders of Parliament, to attend on his execution. "Alas!" he said, "I have given these good folks much trouble while alive, and do I continue to be a terror to them on the day I am to die?"

The clergy importuned him, urging repentance of his sins, and offering, on his expressing such compunction, to relieve him from the sentence of excommunication, under which he laboured. He calmly replied, that though the excommunication had been rashly pronounced, yet it gave him pain, and he desired to be freed from it, if a relaxation could be obtained, by expressing penitence for his offences as a man; but that he had committed none in his duty to his prince and country, and, therefore, had none to acknowledge or repent of.

Johnstone of Warriston, an eminent Covenanter, intruded himself on the noble prisoner, while he was combing the long curled hair which he wore as a cavalier. Warriston, a gloomy fanatic, hinted as if it were but an idle employment at so solemn a time. "I will arrange my head as I please to-day, while it is still my own," answered Montrose; "to-morrow it will be yours, and you may deal with it as you list."

The Marquis walked on foot, from the prison to the Grass-market, the common place of execution for the basest felons, where a gibbet of

---

[1] The following lines were written with the point of a diamond upon the window of his prison:—

> "Let them bestow on every airth* a limb,
> Then open all my veins, that I may swim
> To thee, my Maker, in that crimson lake;
> Then place my parboil'd head upon a stake;
> Scatter my ashes, strew them in the air.
> Lord! since thou knowest where all these atoms are,
> I'm hopeful thou't recover once my dust,
> And confident thou't raise me with the just."
>   *Airt-point of the compass.

extraordinary height, with a scaffold covered with black cloth, was erected. Here he was again pressed by the Presbyterian clergy to own his guilt. Their cruel and illiberal officiousness could not disturb the serenity of his temper. To exaggerate the infamy of his punishment, or rather to show the mean spite of his enemies, a book, containing the printed history of his exploits, was hung around his neck by the hangman. This insult, likewise, he treated with contempt, saying, he accounted such a record of his services to his prince as a symbol equally honourable with the badge of the Garter, which the King had bestowed on him. In all other particulars, Montrose bore himself with the same calm dignity, and finally submitted to execution with such resolved courage, that many, even of his bitterest enemies, wept on the occasion. He suffered on the 21st of May 1650.

Argyle, the mortal foe of Montrose, exulted in private over the death of his enemy, but abstained from appearing in Parliament when he was condemned, and from witnessing his execution. He is even said to have shed tears when he heard the scene rehearsed. His son, Lord Lorn, was less scrupulous; he looked on his feudal enemy's last moments, and even watched the blows of the executioner's axe, while he dissevered the head from the body. His cruelty was requited in the subsequent reign; and indeed Heaven soon after made manifest the folly, as well as guilt, which destroyed this celebrated commander, at a time when approaching war might have rendered his talents invaluable to his country.

Other noble Scottish blood was spilt at the same time, both at home and in England. The Marquis of Huntly, who had always acted for the King, though he had injured his affairs by his hesitation to co-operate with Montrose, was beheaded at Edinburgh; and Urry, who had been sometimes the enemy, sometimes the follower of Montrose, was executed with others of the Marquis's principal followers.

The unfortunate Duke of Hamilton, a man of a gentle but indecisive character, was taken, as I have told you, in his attempt to invade England and deliver the King, whom he seems to have served with fidelity, though he fell under his suspicion, and even suffered a long imprisonment by the Royal order. While he was confined at Windsor, Charles, previous to his trial, was brought there by the soldiers. The dethroned King was permitted a momentary interview with the subject, who had lost fortune and liberty in his cause. Hamilton burst into tears, and flung himself at the King's feet, exclaiming, "My dear master!"—"I have been a *dear* master to you indeed," said Charles, kindly raising him. After the execution of the King, Hamilton, with the Earl of Holland, Lord Capel, and others, who had promoted the rising of the Royalists on different points, were condemned to be beheaded. A stout old cavalier, Sir John Owen, was one of the number. When the sentence was pronounced, he exclaimed it was a great honour to a poor Welsh knight to be beheaded with so many nobles, adding, with an oath, "I thought they would have hanged me." This gallant old man's life was spared, when his companions in misfortune were executed.

While these bloody scenes were proceeding, the Commissioners of the Scottish Parliament continued to carry on the treaty with Charles II. He had nearly broken it off, when Montrose's execution was reported to him; but a sense of his own duplicity in maintaining a treaty with the Parliament, while he gave Montrose a commission to invade and make war on them, smothered his complaints on the subject. At length Charles, seeing no other resource, agreed to accept the crown of Scotland on the terms offered, which were those of the most absolute compliance with the will of the Scottish Parliament in civil affairs, and with the pleasure of the General Assembly of the Kirk in ecclesiastical concerns. Above all, the young King promised to take upon him the obligations of the Solemn League and Covenant, and to further them by every means in his power. On these conditions the treaty was concluded; Charles sailed from Holland, and arriving on the coast of Scotland, landed near the mouth of the river Spey, and advanced to Stirling.

Scotland was at this time divided into three parties, highly inimical to each other. There was, FIRST, the rigid Presbyterians, of whom Argyle was the leader. This was the faction which had, since the Whigamores' Raid, been in possession of the supreme power of government, and with its leaders the King had made the treaty in Holland. SECONDLY, the moderate Presbyterians, called the Engagers, who had joined with Hamilton in his incursion into England. These were headed by the Earl of Lanark, who succeeded to the dukedom of Hamilton on the execution of his brother; by Lauderdale, a man of very considerable talents; Dunfermline and others. THIRDLY, there was the party of the Absolute Loyalists, friends and followers of Montrose; such as the Marquis of Huntly, Lord Ogilvy, a few other nobles and gentlemen, and some Highland chiefs, too ignorant and too remotely situated to have any influence in state affairs.

As all these three parties acknowledged, with more or less warmth, the sovereignty of King Charles, it might have seemed no very difficult matter to have united them in the same patriotic purpose of maintaining the national independence of the kingdom. But successful resistance to the English was a task to which the high Presbyterians, being the ruling party, thought themselves perfectly competent. Indeed they entertained the most presumptuous confidence in their own strength, and their clergy assured them, that so far from the aid of either Engagers or Malignants being profitable to them in the common defence, the presence of any such profane assistants would draw down the curse of Heaven on the cause, which, if trusted to the hands of true Covenanters only, could not fail to prosper.

Argyle, therefore, and his friends, received the young King with all the outward marks of profound respect. But they took care to give him his own will in no one particular. They excluded from attendance on his person all his English adherents, suspicious of their attachment to Prelacy and malignant opinions. The ministers beset him with exhortations and sermons of immoderate length, introduced on all occasions, and exhausting the patience of a young prince, whose strong sense of the ridiculous, and impatience of serious subjects, led him to receive with heartfelt contempt and disgust the homely eloquence of the long-winded orators. The preachers also gave him offence, by choosing frequently for their themes the sins of his father, the idolatry of his mother, who was a Catholic, and what they frankly termed his own ill-disguised disposition to malignity. They numbered up the judgments which, they affirmed, these sins had brought on his father's house, and they prayed that they might not be followed by similar punishments upon Charles himself. These ill-timed and ill-judged admonitions were so often repeated, as to impress on the young King's mind a feeling of dislike and disgust, with which he remembered the Presbyterian preachers and their doctrines as long as he lived.

Sometimes their fanaticism and want of judgment led to ridiculous scenes. It is said, that on one occasion a devout lady, who lived opposite to the Royal lodgings, saw from her window the young King engaged in a game at cards, or some other frivolous amusement, which the rigour of the Covenanters denounced as sinful. The lady communicated this important discovery to her minister, and it reached the ears of the Commission of the Kirk, who named a venerable member of their body to rebuke the monarch personally for this act of backsliding.

The clergyman to whom this delicate commission was entrusted was a shrewd old man, who saw no great wisdom in the proceedings of his brethren, but executed their commands with courtly dexterity, and summed up his ghostly admonition with a request, that when his Majesty indulged in similar recreations, he would be pleased to take the precaution of shutting the windows. The King laughed, and was glad to escape so well from the apprehended lecture. But events were fast approaching which had no jesting aspect.

England, to which you must now turn your attention, had totally changed its outward constitution since the death of the King. Cromwell, who, using the victorious army as his tools, was already in the real possession of the supreme power, had still more tasks than one to accomplish before he dared venture to assume the external appearance of it. He suffered, therefore, the diminished and mutilated House of Commons to exist for a season, during which the philosophical Republicans of the party passed resolutions that monarchy should never be again established in England; that the power of the Executive Government should be lodged in a Council of State; and that the House of Lords should be abolished.

Meantime, Cromwell led in person a part of his victorious army to Ireland, which had been the scene of more frightful disorders than England, or even Scotland. These had begun by the Catholic inhabitants rising upon the Protestants, and murdering many thousands of them in what is termed the Irish Massacre. This had been followed by a general war between the opposite parties in religion, but at length the address of the Duke of Ormond, as devoted a loyalist as Montrose, contrived to engage a large portion of the Catholics on the side of Charles; and Ireland became the place of refuge to all the Cavaliers, or remains of the Royal party, who began to assume a formidable appearance in that island. The arrival of Cromwell suddenly changed this gleam of fortune into cloud and storm. Wherever this fated general appeared he was victorious; and in Ireland, in order perhaps to strike terror into a fierce people (for Oliver Cromwell was not bloodthirsty by disposition), he made dreadful execution among the vanquished, particularly at the storming of the town of Drogheda, where his troops spared neither sex nor age. He now returned to England, with even greater terror attached to his name than before.

The new Commonwealth of England had no intention that the son of the King whom they had put to death should be suffered to establish himself quietly in the sister kingdom of Scotland, and enjoy the power, when opportunity offered, of again calling to arms his numerous adherents in England, and disturbing, or perhaps destroying, their new-modelled republic. They were resolved to prevent this danger by making war on Scotland, while still weakened by her domestic dissensions; and compelling her to adopt the constitution of a republic, and to become confederated with their own. This proposal was of course haughtily rejected by the Scots, as it implied a renunciation at once of king and kirk, and a total alteration of the Scottish Constitution in civil and ecclesiastical government. The ruling parties of both nations, therefore, prepared for the contest.

The rigid Presbyterians in Scotland showed now a double anxiety to exclude from their army all, however otherwise well qualified to assist in such a crisis, whom they regarded as suspicious, whether as absolute malignants, or as approaching nearer to their own doctrines, by professing only a moderate and tolerant attachment to Presbytery.

Yet even without the assistance of these excluded parties, the Convention of Estates assembled a fine army, full of men enthusiastic in the cause in which they were about to fight; and feeling all the impulse which could be given by the rude eloquence of their favourite ministers. Unfortunately the preachers were not disposed to limit themselves to the task of animating the courage of the soldiers; but were so presumptuous as to interfere with and control the plans of the general, and movements of the army.

The army of England, consisting almost entirely of Independents, amongst whom any man who chose might assume the office of a clergyman, resembled the Presbyterian troops of Scotland; for both armies professed to appeal to Heaven for the justice of their cause, and both resounded with psalms, prayers, exhortations, and religious exercises, to confirm the faith, and animate the zeal of the soldiers. Both likewise used the same language in their proclamations against each other, and it was such as implied a war rather on account of religion than of temporal interests. The Scottish proclamations declared the army commanded by Cromwell to be a union of the most perverse heretical sectaries, of every different persuasion, agreeing in nothing, saving their desire to effect the ruin of the unity and discipline of the Christian Church, and the destruction of the Covenant, to which most of their leaders had sworn fidelity. The army of Cromwell replied to them in the same style. They declared that they valued the Christian Church ten thousand times more than their own lives. They protested that they were not only a rod of iron to dash asunder the common enemies, but a hedge (though unworthy) about the divine vineyard. As for the Covenant, they protested that, were it not for making it an object of idolatry, they would be content, if called upon to encounter the Scots in this quarrel, to place that national engagement on the point of their pikes, and let God himself judge whether they or their opponents had best observed its obligations.

Although the contending nations thus nearly resembled each other in their ideas and language, there was betwixt the Scottish and English soldiers one difference, and it proved a material one. In the English army the officers insisted upon being preachers, and though their doctrine was wild enough, their ignorance of theology had no effect on military events. But with the Scots, the Presbyterian clergy were unhappily seized with the opposite rage of acting as officers and generals, and their skill in their own profession of divinity could not redeem the errors which they committed in the art of war.

Fairfax having declined the command of the English army, his conscience (for he was a Presbyterian) not permitting him to engage in the war, Cromwell accepted with joy the supreme military authority, and prepared for the invasion of Scotland.

The wars between the sister kingdoms seemed now about to be rekindled, after the interval of two-thirds of a century; and notwithstanding the greatly superior power of England, there was no room for absolute confidence in her ultimate success. The Scots, though divided into parties, so far as church government was concerned, were unanimous in acknowledging the right of King Charles, whereas the English were far from making common cause against his claims. On the contrary, if the stern army of sectaries, now about to take the field, should sustain any great disaster, the Cavaliers of England, with great part of the Presbyterians in that country, were alike disposed to put the King once more at the head of the government; so that the fate not of Scotland alone, but of England also, was committed to the event of the present war.

Neither were the armies and generals opposed to each other unworthy of the struggle. If the army of Cromwell consisted of veteran soldiers, inured to constant victory, that of Scotland was fresh, numerous, and masters of their own strong country, which was the destined scene of action. If Cromwell had defeated the most celebrated generals

of the Cavaliers, David Lesley, the effective commander-in-chief in
Scotland, had been victor over Montrose, more renowned perhaps
than any of them. If Cromwell was a general of the most decisive character, celebrated for the battles which he had won, Lesley was, by early
education, a trained soldier, more skillful than his antagonist in taking
positions, defending passes, and all the previous arrangements of a
campaign. With these advantages on the different sides, the eventful
struggle commenced.

Early in the summer of 1650 Cromwell invaded Scotland at the
head of his veteran and well-disciplined troops. But, on marching
through Berwickshire and East Lothian, he found that the country was
abandoned by the population, and stripped of everything which could
supply the hostile army. Nothing was to be seen save old spectre-look-
ing women, clothed in white flannel, who told the English officers that
all the men had taken arms, under command of the barons.

Subsisting chiefly on the provisions supplied by a fleet, which, sail-
ing along the coast, accompanied his movements, the English general
approached the capital, where Lesley had fixed his headquarters. The
right wing of the Scottish army rested upon the high grounds at the
rise of the mountain called Arthur's Seat, and the left wing was posted
at Leith; while the high bank, formerly called Leith Walk, made a part
of his lines, which, defended by a numerous artillery, completely protected the metropolis. Cromwell skirmished with the Scottish
advanced posts near to Restalrig, but his cuirassiers were so warmly
encountered that they gained no advantage, and their general was
obliged to withdraw to Musselburgh. His next effort was made from
the westward.

The English army made a circuit from the coast, proceeding inland
to Colinton, Redhall, and other places near to the eastern extremity of
the Pentland hills, from which Cromwell hoped to advance on Edinburgh. But Lesley was immediately on his guard. He left his position
betwixt Edinburgh and Leith, and took up one which covered the city
to the westward, and was protected by the Water of Leith, and the several cuts, drains, and mill-leads, at Saughton, Coltbridge, and the
houses and villages in that quarter. Here Cromwell again found the
Scots in order of battle, and again was obliged to withdraw after a distant cannonade.

The necessity of returning to the neighbourhood of his fleet
obliged Cromwell to march back to his encampment at Musselburgh.

Nor was he permitted to remain there in quiet. At the dead of night a strong body of cavalry, called the regiment of the Kirk, well armed at all points, broke into the English lines, with loud cries of "God and the Kirk! all is ours!" It was with some difficulty that Cromwell rallied his soldiers upon this sudden alarm, in which he sustained considerable loss, though the assailants were finally compelled to retreat.

The situation of the English army now became critical; their provisions were nearly exhausted, the communication with the fleet grew daily more precarious, while Lesley, with the same prudence which had hitherto guided his defence, baffled all the schemes of the English leader, without exposing his army to the risk of a general action; until Cromwell, fairly outgeneralled by the address of his enemy, was compelled to retire towards England.

Lesley, on his part, left his encampment without delay, for the purpose of intercepting the retreat of the English. Moving by a shorter line than Cromwell, who was obliged to keep the coast, he took possession with his army of the skirts of Lammermoor, a ridge of hills terminating on the sea near the town of Dunbar, abounding with difficult passes, all of which he occupied strongly. Here he proposed to await the attack of the English, with every chance, nay, almost with the certainty, of gaining a great and decisive victory.

Cromwell was reduced to much perplexity. To force his way, it was necessary to attack a tremendous pass called Cockburn's path, where, according to Cromwell's own description, one man might do more to defend than twelve to make way. And if he engaged in this desperate enterprise, he was liable to be assaulted by the numerous forces of Lesley in flank and rear. He saw all the danger, and entertained thoughts of embarking his foot on board of his ships, and cutting his own way to England as he best could, at the head of his cavalry.

At this moment, the interference of the Presbyterian preachers, and the influence which they possessed over the Scottish army and its general, ruined this fair promise of success. In spite of all the prudent remonstrances of Lesley, they insisted that the Scottish army should be led from their strong position, to attack the English upon equal ground. This, in the language of Scripture, they called going down against the Philistines at Gilgal.

Cromwell had slept at the Duke of Roxburghe's house, called Broxmouth, half a mile east of Dunbar, and his army was stationed in the park there, when he received news that the Scots were leaving their fastnesses, and about to hazard a battle on the level plain. He exclaimed, "That God had delivered them into his hands;" and calling for his horse, placed himself at the head of his troops. Coming to the head of a regiment of Lancashire men, he found one of their officers, while they were in the act of marching to battle, in a fit of sudden enthusiasm holding forth or preaching to the men. Cromwell also listened, and seemed affected by his discourse. At this moment the sun showed his broad orb on the level surface of the sea, which is close to the scene of action. "Let the Lord arise," he said, "and let his enemies be scattered;" and presently after, looking upon the field where the battle had now commenced, he added, "I profess they flee."

Cromwell's hopes did not deceive him. The hastily raised Scottish levies, thus presumptuously opposed to the veteran soldiers of the English commander, proved unequal to stand the shock. Two regiments fought bravely and were almost all cut off; but the greater part of Lesley's army fell into confusion without much resistance. Great slaughter ensued, and many prisoners were made, whom the cruelty of the English government destined to a fate hitherto unknown in Christian warfare. They transported to the English settlements in America those unfortunate captives, subjects of an independent kingdom, who bore arms by order of their own lawful government, and there sold them for slaves.

The decisive defeat at Dunbar opened the whole of the south of Scotland to Cromwell. The Independents found a few friends and brother sectaries among the gentry, who had been hitherto deterred, by the fear of the Presbyterians, from making their opinions public. Almost all the strong places on the south side of the Forth were won by the arms of the English or yielded by the timidity of their defenders. Edinburgh Castle was surrendered, not without suspicion of gross treachery; and Tantallon, Hume, Roslin, and Borthwick, with other fortresses, fell into their hands.

Internal dissension added to the calamitous state of Scotland. The Committee of Estates, with the King, and the remainder of Lesley's army, retreated to Stirling, where they still hoped to make a stand, by defending the passes of the Forth. A Parliament, held at Perth, was in this extremity disposed to relax in the extreme rigour of its exclusive doctrines, and to admit into the army, which it laboured to reinforce, such of the moderate Presbyterians, or Engagers, and even of the Royalists and Malignants, as were inclined to make a formal confession of their former errors. The Royalists readily enough complied with this requisition; but as their pretended repentance was generally regarded as a mere farce, submitted to that they might obtain leave to bear arms for the King, the stricter Presbyterians looked upon this compromise with Malignants as a sinful seeking for help from Egypt. The Presbyterians of the western counties, in particular, carried this opinion so far, as to think this period of national distress an auspicious time for disclaiming the King's interest and title. Refusing to allow that the victory of Dunbar was owing to the military skill of Cromwell and the disciplined valour of his troops, they set it down as a chastisement justly inflicted on the Scottish nation for espousing the Royal cause. Under this separate banner there assembled an army of about four thousand men, commanded by Kerr and Strachan. They were resolved, at the same time, to oppose the English invasion, and to fight with the King's forces, and thus embroil the kingdom in a threefold war. The leaders of this third party, who were called Remonstrators, made a smart attack on a large body of English troops, stationed in Hamilton under General Lambert, and were at first successful; but falling into disorder, owing to their very success, they were ultimately defeated. Kerr, one of their leaders, was wounded, and made prisoner; and Strachan soon afterwards revolted, and joined the English army.

Cromwell, in the meanwhile, made the fairest promises to all who would listen to him, and laboured, not altogether in vain, to impress the rigid Presbyterian party with a belief, that they had better join with the Independents, although disallowing of church-government, and thus obtain peace and a close alliance with England, than adhere to the cause of the King, who, with his father's house, had, he said, been so long the troublers of Israel. And here I may interrupt the course of public events, to tell you an anecdote not generally known, but curious as illustrating the character of Cromwell.

Shortly after the battle of Dunbar, Cromwell visited Glasgow; and on Sunday attended the Presbyterian service in the principal church of that city. The preacher, a rigid Presbyterian, was nothing intimidated by the presence of the English general; but entering freely upon state affairs, which were then a common topic in the pulpit, he preached boldly on the errors and heresies of the Independent sectaries, insisted on the duty of resisting their doctrines, and even spoke with little respect of the person of Cromwell himself. An officer who sat behind Cromwell whispered something in his ear more than once, and the general as often seemed to impose silence upon him. The curiosity of the congregation was strongly excited. At length the service was ended, and Cromwell was in the act of leaving the church, when he cast his eyes on one Wilson, a mechanic who had long resided at Glasgow, and called on him by name. The man no sooner saw the general take notice of him than he ran away. Cromwell directed that he should be followed and brought before him, but without injury. At the same time he sent a civil message to the clergyman who had preached, desiring to see him at his quarters. These things augmented the curiosity of the town's people; and when they saw Wilson led as prisoner to the general's apartments, many remained about the door, watching the result. Wilson soon returned, and joyfully showed his acquaintances some money which the English general had given him to drink his health. His business with Cromwell was easily explained. This man had been son of a footman who had attended James VI. to England. By some accident Wilson had served his apprenticeship to a shoemaker in the same town where Cromwell's father lived, had often played with Master Oliver while they were both children, and had obliged him by making balls and other playthings for him. When Wilson saw that his old companion recognised him, he ran away, because, recollecting his father had been a servant of the Royal family, he thought the general, who was known to have brought the late King to the block, might nourish ill-will against all who were connected with him. But Cromwell had received him kindly, spoken of their childish acquaintance, and gave him some money. The familiarity with which he seemed to treat him encouraged Wilson to ask his former friend what it was that passed betwixt the officer and him, when the preacher was thundering from the pulpit against the sectaries and their general. "He called the clergyman an insolent rascal," said Cromwell, not unwilling, perhaps, that his forbearance should be made public, "and asked my leave to pull him out of the pulpit by the ears; and I commanded him to sit still, telling him the minister was one fool, and he another." This anecdote serves to show Cromwell's recollection of persons and faces. He next gave audience to the preacher, and used arguments with him which did not reach the public; but were so convincing, that the minister pronounced a second discourse in the evening, in a tone much mitigated towards Independency and its professors.

While the south of Scotland was overawed, and the Western Remonstrators were dispersed by Cromwell, the Scottish Parliament, though retired beyond the Forth, still maintained a show of decided opposition. They resolved upon the coronation of Charles, a ceremony hitherto deferred, but which they determined now to perform, as a solemn pledge of their resolution to support the constitution and religion of Scotland to the last.

But the melancholy solemnity had been nearly prevented by the absence of the principal personage. Charles, disgusted with the invectives of the Presbyterian clergy, and perhaps remembering the fate of his father at Newcastle, formed a hasty purpose of flying from the Presbyterian camp. He had not been sufficiently aware of the weakness of the Royalists, who recommended this wild step, and he actually went off to the hills. But he found only a few Highlanders at Clova,[1] without the appearance of an army, which he had promised himself, and was easily induced to return to the camp with a party who had been despatched in pursuit of him.

This excursion, which was called the *Start,* did not greatly tend to increase confidence betwixt the young King and his Presbyterian counsellors. The ceremony of the coronation was performed with such solemnities as the time admitted, but mingled with circumstances which must have been highly disgusting to Charles. The confirmation of the Covenant was introduced as an essential part of the solemnity; and the coronation was preceded by a national fast and humiliation, expressly held on account of the sins of the Royal family. A suspected hand, that of the Marquis of Argyle, placed an insecure crown on the head of the son,[2] whose father he had been one of the principal instruments in dethroning.

These were bad omens. But, on the other hand, the King enjoyed more liberty than before; most of the Engagers had resumed their seats in Parliament; and many Royalist officers were received into the army.

---

[1] The village of Clova is situated in the northern extremity of Forfarshire, near to the source of the South Esk, in a glen of the Grampians, along which that river flows in a south-eastward direction for upwards of ten miles, issuing at length into a more open course in the romantic vicinity of Cortachy Castle, a seat of the Earl of Airlie.

[2] "Upon that occasion, the King, clad in a prince's robe walked in procession from the hall of the palace to the church, the spurs, sword of state, sceptre, and crown being carried before him by the principal nobility. It was remarkable, that upon this occasion the crown was borne by the unhappy Marquis of Argyle, who was put to death in no very legal manner immediately after the Restoration, using upon the scaffold these remarkable words, 'I placed the crown on the King's head, and in reward he brings mine to the block.'"—See *History of the Regalia of Scotland.*

Determined at this time not to be tempted to a disadvantageous battle, the King, who assumed the command of the army in person, took up a line in front of Stirling, having in his front the river of Carron. Cromwell approached, but could neither with prudence attack the Scots in their lines, nor find means of inducing them to hazard a battle, unless on great advantage. After the armies had confronted each other for more than a month, Cromwell despatched Colonel Overton into Fife, to turn the left flank of the Scottish army, and intercept their supplies. He was encountered near the town of Inverkeithing by the Scots, commanded by Holborn and Brown. The first of these officers behaved basely, and perhaps treacherously. Brown fought well and bravely, but finally sustaining a total defeat, was made prisoner, and afterwards died of grief.

The situation of the main Scottish army, under Charles, became hazardous after this defeat, for their position was rendered precarious by the footing which the English obtained in the counties of Fife and Kinross, which enabled them to intercept the King's supplies and communications from the north. In this distressed situation Charles adopted a bold and decisive measure. He resolved to transfer the war from Scotland to England and suddenly raising his camp, he moved to the south-westward by rapid marches, hoping to rouse his friends in England, to arms, before Cromwell could overtake him. But the Cavaliers of England where now broken and dispirited, and were, besides, altogether unprepared for this hasty invasion, which seemed rather the effect of despair than the result of deliberate and settled resolution. The Presbyterians, though rather inclined to the Royal cause, were still less disposed to hazard a junction with him, until terms of mutual accommodation could be settled. They were divided and uncertain, while the republicans were resolved and active.

The English militia assembled under Lambert to oppose Charles in front, and Cromwell followed close in his rear, to take every advantage that could offer. The Scots reached the city of Worcester without much opposition, where the militia, commanded by Lambert, and the regular forces under Cromwell, attacked the Royalists with a force double their number. Clarendon and other English authors represent the Scottish army as making little resistance. Cromwell, on the contrary, talks of the battle of Worcester, in his peculiar phraseology, as "a stiff business—a very glorious mercy—as stiff a contest as he had ever beheld." But, well or ill disputed, the day was totally lost. Three thousand men were slain in the field, ten thousand were taken, and such of them as survived their wounds, and the horrors of overcrowded jails, were shipped off to the plantations as slaves.

Charles, after beholding the ruin of his cause, and having given sufficient proofs of personal valour, escaped from the field, and concealed himself in obscure retreats, under various disguises. At one time he was obliged to hide himself in the boughs of a spreading oak-tree; hence called the Royal Oak. At another time he rode before a lady, Mrs. Lane, in the quality of a groom; and in this disguise passed through a part of the Parliament forces. After infinite fatigue, many romantic adventures, and the most imminent risk of discovery, he at length escaped by sea, and for eight years continued to wander from one foreign court to another, a poor, neglected, and insulted adventurer, the claimant of thrones which he seemed destined never to possess.

The defeat at Worcester was a deathblow to the resistance of the King's party in Scotland. The Parliament, driven from Stirling to the Highlands, endeavoured in vain to assemble new forces. The English troops, after Cromwell's departure, were placed under the command of General Monk, who now began to make a remarkable figure in those times. He was a gentleman of good birth, had been in arms for the King's service, but being made prisoner, had finally embraced the party of the Parliament, and fought for them in Ireland. He was accounted a brave and skillful commander, totally free from the spirit of fanaticism so general in the army of Cromwell, and a man of deep sagacity, and a cold reserved temper. Under Monk's conduct, seconded by that of Overton, Alured, and other Parliamentary officers, the cities, castles, and fortresses of Scotland were reduced one after another. The partial resistance of the wealthy seaport of Dundee, in particular, was punished with the extremities of fire and sword, so that Montrose, Aberdeen, and St. Andrews became terrified, and surrendered without opposition.

The castle of Dunottar, in Kincardineshire, the hereditary fortress of the Earls Marischal, made an honourable defence under George Ogilvy of Barras. It is situated upon a rock, almost separated from the land by a deep ravine on the one side, and overhanging the ocean on the other.[1] In this strong fortress the Honours of Scotland, as they were called, had been deposited after the battle of Dunbar. These were the

---

[1] On the Eastern coast, nigh to the town of Stonehaven, and seventeen miles south of Aberdeen.

crown, sceptre, and sword of state, the symbols of Scottish sovereignty, which were regarded by the nation with peculiar veneration. The terror was great lest pledges, with which the national honour was so intimately connected, should fall into the hands of foreign schismatics and republicans. On the other hand, the English, ardently desirous to possess themselves of these trophies (the rather that they had formed a disproportioned idea of their intrinsic value), besieged the castle closely, and blockaded it by sea and land. As provisions began to fail, the governor foresaw that further defence must speedily become impossible; and, with the assistance of Mr. Granger, minister of Kinneff, he formed a stratagem for securing the ancient and venerable *regalia* from the threatened dishonour. The first preparation was to spread a report that these national treasures had been carried abroad by Sir John Keith, a younger son of the Earl Marischal, ancestor of the family of Kintore. Mrs. Granger, the minister's wife, was the principal agent in the subsequent part of the scheme. Having obtained of the English general the permission to bring out of the castle some *hards* (or bundles) of lint, which she said was her property, she had the courage and address to conceal the regalia within the hards of lint, and carried them boldly through the English camp, at the risk of much ill-usage, had she been discovered in an attempt to deprive the greedy soldiery of their prey. Mrs. Granger played her part so boldly, that she imposed on the general himself, who courteously saluted her, and helped her to mount on horseback as she left the encampment, little guessing with what a valuable part of his expected booty she was loaded. Arriving with her precious charge at Kinneff, the minister buried the relics of royalty under the pulpit of his church, and visited them from time to time, in order to wrap them in fresh packages, and preserve them from injury. Suspicion attached to the Governor of Dunottar; and when the castle was finally surrendered, for want of provisions, he was rigorously dealt with, imprisoned, and even tortured, to make him discover where the regalia were concealed. His lady, who had been active in the stratagem, was subjected to similar severities, as were also the minister of Kinneff and his courageous spouse. All, however, persisted in keeping the secret. Rewards were distributed, after the Restoration, to those who had been concerned in saving the Honours, but they do not appear to have been very accurately accommodated to the merits of the parties. Sir John Keith, whose name had only been used in the transaction as a blind, to put the English on a wrong scent, was created Earl of Kintore, and Ogilvy was made a baronet; but the courageous minister, with his heroic wife, were only rewarded with a pension in money.

The towns and castles of Scotland being thus reduced, the national resistance was confined to a petty warfare, carried on by small bands, who lurked among the mountains and morasses, and took every advantage which these afforded to annoy the English troops, and cut off small parties, or straggling soldiers. These were called Mosstroopers, from a word formerly appropriated to the freebooters of the Border. But the English, who observed a most rigid discipline, were not much in danger of suffering from such desultory efforts; and as they seldom spared the prisoners taken in the skirmishes, the Scots found themselves obliged to submit, for the first time, to an invader more fortunate than all the preceding riders of England. Their resistance ceased, but their hatred watched for a safer opportunity of vengeance. The Highlanders, however, being strong in the character of the country and its inhabitants, continued refractory to the English authority, and if the soldiery ventured to go through the country alone, or in small parties, they were sure to be surprised and slain, without its being possible to discover the actors. The English officers endeavoured to obtain from the neighbouring chiefs, who pretended complete ignorance of these transactions, such redress as the case admitted of, but their endeavours were in general ingeniously eluded.

For example, an English garrison had lost cattle, horses, and even men, by the incursion of a Highland clan who had their residence in the neighbouring mountains, so that the incensed governor demanded peremptorily, that the actors of these depredations should be delivered up to him to suffer punishment. The chief was in no condition to resist, but was not the less unwilling to deliver up the men actually concerned in the *creagh,* who were probably the boldest, or, as it was then termed, the *prettiest,* men of his name. To get easily out of the dilemma, he is said to have selected two or three old creatures, past all military service, whom he sent down to the English commandant, as if they had been the caterans, or plunderers, whom he wanted. The English officer caused them instantly to be hanged *in terrorem,* which was done accordingly, no protestations which they might make of their innocence being understood or attended to. It is to be hoped that other refractory chiefs found more justifiable means of preserving their authority.

In the meantime, Oliver Cromwell accomplished an extraordinary revolution in England, which I can here but barely touch upon. He and his council of officers, who bad so often offered violence to the Parliament, by excluding from the sittings such members as were obnoxious to them, now resolved altogether to destroy the very remnant of this body. For this purpose Cromwell came to the house while it was sitting, told them, in a violent manner, that they were no longer a Parliament, and, upbraiding several individuals with injurious names, he called in a body of soldiers, and commanded one of them to "take away that bauble," meaning the silver mace, which is an emblem of the authority of the House. Then turning the members forcibly out of the hall, he locked the doors, and thus dissolved that memorable body, which had made war against the King, defeated, dethroned, and beheaded him, yet sunk at once under the authority of one of their own members, and an officer of their own naming, who had, in the beginning of these struggles, been regarded as a man of very mean consideration. Oliver Cromwell now seized the supreme power into his hands, with the title of Protector of the Republics of Great Britain and Ireland, under which he governed these islands till his death, with authority more ample than was ever possessed by any of their lawful monarchs.

The confusion which the usurpation of Cromwell was expected to have occasioned in England, determined the Royalists to attempt a general rising, in which it was expected that great part of the Highland chieftains would join. The successes of Montrose were remembered, although it seems to have been forgotten that it was more his own genius than his means, that enabled him to attain them. The Earl of Glencairn was placed by the King's commission at the head of the insurrection; he was joined by the Earl of Athole, by the son of the heroic Montrose, by Lord Lorn, the son of the Marquis of Argyle, and other nobles. A romantic young English cavalier, named Wogan, joined this insurgent army at the head of a body of eighty horse, whom he brought by a toilsome and dangerous march through England and the Lowlands of Scotland. This gallant troop was frequently engaged with the Republican forces, and particularly with a horse regiment, called "the Brazen Wall," from their never having been broken. Wogan defeated, however, a party of these invincibles, but received several wounds, which, though not at first mortal, became so for want of good surgeons; and thus, in an obscure skirmish, ended the singular career of an enthusiastic Royalist.

The army under Glencairn increased to five thousand men, numbers much greater than Montrose usually commanded. Their leader, however, though a brave and accomplished nobleman, seems to have been deficient in military skill, or, at any rate, in the art of securing the good-will and obedience of the various chiefs and nobles who acted under him. It was in vain that Charles, to reconcile their feuds, sent over, as their commander-in-chief, General Middleton, who, after having fought against Montrose in the cause of the Covenant, had at length become an entire Royalist, and was trusted as such. But his military talents were not adequate to surmount the objections which were made to his obscure origin, and the difficulties annexed to his situation.

General Middleton met with but an indifferent welcome from the Highland army, as the following scene, which took place at an entertainment given by him on taking the command, will show. Glencairn had spoken something in praise of the men he had assembled for the King's service, especially the Highlanders. In reply, up started Sir George Munro, an officer of some reputation, but of a haughty and brutal temper, and who, trained in the wars of Germany, despised all irregular troops, and flatly swore that the men of whom the Earl thus boasted, were a pack of thieves and robbers, whose place he hoped to supply with very different soldiers. Glengarry, a Highland chief who was present, arose to resent this insolent language; but Glencairn, preventing him, replied to Munro, "You are a base liar!—these men are neither thieves nor robbers, but gallant gentlemen, and brave soldiers."

In spite of Middleton's attempts to preserve peace, this altercation led to a duel. They fought on horseback, first with pistols, and then with broadswords. Sir George Munro having received a wound on the bridle hand, called to the Earl that he was unable to command his horse, and therefore desired to continue the contest on foot. "You base churl," answered Glencairn, "I will match you either on foot or on horseback." Both dismounted, and encountered fiercely on foot, with their broadswords, when Munro received a wound across his forehead, from which the blood flowed so fast into his eyes, that he could not see to continue the combat. Glencairn was about to thrust his enemy through the body, when the Earl's servant struck up the point of his master's sword, saying, "You have enough of him, my Lord—you have gained the day." Glencairn, still in great anger, struck the intrusive peacemaker across the shoulders, but returned to his quarters, where he was shortly after laid under arrest, by order of the general.

Ere this quarrel was composed, one Captain Livingstone, a friend of Munro's, debated the justice of the question betwixt the leaders so keenly with a gentleman, named Lindsay, that they must needs fight a duel also, in which Lindsay killed Livingstone on the spot. General Middleton, in spite of Glencairn's intercessions, ordered Lindsay to be executed by martial law, on which Glencairn left the army with his own immediate followers, and soon after returning to the Lowlands, made peace with the English. His example was followed by most of the Lowland nobles, who grew impatient of long marches, Highland quarters, and obscure skirmishes, which were followed by no important result.

Middleton still endeavoured to keep the war alive, although Cromwell had sent additional forces into the Highlands. At length he sustained a defeat at Loch Garry, 26th July 1654, after which his army dispersed, and he himself retired abroad. The English forces then marched through the Highlands, and compelled the principal clans to submit to the authority of the Protector. And here I may give you an account of one individual chieftain, of great celebrity at that time, since you will learn better the character of that primitive race of men from personal anecdotes than from details of obscure and petty contests, fought at places with unpronounceable names.

Evan Cameron of Lochiel, chief of the numerous and powerful clan of Cameron, was born in 1629. He was called MacConnuill Dhu (the son of Black Donald), from the patronymic that marked his descent, and Evan Dhu, or Black Evan, a personal epithet derived from his own complexion. Young Lochiel was bred up under the directions of the Marquis of Argyle, and was in attendance on that nobleman, who regarded him as a hostage for the peaceable behaviour of his clan. It is said, that in the civil war the young chief was converted to the side of the King by the exhortations of Sir Robert Spottiswood, then in prison at St. Andrews, and shortly afterwards executed, as we have elsewhere noticed, for his adherence to Montrose.

Evan Dhu, having embraced these principles, was one of the first to join in the insurrection of 1652, of which I have just given a short account. During the best part of two years he was always with his clan, in the very front of battle, and behaved gallantly in the. various skirmishes which took place. He was compelled, however, on one occasion, to withdraw from the main body, on learning that the English were approaching Lochaber, with the purpose of laying waste the country of Lochiel. He hastened thither to protect his own possessions, and those of his clan.

On returning to his estates, Lochiel had the mortification to find that the English had established a garrison at Inverlochy, with the purpose of reducing to submission the Royalist clans in the neighbourhood, particularly his own, and the MacDonalds of Glengarry and Keppoch. He resolved to keep a strict watch on their proceedings, and dismissing the rest of his followers, whom he had not the means of maintaining without attracting attention to his motions, he lay in the woods with about fifty chosen men, within a few miles of Inverlochy.

It was the constant policy of Cromwell and his officers, both in Ireland and Scotland, to cut down and destroy the forests in which the insurgent natives found places of defence and concealment. In conformity with this general rule, the commandant of Inverlochy embarked three hundred men in two light-armed vessels, with directions to disembark at a place called Achdelew, for the purpose of destroying Lochiel's cattle and felling his woods. Lochiel, who watched their motions closely, saw the English soldiers come ashore, one-half having hatchets and other tools as a working party, the other half under arms, to protect their operations. Though the difference of numbers was so great, the chieftain vowed that he would make the red soldier (so the English were called from their uniform) pay dear for every bullock or tree which he should destroy on the black soldier's property (alluding to the dark colour of the tartan, and perhaps to his own complexion). He then demanded of some of his followers who had served under Montrose, whether they had ever seen the Great Marquis, encounter with such unequal numbers. They answered, they could recollect no instance of such temerity. "We will fight, nevertheless," said Evan Dhu, "and if each of us kill a man, which is no mighty matter, I will answer for the event." That his family might not be destroyed in so doubtful an enterprise, he ordered his brother Allan to be bound to a tree, meaning to prevent his interference in the conflict. But Allan prevailed on a little boy, who was left to attend him, to unloose the cords, and was soon as deep in the fight as Evan himself.

The Camerons, concealed by the trees, advanced so close on the enemy as to pour on them an unexpected and destructive shower of shot and arrows, which slew thirty men; and ere they could recover from their surprise, the Highlanders were in the midst of them, laying about them with incredible fury with their ponderous swords and axes. After a gallant resistance, the mass of the English began to retire towards their vessels, when Evan Dhu commanded a piper and a small party to go betwixt the enemy and their barks, and then sound his pibroch and war-cry, till their clamour made it seem that there was another body of Highlanders in ambush to cut off their retreat. The English, driven to fury and despair by this new alarm, turned back, like brave men, upon the first assailants, and, if the working party had possessed military weapons, Lochiel might have had little reason to congratulate himself on the result of this audacious stratagem.

He himself had a personal rencontre, strongly characteristic of the ferocity of the times. The chief was singled out by an English officer of great personal strength, and, as they were separated from the general strife, they fought in single combat for some time. Lochiel was dexterous enough to disarm the Englishman; but his gigantic adversary suddenly closed on him, and in the struggle which ensued both fell to the ground, the officer uppermost. He was in the act of grasping at his sword, which had fallen near the place where they lay in deadly struggle, and was naturally extending his neck in the same direction, when the Highland chief, making a desperate effort, grasped his enemy by the collar, and snatching with his teeth at the bare and outstretched throat, he seized it as a wild-cat might have done, and kept his hold so fast as to tear out the windpipe. The officer died in this singular manner. Lochiel was so far from disowning, or being ashamed of this extraordinary mode of defence, that he was afterwards heard to say, it was the sweetest morsel he had ever tasted.

When Lochiel, thus extricated from the most imminent danger, was able to rejoin his men, he found they had not only pursued the English to the beach, but even into the sea, cutting and stabbing whomsoever they could overtake. He himself advanced till he was chin-deep, and observing a man on board one of the armed vessels take aim at him with a musket, he dived under the water, escaping so narrowly that the bullet grazed his head. Another marksman was foiled by the affection of the chief's foster-brother, who threw himself betwixt the Englishman and the object of his aim, and was killed by the ball designed for his lord.

Having cut off a second party, who ventured to sally from the fort, and thus, as he thought, sufficiently chastised the garrison of

Inverlochy, Lochiel again joined Middleton, but was soon recalled to Lochaber, by new acts of devastation. Leaving most of his men with the Royalist general, Evan Dhu returned with such speed and secrecy, that he again surprised a strong party when in the act of felling his woods, and assaulting them suddenly, killed on the spot a hundred men, and all the officers, driving the rest up to the very walls of the garrison.

Middleton's army being disbanded, it was long ere Lochiel could bring himself to accept of peace from the hands of the English. He continued to harass them by attacks on detached parties who straggled from the fort,—on the officers who went out into the woods in hunting-parties,—on the engineer officers who were sent to survey the Highlands, of whom he made a large party prisoners, and confined them in a desolate island, on a small lake called Loch Ortuigg. By such exploits he rendered himself so troublesome, that the English were desirous to have peace with him on any moderate terms. Their overtures were at first rejected, Evan Dhu returning for answer, that he would not abjure the King's authority, even although the alternative was to be his living and dying in the condition of an exile and outlaw. But when it was hinted to him that no express renunciation of the King's authority would be required, and that he was only desired to live in peace under the existing government, the chief made his submission to the existing powers with much solemnity.

Lochiel came down on this occasion at the head of his whole clan in arms, to the garrison of Inverlochy. The English forces being drawn up in a line opposite to them, the Camerons laid down their arms in the name of King Charles, and took them up again in that of the States, without any mention of Cromwell, or any disowning of the King's authority. In consequence of this honourable treaty, the last Scotsman who maintained the cause of Charles Stewart submitted to the authority of the republic.

It is related of this remarkable chieftain, that he slew with his own hand the last wolf that was ever seen in the Highlands of Scotland. Tradition records another anecdote of him. Being benighted, on some party for the battle or the chase, Evan Dhu laid himself down with his followers to sleep in the snow. As he composed himself to rest, he observed that one of his sons, or nephews, had rolled together a great snow-ball, on which he deposited his head. Indignant at what he considered as a mark of effeminacy, he started up and kicked the snow-ball

from under the sleeper's head, exclaiming,—"Are you become so luxu-
rious that you cannot sleep without a pillow?"

After the accession of James II., Lochiel came to court to obtain
pardon for one of his clan, who, being in command of a party of
Camerons, had fired by mistake on a body of Athole men, and killed
several. He was received with the most honourable distinction, and his
request granted. The King desiring to make him a knight, asked the
chieftain for his own sword, in order to render the ceremony still more
peculiar. Lochiel had ridden up from Scotland, being then the only
mode of travelling, and a constant rain had so rusted his trusty
broadsword, that at the moment no man could have unsheathed it.
Lochiel, affronted at the idea which the courtiers might conceive from
his not being able to draw his own sword, burst into tears.

"Do not regard it, my faithful friend," said King James, with ready
courtesy—"your sword would have left the scabbard of itself had the
Royal cause required it."

With that he bestowed the intended honour with his own sword,
which he presented to the new knight as soon as the ceremony was
performed.

Sir Evan Dhu supported the cause of the Stewart family, for the last
time, and with distinguished heroism, in the battle of Killiecrankie.
After that civil strife was ended, he grew old in peace, and survived
until 1719, aged about ninety, and so much deprived of his strength
and faculties, that this once formidable warrior was fed like an infant,
and like an infant rocked in a cradle.

XLVII

Cromwell's Subjugation

1655-1658

W E will now take a general glance of Scotland, reduced as the country was to temporary submission to Cromwell, whose power there
and elsewhere was founded upon military usurpation only. He built
strong citadels at Leith, Ayr, Inverness, and Glasgow. Eighteen garrisons were maintained throughout the kingdom, and a standing army
of ten thousand men kept the country in subjection. Monk, so often
mentioned, commanded this army, and was, besides, member of a
Council of State, to whom the executive government was committed.
Lord Broghill was President of this body, and out of nine members two
only, Swinton and Lockhart, were natives of Scotland.

To regulate the administration of public justice, four English, and
three Scottish judges, were appointed to hear causes, and to make cir-
cuits for that purpose. The English judges, it may be supposed, were
indifferently versed in the law of Scotland; but they distributed justice
with an impartiality to which the Scottish nation had been entirely a
stranger, and which ceased to be experienced from the native judges
after the Restoration. The peculiar rectitude of the men employed by
Cromwell being pointed out to a learned judge, in the beginning of the
next century, his lordship composedly answered, "Devil thank them for

271

their impartiality! a pack of kinless loons—for my part, I can never see a cousin or friend in the wrong."

This shameful partiality in the Scottish courts of justice revived, as just noticed, with the Restoration, when the judges were to be gained, not only by the solicitation of private friends, and by the influence of kinsfolk, but by the interference of persons in power, and the application of downright bribery.

In point of taxation, Oliver Cromwell's Scottish government was intolerably oppressive, since he appears to have screwed out of that miserable country an assessment of £10,000 per month, which, even when gradually diminished to £72,000 yearly, was paid with the utmost difficulty. Some alleviation was indeed introduced by the circulation of the money with which England paid her soldiers and civil establishment, which was at one time calculated at half a million yearly, and was never beneath the moiety of that sum.

With regard to the Presbyterian Church, Cromwell prudently foresaw, that the importance of the preachers would gradually diminish if they were permitted to abuse each other, but prevented from stirring up their congregations to arms. They continued to be rent asunder by the recent discord, which had followed upon the King's death. The majority were Resolutionists, who owned the King's title, and would not be prohibited from praying for him at any risk. The Remonstrants, who had never been able to see any sufficient reason for embracing the cause, or acknowledging the right, of Charles the Second, yielded obedience to the English government, and disowned all notice of the King in their public devotions. The Independents treated both with contemptuous indifference, and only imposed on them the necessity of observing toleration towards each other.

But though divided into different classes, Presbyterianism continued on the whole predominant. The temper of the Scottish nation seemed altogether indisposed to receive any of the various sects which had proved so prolific in England. The quiet and harmless Quakers were the only sectaries who gained some proselytes of distinction. Independents of other denominations made small progress, owing to the vigilance with which the Presbyterian clergy maintained the unity of the Church.

Even Cromwell was compelled to show deference to the prevailing opinions in favour of Presbytery in Scotland, though contrary to his principles as an Independent. He named a commission of about thirty ministers from the class of Remonstrators, and declared that, without certificates from three or four of these select persons, no minister, though he might be called to a church, should enjoy a stipend. This put the keys of the Church (so far as emolument was concerned) entirely into the hands of the Presbyterians; and it may be presumed, that such of the Commissioners as acted (for many declined the office, thinking the duties of the Ecclesiastical Commission too much resembled the domination of Episcopacy) took care to admit no minister whose opinions did not coincide with their own. The sectaries who were concerned in civil affairs were also thwarted and contemned; and on the whole, in spite of the victories of the Independents in the field, their doctrines made little progress in Scotland.

During the four years which ensued betwixt the final cessation of the Civil War, by the dispersion of the Royalist army, and the Restoration of Monarchy, there occurred no public event worthy of notice. The spirit of the country was depressed and broken. The nobles, who hitherto had yielded but imperfect obedience to their native monarchs, were now compelled to crouch under the rod of an English usurper. Most of them retired to their country seats, or castles, and lived in obscurity, enjoying such limited dominion over their vassals as the neighbourhood of the English garrisons permitted them to retain. These, of course, precluded all calling of the people to arms, and exercise of the privilege, on the part of the barons, of making open war on each other.

Thus far the subjection of the country was of advantage to the tenantry and lower classes, who enjoyed more peace and tranquillity during this period of national subjugation than had been their lot during the civil wars. But the weight of oppressive taxes, collected by means of a foreign soldiery, and the general sense of degradation arising from the rule of a foreign power, counterbalanced for the time the diminution of feudal oppression.

In the absence of other matter, I may here mention a subject which is interesting, as peculiarly characteristic of the manners of Scotland. I mean the frequent recurrence of prosecutions for witchcraft, which distinguishes this period.

Scripture refers more than once to the existence of witches; and though divines have doubted concerning their nature and character, yet most European nations have, during the darker periods of their history, retained in their statutes laws founded upon the text of Exodus,

"Thou shalt not suffer a witch to live."[1] The Reformers, although reject-
ing the miracles of the Catholic Church, retained with tenacity the
belief of the existence of such sorceresses, and zealously enforced the
penalties against all unfortunate creatures whom they believed to fall
under the description of witches, wizards, or the like. The increase of
general information and common sense has, at a later period, occasioned the annulling of those cruel laws in most countries of Europe. It
has been judiciously thought that, since the Almighty has ceased to
manifest His own power by direct and miraculous suspension of the
ordinary laws of nature, it is inconsistent to suppose that evil spirits
should be left at liberty in the present day to form a league with
wretched mortals, and impart to them supernatural powers of injuring
or tormenting others. And the truth of this reasoning has been proved
by the general fact, that where the laws against witchcraft have been
abolished, witches are rarely heard of, or thought of, even amongst the
lowest vulgar.

But in the seventeenth century, the belief in this imaginary crime
was general, and the prosecutions, especially in Scotland, were very
frequent. James VI., who often turned the learning he had acquired to
a very idle use, was at the trouble to write a treatise against witchcraft,
as he composed another against smoking tobacco; and the Presbyterian
clergy, however little apt to coincide with that monarch's sentiments,
gave full acceptation to his opinion on the first point of doctrine, and
very many persons were put to death as guilty of this imaginary crime.

I must, however, observe that some of those executed for witchcraft well deserved their fate. Impostors of both sexes were found, who
deluded credulous persons by pretending an intercourse with supernatural powers, and furnished those who consulted them with potions,
for the purpose of revenging themselves on their enemies, which were
in fact poisonous compounds sure to prove fatal to those who partook
of them.

Among many other instances, I may mention that of a lady of high
rank, the second wife of a northern earl, who, being desirous of

---

[1] "In the Law of Moses, dictated by the Divinity himself, was announced a text, which,
as interpreted literally, having been inserted into the Criminal Code of all Christian
nations, has occasioned much cruelty and bloodshed, either from its tenor being mis-
understood, or that, being exclusively calculated for the Israelites, it made part of the
judicial Mosaic dispensation, and was abrogated, like the greater part of that law, by
the more benign and element dispensation of the Gospel."—*Letters on Demonology*.

destroying her husband's eldest son by the former marriage, in order that her own son might succeed to the father's title and estate, procured drugs to effect her purpose from a Highland woman, who pretended to be a witch or sorceress. The fatal ingredients were mixed with ale, and set aside by the wicked countess, to be given to her victim on the first fitting opportunity. But Heaven disappointed her purpose, and, at the same time, inflicted on her a dreadful punishment. Her own son, for whose advantage she meditated this horrible crime, returning fatigued and thirsty from hunting, lighted by chance on this fatal cup of liquor, drank it without hesitation, and died in consequence. The wretched mixer of the poison was tried and executed; but, although no one could be sorry that the agent in such a deed was brought to punishment, it is clear she deserved death, not as a witch, but as one who was an accomplice in murder by poison.

But most of the poor creatures who suffered death for witchcraft were aged persons, usually unprotected females, living alone, in a poor and miserable condition and disposed, from the peevishness of age and infirmity, to rail against or desire evil, in their froward humour, to neighbours by whom they were abused or slighted. When such unhappy persons had unwittingly given vent to impotent anger in bad wishes or imprecations, if a child fell sick, a horse became lame, a bullock died, or any other misfortune chanced in the family against which the ill-will had been expressed, it subjected the utterer instantly to the charge of witchcraft, and was received by judges and jury as a strong proof of guilt. If, in addition to this, the miserable creature had, by the oddity of her manners, the crossness of her temper, the habit of speaking to herself, or any other signs of the dotage which attends comfortless old age and poverty, attracted the suspicions of her credulous neighbours, she was then said to have been held and reputed a witch, and was rarely permitted to escape being burnt to death at the stake.

It was equally fatal for an aged person of the lower ranks, if, as was frequently the case, she conceived herself to possess any peculiar receipt or charm for curing diseases, either by the application of medicines, of which she had acquired the secret, or by repeating words, or using spells and charms, which the superstition of the time supposed to have the power of relieving maladies that were beyond the skill of medical practitioners.

Such a person was accounted a *white* witch; one who employed her skill for the benefit, not the harm, of her fellow creatures. But still she was a sorceress, and, as such, was liable to be brought to the stake. A doctress of this kind was equally exposed to a like charge, whether her patient died or recovered; and she was, according to circumstances, condemned for using sorcery whether to cure or to kill. Her allegation that she had received the secret from family tradition, or from any other source, was not admitted as a defence; and she was doomed to death with as little hesitation for having attempted to cure by mysterious and unlawful means, as if she had been charged, as in the instance already given, with having assisted to commit murder.

The following example of such a case is worthy of notice. It rests on tradition, but is very likely to be true. An eminent English judge was travelling the circuit when an old woman was brought before him for using a spell to cure dimness of sight, by hanging a clew of yarn round the neck of the patient. Marvellous things were told by the witnesses of the cures which this spell had performed on patients far beyond the reach of ordinary medicine. The poor woman made no other defence than by protesting, that if there was any witchcraft in the ball of yarn, she knew nothing of it. It had been given her, she said, thirty years before, by a young Oxford student, for the cure of one of her own family, who having used it with advantage for a disorder in her eyes, she had seen no harm in lending it for the relief of others who laboured under similar infirmity, or in accepting a small gratuity for doing so. Her defence was little attended to by the jury; but the judge was much agitated. He asked the woman where she resided when she obtained possession of this valuable relic. She gave the name of a village, in which she had in former times kept a petty alehouse. He then looked at the clew very earnestly, and at length addressed the jury. "Gentlemen," he said, "we are on the point of committing a great injustice to this poor old woman; and to prevent it, I must publicly confess a piece of early folly, which does me no honour. At the time this poor creature speaks of, I was at college, leading an idle and careless life, which, had I not been given grace to correct it, must have made it highly improbable that ever I should have attained my present situation. I chanced to remain for a day and night in this woman's alehouse, without having money to discharge my reckoning. Not knowing what to do, and seeing her much occupied with a child who had weak eyes, I had the meanness to pretend that I could write out a spell that would mend her daughter's sight, if she would accept it instead of her bill. The ignorant woman readily agreed; and I scrawled some figures on a piece of parchment, and added two lines of nonsensical doggerel, in ridicule of her credulity, and caused her to make it up in that clew which has so nearly cost her her life. To prove the truth of this, let the yarn be unwound, and you may judge of the efficacy of the spell." The clew was unwound accordingly; and the following pithy couplet was found on the enclosed bit of parchment—

> "The devil scratch out both thine eyes,
> And spit into the holes likewise."

It was evident that those who were cured by such a spell, must have been indebted to nature, with some assistance, perhaps, from imagination. But the users of such charms were not always so lucky as to light upon the person who drew them up; and doubtless many innocent and unfortunate creatures were executed, as the poor alewife would have been, had she not lighted upon her former customer in the unexpected character of her judge.

Another old woman is said to have cured many cattle of the murrain, by a repetition of a certain verse. The fee which she required, was a loaf of bread and a silver penny; and when she was commanded to reveal the magical verses which wrought such wonders, they, were found to be the following jest on the credulity of her customers:—

> "My loaf in my lap, and my penny in my purse,
> Thou art never the better, and I never the worse."

It was not medicine only which witchery was supposed to mingle with; but any remarkable degree of dexterity in an art or craft, whether attained by skill or industry, subjected those who possessed it to similar suspicion. Thus it was a dangerous thing to possess more thriving cows than those of the neighbourhood, though their superiority was attained merely by paying greater attention to feeding and cleaning the animals. It was often an article of suspicion, that a woman had spun considerably more thread than her less laborious neighbours chose to think could be accomplished by ordinary industry; and, to crown these absurdities, a yeoman of the town of Malling, in Kent, was accused before a justice of peace as a sorcerer, because he used more frequently than his companions to hit the mark which he aimed at. This dexterity, and some idle story of the archer's amusing himself with letting a fly hum and buzz around him, convinced the judge that the poor man's skill in his art was owing to the assistance of some imp of Satan. So he punished the marksman severely, to the great encouragement of archery, and as a wise example to all justices of the peace.

Other charges, the most ridiculous and improbable, were brought against those suspected of witchcraft. They were supposed to have power, by going through some absurd and impious ceremony, to summon to their presence the Author of Evil, who appeared in some mean or absurd shape, and, in return for the invokers renouncing their redemption, gave them the power of avenging themselves on their enemies; which privilege, with that of injuring and teasing their fellow-creatures, was almost all they gained from their new master. Sometimes, indeed, they were said to obtain from him the power of flying through the air on broomsticks, when the Foul Fiend gave public parties; and the accounts given of the ceremonies practised on such occasions are equally disgusting and vulgar, totally foreign to any idea we can have of a spiritual nature, and only fit to be invented and believed by the most ignorant and brutal of the human species.

Another of these absurdities was, the belief that the evil spirits would attend if they were invoked with certain profane and blasphemous ceremonies, such as reading the Lord's Prayer backwards, or the like; and would then tell the future fortunes of those who had raised them, as it was called, or inform them what was become of articles which had been lost or stolen. Stories are told of such exploits by grave authors, which are to the full as ridiculous, and indeed more so, than anything that is to be found in fairy tales, invented for the amusement of children. And for all this incredible nonsense, unfortunate creatures were imprisoned, tortured, and finally burnt alive, by the sentence of their judges.

It is strange to find, that the persons accused of this imaginary crime in most cases paved the way for their own condemnation, by confessing and admitting the truth of all the monstrous absurdities which were charged against them by their accusers. This may surprise you; but yet it can be accounted for.

Many of these poor creatures were crazy, and infirm in mind as well as body; and, hearing themselves charged with such monstrous enormities by those whom they accounted wise and learned, became half persuaded of their own guilt, and assented to all the nonsensical questions which were put to them. But this was not all. Very many made these confessions under the influence of torture, which was applied to them with cruel severity.

It is true, the ordinary courts of justice in Scotland had not the power of examining criminals under torture, a privilege which was reserved for the Privy Council. But this was a slight protection; for witches were seldom tried before the ordinary Criminal Courts, because the judges and lawyers, though they could not deny the existence of a crime for which the law had assigned a punishment, yet showed a degree of incredulity respecting witchcraft which was supposed frequently to lead to the escape of those accused of this unpopular crime, when in the management of professional persons. To avoid the ordinary jurisdiction of the Justiciary, and other regular criminal jurisdictions, the trial of witchcraft in the provinces was usually brought before commissioners appointed by the Privy Council. These commissioners were commonly country gentlemen and clergymen, who, from ignorance on the one side, misdirected learning on the other, and bigotry on both, were as eager in the prosecution as the vulgar could desire. By their commission they had the power of torture, and employed it unscrupulously, usually calling in to their assistance a witchfinder; a fellow, that is, who made money by pretending to have peculiar art and excellence in discovering these offenders, and who sometimes undertook to rid a parish or township of witches at so much a-head, as if they had been foxes, wild-cats, or other vermin. These detestable impostors directed the process of the torture, which frequently consisted in keeping the aged and weary beings from sleep, and compelling them to walk up and down their prison, whenever they began to close their eyes, and in running needles into their flesh, under pretence of discovering a mark, which the witch-finders affirmed the devil had impressed on their skin, in token that they were his property and subjects. It is no wonder that wretched creatures, driven mad by pain and want of sleep, confessed anything whatever to obtain a moment's relief, though they were afterwards to die for it.

But besides the imbecility of such victims, and the torture to which they were subjected, shame and weariness of life often caused their pleading guilty to accusations in themselves absurd and impossible. You must consider that the persons accused of witchcraft were almost always held guilty by the public and by their neighbours, and that if the court scrupled to condemn them, it was a common thing for the mob to take the execution into their own hands, and duck the unhappy wretches to death, or otherwise destroy them. The fear of such a fate might determine many of the accused, even though they were in their sound mind, and unconstrained by bodily torture, to plead guilty at once, and rather lose their wretched life by the sentence of the law, than expose themselves to the fury of the prejudiced multitude. A singular story is told to this effect.

An old woman and her daughter were tried as witches at Haddington. The principal evidence of the crime was that, though miserably poor, the two females had contrived to look "fresh and fair," during the progress of a terrible famine, which reduced even the better classes to straits, and brought all indigent people to the point of starving; while, during the universal distress, these two women lived on in their usual way, and never either begged for assistance or seemed to suffer by the general calamity. The jury were perfectly satisfied that this could not take place by any natural means; and, as the accused persons, on undergoing the discipline of one Kincaid, a witch-finder, readily admitted all that was asked about their intercourse with the devil, the jury, on their confession, brought them in guilty of witchcraft without hesitation.

The King's Advocate for the time (I believe Sir George Mackenzie is named) was sceptical on the subject of witchcraft. He visited the women in private, and urged them to tell the real truth. They continued at first to maintain the story they had given in their confession. But the Advocate, perceiving them to be women of more sense than ordinary, urged upon them the crime of being accessary to their own death, by persisting in accusing themselves of impossibilities, and promised them life and protection, providing they would unfold the true secret which they used for their subsistence. The poor women looked wistfully on each other, like people that were in perplexity. At length, the mother said, "You are very good, my lord, and I daresay your power is very great, but you cannot be of use to my daughter and me. If you were to set us at liberty from the bar, you could not free us from the suspicion of being witches. As soon as we return to our hut, we shall be welcomed by the violence and abuse of all our neighbours, who, if they do not beat our brains out, or drown us on the spot, will retain hatred and malice against us, which will be shown on every occasion, and make our life so miserable, that we have made up our minds to prefer death at once."

"Do not be afraid of your neighbours," said the Advocate. "If you will trust your secret with me, I will take care of you for the rest of your lives, and send you to an estate of mine in the north, where nobody can know anything of your history, and where, indeed, the people's ideas are such, that, if they even thought you witches, they would rather regard you with fear and respect than hatred."

The women, moved by his promises, told him that, if he would cause to be removed an old empty trunk which stood in the corner of their hut, and dig the earth where he saw it had been stirred, he would find the secret by means of which they had been supported through the famine; protesting to Heaven, at the same time, that they were totally innocent of any unlawful arts, such as had been imputed them, and which they had confessed in their despair. Sir George Mackenzie hastened to examine the spot, and found concealed in the earth two firkins of salted snails, one of them nearly empty. On this strange food the poor women had been nourished during the famine. The Advocate was as good as his word; and the story shows how little weight is to be laid on the frequent confessions of the party in cases of witchcraft.

As this story is only traditional, I will mention two others of the same kind, to which I can give a precise date.

The first of these instances regards a woman of rank, much superior to those who were usually accused of this imaginary crime. She was sister of Sir John Henderson of Fordel, and wife to the Laird of Pittardo, in Fife. Notwithstanding her honourable birth and connections, this unfortunate matron was, in the year 1649, imprisoned in the common jail of Edinburgh, from the month of July till the middle of the month of December, when she was found dead, with every symptom of poison. Undoubtedly the infamy of the charge, and the sense that it must destroy her character and disgrace her family, was the cause which instigated her to commit suicide.

The same sentiment which drove this poor lady to her death was expressed by a female, young and handsome, executed at Paisley in 1697, in the following short answer to some of her friends, who were blaming her for not being sufficiently active in defending herself upon her trial. "They have taken away my character," she said, "and my life is not worth preserving."

But the most affecting instance of such a confession being made, and persisted in to the last, by an innocent person, is recorded by one who was a diligent collector of witch stories, and a faithful believer in them. He says, that in the village of Lauder, there was a certain woman accused of witchcraft, who for a long time denied her guilt. At length when all her companions in prison had been removed, and were

appointed for execution, and she herself about to be left to total soli-
tude, the poor creature became weary of life, and made a false confession, avowing that she was guilty of certain facts, which, in the opinion
of the times, amounted to witchcraft. She, therefore, made it her petition that she should be put to death with the others on the day
appointed for their execution. Her clergyman and others, on considering this young woman's particular case, entertained, for once, some
doubts that her confession was not sincere, and remonstrated strongly
with her upon the wickedness of causing her own death by a false
avowal of guilt. But as she stubbornly adhered to her confession, she
was condemned, and appointed to be executed with the rest, as she
had so earnestly desired. Being carried forth to the place of execution,
she remained silent during the first, second, and third prayer, and then
perceiving that there remained no more but to rise and go to the stake,
she lift up her body, and with a loud voice cried out, "Now, all you that
see me this day, know that I am now to die as a witch, by my own confession: and I free all men, especially the ministers and magistrates, of
the guilt of my blood. I take it wholly upon myself—my blood be upon
my own head; and, as I must make answer to the God of Heaven
presently, I declare I am as free of witchcraft as any child; but being
delated by a malicious woman, and put in prison under the name of a
witch,—disowned by my husband and friends,—and seeing no
ground of hope of my coming out of prison, or ever coming in credit
again, through the temptation of the devil I made up that confession,
on purpose to destroy my own life, being weary of it, and choosing
rather to die than live."—And so died.

It was remarkable that the number of supposed witches seemed to
increase in proportion to the increase of punishment. On the 22d of
May 1650 the Scottish Parliament named a committee for inquiry into
the depositions of no less than fifty-four witches, with power to grant
such commissions as we have already described, to proceed with their
trial, condemnation, and execution. Supposing these dreaded sorceresses to exist in such numbers, and to possess the powers of injury
imputed to them, it was to be expected, as Reginald Scott expresses
himself, that "there would neither be butter in the churn, nor cow in
the close, nor corn in the field, nor fair weather without, nor health
within doors." Indeed the extent to which people indulged their horrors and suspicions was in itself the proof of their being fanciful. If, in a
small province, or even a petty town, there had existed scores of people

possessed of supernatural power, the result would be that the laws of nature would have been liable to constant interruption.

The English judges appointed for Scotland in Cromwell's time saw the cruelty and absurdity of witch-trials, and endeavoured to put a stop to them; but the thanks which they received were only reflections on their principles of toleration the benefit of which, in the opinion of the Scots, was extended, by this lenity, not only to heretics of every denomination, but even to those who worshipped the devil. Some went still farther, and accused the sectaries of holding intercourse with evil spirits in their devotions. This was particularly reported and believed of the Quakers, the most simple and moral of all dissenters from the Church.

Wiser and better views on the subject began to prevail in the end of the seventeenth century, and capital prosecutions for this imaginary crime were seen to decrease. The last instance of execution for witch-craft took place in the remote province of Sutherland in 1722, under the direction of an ignorant provincial judge, who was censured by his superiors for the proceeding. The victim was an old woman in her last dotage, so silly that she was delighted to warm her wrinkled hands at the fire which was to consume her; and who, while they were preparing for her execution, repeatedly said, that so good a blaze, and so many neighbours gathered round it, made the most cheerful sight she had seen for many years![1]

The laws against witchcraft, both in England and Scotland, were abolished; and persons who pretend to fortune-telling, the use of spells, or similar mysterious feats of skill, are now punished as common knaves and impostors. Since this has been the case, no one has ever heard of witches or witchcraft, even among the most ignorant of the vulgar; so that the crime must have been entirely imaginary, since it ceased to exist so soon as men ceased to hunt it out for punishment.

---

[1] "The last person who was prosecuted before the *Lords of Justiciary* for witchcraft was *Elspeth Rule,* who was tried before Lord Anstruther at the Dumfries circuit, on the 3d of May 1709. No special act of witchcraft was charged against her; the indictment was of a very general nature, that the prisoner was *habit and repute* a witch, and that she had used threatening expressions against persons at enmity with her, who were afterwards visited with the loss of cattle, or the death of friends, and one of whom ran mad. The jury by a majority of voices found these articles proved, and the judge ordained the prisoner to be burned on the cheek, and to be banished Scotland for life."—ARNOT.

KINGS OF SCOTLAND

Dep. indicates *deposed*—Ab. *abdicated*—Res. *resigned*—d. *daughter*

Name	Parentage	Marriage	Accession (A.D.)	Death (A.D.)	Reign (Yrs.)	Children
Duncan I.	Crinan, Abbot of Dunkeld, and Beatrice, d. of Malcolm II.	With the sister of Seward, Earl of Northumberland.	1034	1039	6	1. Malcolm Canmore; 2. Donald Bane.
Macbeth.	Finlegh, Thane of Ross and Doada, d. of Malcolm II.	The Lady Gruach, granddaughter of Kenneth IV.	1039	1056	17	
Malcolm III. (Canmore.)	Duncan I.	Margaret of England.	1057	1093	36	1. Edward; 2. Ethelred; 3. Edmund; 4. Edgar; 5. Alexander; 6. David; 7. Matilda; 8. Mary.
Donald Bane.	Duncan I.		1093	1094	1	
Duncan II.	Grandson of Malcolm III.	Ethreda, daughter of Gosspatric.	1094	1095	1	William.
Donald (restored).			1095	Dep 1097	2	Madach, 1st Earl of Athole.
Edgar.	Malcolm III.		1097	1107	10	
Alexander I.	Malcolm III.	Sibilla, natural d. of Henry I. of England.	1107	1124	18	
David I.	Malcolm III.	Matilda, d. of Waltheof, Earl of Northumberland.	1124	1153	30	Henry[1].
Malcolm IV.	Henry, son of David I. and Ada, d. of the Earl of Warrne and Surrey.		1153	1165	13	
William the Lion.	The same.	Ermengarde, d. of Viscount Beaumont.	1165	1214	49	1. Alexander; 2. Margaret; 3. Isabella; 4. Marjory.
Alexander II.	William.	I. Joan, d. of King John of England, no issue; II. Mary of Picardy.	1214	1249	35	Alexander.

[1] Prince Henry who died before his father, 12th June 1152, married Ada, d. of Earl of Warrene and Surrey. Issue: 1. Malcolm; 2. William, afterwards Kings; 3. David, Earl of Huntington, and three daughters.

Name	Parentage	Marriage	Accession (A.D.)	Death (A.D.)	Reign (Yrs.)	Children
Alexander III.	Alexander II.	I. Margaret, d. of King Henry III. of England, issue; II. Joleta, d. of the Count de Dreux, no issue.	1249	1286	37	1. Alexander; 2. David; 3. Margaret.
Margaret.	Eric, King of Norway, and Margaret, d. of Alexander III.		1286	1290	5	
Interregnum.					2	
John Baliol.	John Baliol of Barnard Castle, and Devorgoil, gr. d. of David, Earl of Huntington, gr. son of David I. Marriage: Isabella, d. of John de Warren, Earl of Surrey.	Isabella, d. of John de Warren, Earl of Surrey.	1292	Res. 1296 died 1314	4	1. Edward; 2. Henry.
Interregnum.					10	
Robert I. The Bruce.	The grandson of Bruce, Baliol's competitor.	I. Isabella, d. of Donald, tenth Earl of Mar; II. Elizabeth, d. of the Earl of Ulster.	1306	1329	24	I. Marjory. II. 1. DAVID; 2. Margaret; 3. Matilda; 4. Elizabeth.
David II.	Robert Bruce.	I. Johanna, d. of King Edward II. of England; II. Margaret, d. of Sir J. Logie.	1329	1371	42	

HOUSE OF STEWART

Name	Parentage	Marriage	Accession (A.D.)	Death (A.D.)	Reign (Yrs.)	Children
Robert II.	Walter, Steward of Scotland, and Marjory, d. of Robert Bruce.	I. Elizabeth, d. of Sir Adam More of Rowallan; II. Euphemia, d. of the Earl of Ross.	1371	1390	19	I. 1. John, afterwards named ROBERT; 2. Walter; 3. Robert; 4. Alexander; and six daughters. II. 1. David; 2. Walter; and four daughters.
Robert III.	Robert II.	Annabella, d. of Sir John Drummond of Stobhall.	1390	1406	17	1. David, Duke of Rothsay; 2. James; and three daughters.
Regencies of the Dukes of Albany, 1406 to 1424			1406	1424	18	
James I.	Robert III.	Joanna, d. of John, Duke of Somerset, gr. Grandson of King Edward III.	1424	1437	13	1. JAMES; and five daughters.
James II.	James I.	Mary, d. of Arnold, Duke of Guelderland.	1437	1460	24	1. JAMES; 2. Alexander; 3. John; 4. Mary; 5. Margaret.

Name	Parentage	Marriage	Accession (A.D.)	Death (A.D.)	Reign (Yrs.)	Children
James III.	James II.	Margaret of Denmark.	1460	1488	28	1. JAMES; 2. James, Marquis of Ormond; 3. John, Earl of Mar.
James IV.	James III.	Margaret, d. of King Henry VII. of England.	1488	1513	26	1. JAMES; 2. Alexander.
James V.	James IV.	I. Magdalen, d. of King Francis I. of France; II. Mary, d. of the Duke of Guise.	1513	1542	29	MARY.
Regency.			1542	1561	19	
Mary.	James V.	I. Francis, son of King Henry II. of France; II. Henry, Lord Darnley; III. Hepburn, E. of Bothwell.	1561 Res. 1567	1587	6	JAMES.
James VI.	Mary.	Anne of Denmark.	1567		36	
Union of the Crowns. James VI. now James. I. of England.			1603	1625	22	1. Henry; 2. CHARLES; 3. Elizabeth.
Charles I.	James VI.	Henrietta of France.	1625	1649	24	1. CHARLES; 2. JAMES; 3. Henry; 4. Mary; 5. Elizabeth; 6. Henrietta.
Charles II.	Charles I.	Catherine of Portugal.	1649		2	
The Commonwealth			1651	1660	9	
Charles II. restored.			1660	1685	25	
James VII. and II. of England[1].	Charles I.	I. Anne Hyde, d. of the Earl of Clarendon; II. Mary of Este.	1685	Abd. 1688	4	I. 1. MARY; 2. ANNE. II. James, afterwards known as the Pretender.
William III. and Mary	Prince of Orange James VII.	Mary, d. of King James VII. William, Prince of Orange.	1689 —	M. 1694 W. 1701	6 13	
Anne.	James VII.	Prince George of Denmark.	1701	1714	14	

[1] The last Sovereign of the House of Stewart, in the male line.

Name	Parentage	Marriage	Accession (A.D.)	Death (A.D.)	Reign (Yrs.)	Children
Union of Parliaments (1707)						
George I.	Sophia, grand d. of James VI.	Sophia, d. of the Duke of Zell.	1714	1727	13	1. GEORGE; 2. Sophia.
George II.	George I.	Caroline of Anspach.	1727	1760	34	1. Frederick, father of George III.; 2. William, Duke of Cumberland; and five daughters.

INDEX